Gender and Ethnicity in Contemporary Europe

**Edited by
Jacqueline Andall**

Oxford • New York

First published in 2003 by
Berg
Editorial offices:
1st Floor, Angel Court, 81 St Clements Street, Oxford, OX4 1AW, UK
838 Broadway, Third Floor, New York, NY 10003-4812, USA

Berg is an imprint of Oxford International Publishers Ltd.

Library of Congress Cataloging-in-Publication Data
Gender and ethnicity in contemporary Europe / edited by Jacqueline
Andall.
  p. cm.
Includes bibliographical references and index.
  ISBN 1-85973-647-5 — ISBN 1-85973-652-1 (pbk.)
  1. Minority women—Europe. 2. Women immigrants—Europe. 3.
Ethnicity—Europe. 4. Women—Europe—Identity. I. Andall, Jacqueline.
HQ1587 .G45 2003
305.48'8'0094—dc21

                                                        2002151688

British Library Cataloguing-in-Publication Data
A catalogue record for this book is available from the British Library.

ISBN 1 85973 647 5 (Cloth)
      1 85973 652 1 (Paper)

Typeset by JS Typesetting Ltd, Wellingborough, Northants.
Printed in the United Kingdom by Biddles Ltd, King's Lynn.

This book is dedicated to my grandmothers,
Elvira St Phillip and Veronica Britton.
To my mother, Joan Andall and to my aunts,
Diana Otten and Cynthia Mitchell – for their
strength, determination and inspiration.

Contents

Contents

Acknowledgements

This book started life during an ESRC-sponsored seminar series on 'Women's Search for Identity in Contemporary Europe'. The series was held at the University of Bath at the Centre for Women's Studies between 1995 and 1997. The fifth seminar addressed the issue of gender and ethnicity and I would like to acknowledge the support of the ESRC in facilitating what proved to be a lively and stimulating seminar. Although only a minority of the papers presented at the seminar are included in this volume, the original seminar contributed to the shape of this collection. I would therefore like to thank all those who participated in the seminar at Bath.

I would also like to thank the University of Bath for giving me sabbatical leave during the academic year 2001–2 and University College London for appointing me Senior Research Fellow during this time. At UCL I would like to thank Linda McDowell and Claire Dwyer for commenting on my draft chapters and James Clarke for technical assistance. Finally, I would like to thank Hari Nada for his constant support and enthusiasm for this project.

Notes on Contributors

Jacqueline Andall is Lecturer in Italian Studies at the University of Bath. Her research interests are on migration, domestic work, gender and youth. She has recently published a monograph, *Gender, Migration and Domestic Service: The Politics of Black Women in Italy* (Ashgate 2000). Her current research is on the emergence of a second generation in Italy.

Umut Erel completed her PhD in Cultural Studies at Nottingham Trent University. Her thesis was on 'Subjectivity and Agency in the Life Stories of Migrant Women from Turkey in Britain and in Germany'. Her research interests are on gender, ethnicity, migration and racism, citizenship and cultural theory. She is currently co-editing a book on gender and migration with Mirjana Morokvasic and Kyoko Shinozaki entitled *Gender on the Move! Crossing Borders Shifting Boundaries.*

Raminder Kaur, is Lecturer in Anthropology at the University of Manchester. She is the co-editor of *Travel Worlds: Journeys in Contemporary Cultural Politics* (1999) and author of *A Trunk full of Tales: Performative Politics and Hinduism in Western India* (forthcoming).

Cathie Lloyd is Senior Research Fellow at the International Development Centre, University of Oxford. She is working on the relationship between conflict and globalization with particular reference to North Africa, and has published on antiracism. Her most recent publications are *Rethinking Antiracism* (co-edited with Floya Anthias, Routledge) and a special issue of Oxford Development Studies on 'The Global and the Local: The Cultural Interfaces of Self-Determination Movements'.

Sònia Parella is Assistant Lecturer in Sociology at the Universitat Autònoma de Barcelona (Spain). Her PhD thesis on immigrant women and domestic service in Spain will be published by Ed. Anthropos-Barcelona. She is also researcher at CEDIME (Centre d'Estudis sobre Migracions i Minories Ètniques) and has published several articles and book chapters on migration.

Annie Phizacklea is Professor of Sociology at Warwick University. Her main research interests are on migration, gender and work. Recent publications reflecting this are *Transnationalism and the Politics of Belonging* (with Sallie Westwood) and *Gender and International Migration in Europe* (with Eleonore Kofman, Pavartic Raghuram and Rosemary Sales) both Routledge.

Carlota Solé is Professor of Sociology at the Universitat Autònoma de Barcelona. She has published 23 books and around 150 articles and book chapters on modernization, migrants' integration and business organisations and corporatism. In 1990 she was awarded the National Award of Sociology and Political Science by the Centro de Investigaciones Sociológicas (Madrid). In 1995 she received the Follet Parker Award by the American Political Science Association.

Ruba Salih is a social anthropologist currently based at the University of Bologna, department of Politics, Institutions and History. She has done research in Italy, Morocco and the Palestinian Occupied Territories. A book based on her doctoral dissertation on the gendered dimension of transnational migration is forthcoming with Routledge.

Ravi K Thiara is Research Fellow in the School of Health and Social Studies at the University of Warwick. She has published and carried out extensive research in the area of 'race', ethnicity and gender and has a particular interest in the formation of diasporic communities. Her current work is focused on issues of male violence and service responses as well as the safety and well-being of women and children.

Joke van der Zwaard graduated as a developmental psychologist and holds a PhD in the social sciences on the work and opinions of district nurses on child rearing in migrant households. She has lectured at the universities of Amsterdam and Utrecht. Since 1996, she has worked in Rotterdam as an independent researcher, focusing on education, poverty and social inequality and social networks and strategies of survival in low-income groups.

Anne White is Senior Lecturer in Russian Studies at the University of Bath. Her publications include *Destalinization and the House of Culture: Declining State Control over Leisure in the USSR, Poland and Hungary, 1953–1989* (1990) and *Democratization in Russia under Gorbachev, 1985–1991: The Birth of a Voluntary Sector* (1999).

Introduction: The Space Between – Gender Politics and Immigration Politics in Contemporary Europe

Jacqueline Andall

Questions related to gender and ethnicity have constituted important areas of theoretical and empirical enquiry in a wide range of social science disciplines. Often however, these two areas have been treated separately so that within individual national contexts we find a separate and rich literature on gender and an equally healthy literature on ethnicity, 'race' and immigration (Andall 2000; Lloyd 1998; Rosenberg 1996). This separation of literatures has undoubtedly contributed to ethnic minority women's limited visibility regarding European gender debates. Similarly, within European immigration and ethnicity debates – the normative framework within which ethnic minorities are considered – ethnic minority women have additionally been marginalized.

Gender cannot, of course, simply be reduced to a discussion about women (Anthias 2000). In the same way, ethnicity should not be implicitly understood as synonymous with 'ethnic minority' and recent studies have called for an interrogation of the 'unseen' ethnicity of ethnic majorities (Frankenberg 1993; Mirza 1997a). Nonetheless, given the limited existing material, this book will focus primarily on ethnic minority women in European Union (EU) countries. A report to the European Women's Lobby in the early 1990s not only confirmed the fragmentary information available regarding black and migrant women in Europe but also their exclusion from general research about women at the European level (European Forum of Left Feminists and Others 1993). Afshar and Maynard (1994: 1) have also identified the 'paucity of material concentrating on the interrelationship of "race" and gender, in general, and the consequences of racism, for women of different backgrounds, in particular'. There are now a number of studies that analyse the socio-political situation of women at the European level. However, as with previous trends in national accounts of gender, these tend not to discuss the position of minority women in any substantive way (Rubery, Smith and Fagan 1999; Garcia-Ramon and Monk 1996).

The aim of this book is to give ethnic minority women greater visibility within the European context and to consider the relationship between gender and ethnicity from a number of thematic perspectives. A new space for a discussion of gender and ethnicity in the European context should draw from both second wave European feminisms and postcolonial feminism (see below). However, it also needs to accommodate the specificity of ethnic minority women's social, cultural and political experiences in Europe and give recognition to their own versions of 'Europeanness'. They are able to draw on both what they encounter and transform within the West and what they bring culturally and experientially from outside of the West. In relation to culture and British Asian women, Bhachu (1993: 225) has described this as the ability to be 'cultural entrepreneurs that . . . interpret and reinterpret their cultural systems in the context of their local and national communities'.

An exhaustive account of this vast subject area is naturally beyond the scope of this book. For this work, the focus will be on the feminization of migration flows to Europe; political mobilization by ethnic minority women; gender, ethnicity and Islam; the relationship between gender, ethnicity and identity. This focus on general areas, as opposed to a wider range of specific case studies, allows for a useful comparative framework. It permits us to draw out the significance of both national socio-political cultures as well as wider European trends in relation to gender and ethnicity issues in Europe. Migration, however, is the key broad issue that ties these areas together, whereas the themes in themselves are of particular pertinence to gender and ethnicity debates within many European countries.

Research has pointed to the feminization of migration as an important feature of contemporary global migrations (Castles and Miller 1993; Phizacklea, this volume). Women's participation as active agents in the migration process has often been rendered invisible (Morokvasic 1983, 1991, 1995; Kofman et al. 2000). In the pre-1973 phase of migration to Europe (see below), female migrants occupied a range of low-level service sector work (Bryan, Dadzie and Scafe 1985; Condon 1995). Recently, migration streams to Europe have become increasingly feminized. In Italy, for example, there is virtually single-sex migration within particular ethnic groups (Andall 1999). In contrast to earlier female migrations, women's contemporary migration to Europe has gradually progressed to a close association with the domestic work sector, although the incidence of sex trafficking and mail-order brides to the EU should not be minimized (Truong and Del Rosario 1995). The case studies presented examine this resurgence of domestic service (Andall, Solé and Parella, this volume). These recent female migrations, moreover, raise wider issues concerning gender relations in Europe and suggest that the different European models of female emancipation cannot be heralded an unqualified success. In addition to these new migrations, more established migration has led to the presence of ethnic minority groups who are second- and third-generation European citizens (see Vertovec and Rogers 1998; Andall 2002). This presence raises a different set of issues for ethnic minorities, ethnic majorities and European governments alike.

In new migration settings, 'culture' and ethnicity tend to assume a new signif-icance precisely because ethnic groups are transformed into 'ethnic minorities'. Yuval-Davis (1997: 116) has demonstrated how 'culture' can be mobilised for ethnic or nationalist political projects and has highlighted how 'women are con-structed as symbols of the national 'essence' . . . as well as border guards of ethnic, national and racial difference'. The boundaries and cultural norms of communities are, of course, not static, but rather open to contestation and renegotiation. Never-theless, an understanding of women's roles as cultural reproducers of communities has led some European governments to envisage a very specific role for ethnic minority women. Thus in France, they are expected to facilitate the 'stability of the ethnic minority population and to see to it that their children integrate or assimilate and become "French"' (Freedman 2000: 15). Within their own ethnic minority communities, women are frequently expected to retain and perform a particular version of 'culture', even when this negates their own interests and promotes that of the patriarchal community. This dichotomy of interests is particularly important with regard to ethnic minority women's political mobiliz-ation, whereby activists seek to challenge both gender inequalities within their own communities and the racism, gender inequalities and injustices present in the national community (Thiara, Lloyd, this volume). The political activism of ethnic minority women therefore has to negotiate difficult terrain, with some activists such as Patel (1997: 256) arguing for a need to move away from a 'white majority/ black minority dichotomy' and the adoption of a critical examination of 'the inner dynamics of our communities'. A broader framework is also required to fully incorporate the various manifestations of ethnic minority women's activism. Mirza (1997b) for example, has suggested that although the strategies employed by British African-Caribbean women to succeed educationally might appear as conservative and conformist, they should be re-evaluated as a radical act in the face of institutional expectations of their educational failure.

Patterns of migration to Europe have also contributed to the widespread presence of Muslims in Europe. There are an estimated seven million Muslims in West Europe, from a wide range of ethnic backgrounds (Vertovec and Rogers 1998). Identifications such as 'British Muslim' must therefore be understood as contested categories that attempt to 'subsume the multi-ethnic, multi-linguistic and multi-denominational features of the community' (Samad 1998: 68). In the early 1990s, Castles (1993: 27) suggested that Muslims were becoming the 'main targets of racist discourse' in Europe. The fear of Islam has indeed become an important aspect of European immigration politics and this has assumed much greater resonance since the events of 11 September 2001. It is the migration setting that constructs Muslims as religious and ethnic minorities. Their experiences within Europe have contributed to a form of Islamic revivalism where they consciously seek to 'carve out a social niche for themselves' (Afshar 1998: 107). How do

Muslim women living in Europe fit into this paradigm? Throughout Europe, we find essentialized representations of Muslim women, normatively categorized as either traditional or secular (Salih, Urel, van der Zwaard, this volume). Moreover, there is an exaggerated preoccupation with Muslim women's attire and particularly the cultural and political meanings to be attributed to the wearing of the 'veil' (Dwyer 1999). Qualitative research presents a different perspective and demonstrates the ways in which Muslim European women negotiate new modes of being Muslim in Europe (Dwyer 2000; Morck 1998).

The final section of this book looks at gender and ethnicity in relation to identity, although issues concerning identity permeate many of the other contributions to the book. Ethnic identity constitutes only one of our many social identities, however its significance can be transformed or assume greater prominence as a result of the wider social and political context (Allen 1994). In contrast to the other chapters, the discussion about identity focuses on white, gendered ethnicities and thus on ethnic majorities (White, Kaur, this volume). The case studies presented are again linked to the broad theme of migration. The first case study examines the case of Russia, which has become more ethnically Russian since the demise of the USSR. Ethnic Russians formally living in other parts of the Soviet empire have returned to Russia in large numbers, often adopting a superior attitude to local Russian populations (Pilkington 1998). Thus, here the issue of identity in relation to nationhood is explored from the gendered perspective of local Russians and 'returnees'. The second case study is also framed by the issue of migration. The post-war migration of Asians to Britain has led to the growth of a geographical area of London in which white British residents now constitute an ethnic minority. As well as providing new perspectives on identity, these debates also contribute to ongoing research into the nature of whiteness (see below).

To contextualize the general themes to be addressed in this book, I present an overview of European gender debates in relation to racialized difference and an overview of European immigration debates.

Gender Politics in Europe

There is some consensus that Anglophone accounts of feminist theory and practice have dominated feminist theorizing and that other European feminist accounts have not had the same influence in relation to international feminism (Bulbeck 1998; Afshar and Maynard 2000). Nonetheless, as one would expect, nation-specific feminisms can be identified in a range of European countries (Bull, Diamond and Marsh 2000). Much further elaboration is required, however, of how these various European feminisms have engaged with notions of difference in terms of 'race' and ethnicity.[1] As Braidotti (1992: 8–9) has argued: 'How aware are European feminists of the realities of migrations in our own countries?'

Second-wave feminism in a range of EU countries tended to focus on a similar set of broad issues in the 1960s and 1970s. These included control over reproduction, sexuality and the rejection of an exclusive mothering role for women (Duchen 1986; Birnbaum 1986; Rosenberg 1996). The importance of these mobilizing campaigns for transforming women's lives in general cannot be underestimated. Moreover, the production of second-wave feminist knowledge has challenged theoretical and empirical academic orthodoxies across a range of disciplines (Afshar and Maynard 2000). In the 1980s the perceived decline in autonomous feminist activity in countries like Britain (Hume 2000) or Italy (Ergas 1986) has been paralleled by what is seen as the 'mainstreaming' of feminism (Randall 2000: 149) or its diffusion into institutionalized structures (Calabrò and Grasso 1985).[2] Nonetheless, in some contexts, a covert anti-feminist institutional backlash has been observed (Randall 2000).

Postcolonial feminism centres on extending 'the analytical lens beyond the narrow confines of Western perceptions and ideas' (Afshar and Maynard 2000: 816). Here, the focus is about both recognizing the different forms that feminism can take in a range of countries outside the West, or as Bulbeck (1998: 1) puts it, to 'focus on unfamiliar forms of feminism'. Within this concept, an engagement with the theory and practice of women beyond the Anglophone West is intended to provoke a re-evaluation of some of the common-sense assumptions of contemporary Anglophone feminism (Bulbeck 1998). A version of postcolonial feminism is also seen to lie within the West as a result of global migrations and the presence of women of different ethnicities and cultures *within* the West. However, these perspectives perhaps fail to capture adequately the manner in which migrant women and their descendents as second- and third-generation European citizens will generate new versions of gendered activism, which will be transformed precisely by their engagement with the West. Of course, the different migratory histories of European countries mean that individual countries have adopted various positions. Nonetheless, the emergence of a transnational West European space (Rogers 2000) facilitates relationships between the same ethnic minority groups across European countries. This may mean that new expressions of Europeanness by ethnic minorities may not be defined primarily by the original 'home' culture but also by the type of relationships and exchanges which occur within Brah's (1996) notion of diasporic space, conceptually broadened to a 'transnational diasporic space'.

Within early second-wave European feminism, women's commonality was promoted and contestation around the notion of difference was largely theoretical or to do with political strategies (Duchen 1986; Rosenberg 1996; Beccalli 1994). In the 1980s, one specific aspect of difference that was introduced to the British feminist debate centred on the issue of racism within the feminist movement (Bourne 1983; Amos and Parmar 1984). Drawing on emerging literature in the United

States (hooks 1981; Davis 1982), this would mark the beginning of a new British literature on black feminist thought (Parmar 1989; Brah 1991; Bhavnani 1993; Mirza 1997a). This literature highlighted ethnic minority women's exclusion from mainstream feminism's theory and practice, and mobilized for a more inclusive feminism. Black feminist accounts identified the manner in which black women 'inhabit the margins of the race, gender and class discourse [existing] in a vacuum of erasure and contradiction' (Mirza 1997a: 4). Early responses to British black feminist critiques in the 1980s often side-stepped the issue of racism (Bhavnani and Coulson 1986) and the nature of racialized power was seen to produce a resounding silence (Mirza 1997a). In other European contexts, ethnic minority women also struggled to transform feminist agendas and practice (Rosenberg 1996; Lloyd 1998).

The experiences of ethnic minority women in Europe must be understood as being dynamically shaped by a wide range of factors including access to formal citizenship, immigration regimes, the general status of women in individual European countries and the variety or dominance of particular ethnic minority groups within specific countries. Thus in Britain, women of both Asian and African-Caribbean origin participated in the theoretical development of a black feminist thought (see Mirza 1997a). In Germany and the Netherlands, women involved in feminist and lesbian politics began to organize as black women (Essed 1996). Nonetheless, as with mainstream feminism, Anglophone accounts of black feminism have become dominant and other ethnic minority European voices often struggle to carve out a place within this framework. This is partly a question of language. As the Dutch-Caribbean academic Essed (1996: 133) has written: 'the denial of racism hampered Dutch development of theories in this area for a long time. In classroom discussions, students sometimes had to swallow before they could say "black", "race," or "racism" – terms that were used in the English-language articles but that were taboo in Dutch'.

Watson's (2000: 106) analysis of feminism in postcommunist states suggests that Western feminism still posits itself as the 'unquestioned norm'. As she argues, Western-centredness in the context of Eastern European countries' transition to democracy is akin to the construction of whiteness within European feminism as 'outside relations of power' (p. 101). The resistance to Western feminism in a range of countries in the former Soviet bloc can thus be partially attributed to the difficulties that Eastern Europeans have experienced in articulating their difference to Western feminism. According to Rosenberg (1996: 147): 'Many [West German feminists] refused to believe that anything that could be considered feminist existed in the east and exhibited a surprising hostility toward eastern attempts to address them on an equal basis.' Agendas, priorities and experiences thus lie at the heart of questions of ethnicized difference for women and have been at the root of challenges to some of the orthodoxies of Western feminism. Within black feminist thought, for example, different perspectives on the family have been elaborated (Phoenix 1987). Similar differentiations appear to be emerging from within Eastern European countries where, in relation to the Russian context, Bridger (2000: 119) states that feminism, in the context of chaos and insecurity, is seen as both unnatural and an 'irrelevant luxury'. However, women's ambivalent positioning in terms of nationalism and political mobilization has meant that a rejection of feminism in Eastern Europe can also be connected to the political assertion of cultural and ethnic identities in the Eastern European countries (Charles and Hintjens 1998).

These examples all highlight the difficulties inherent in developing a more inclusive gender politics. There still needs to be greater recognition on the part of those who have a dominant voice in the production of feminist knowledge and activity of wider political power relations and the often unchallenged normalization of Western visions of progress. Mirza's (1997a: 18) vision of the future direction of black feminism is of wider relevance to all those engaged in a feminist praxis. She writes of the need for 'conscious alliances, critical dialogue and intellectual rigor . . . to reveal the operation of power in which we are implicated'. Braidotti (1992: 10), writing from a white feminist perspective, calls for 'multiple literacies', which presuppose 'that feminists relinquish the dream of a common language in favour of the recognition of the complexity of the semiotic and material context in which we operate'.

The concept of racialized difference in relation to gender politics has been problematized by a number of scholars. For example, it has been suggested that difference as an organizational concept can prevent us from considering 'the relationships between things and the possible consequences in terms of domination and control which ensue' (Maynard 1994:18). Mirza (1997a: 13) is similarly critical of difference as an analytical concept because it contributes to 'deflecting attention away from power which is still materially located'. Moreover, in her view, the notion of difference can actually privilege whiteness in the European context given that difference in terms of ethnicity is relationally positioned to the norm of whiteness. The issue of whiteness as a privileged social identity has received growing attention since the 1990s (Frankenberg 1993; Dyer 1997). This research has identified a number of themes in relation to whiteness: 'invisibility; naturalisation; naming; guilt and embarrassment; othering; vacancy or absence; mixing; and problems with definition' (Brown 1999: 6). An awareness of 'race' difference, however, is not tantamount to paying due attention to racism (Maynard 1994). To end this overview of postwar European gender debates and to formulate a link with the review of immigration and ethnicity politics, I now turn to the issue of racism.

Racism – the process by which people constructed as a 'race' are subordinated – forms a constitutive component of the two arenas of debate being addressed in this book. Racism is present in many forms in Europe and individual countries approach the topic in a variety of ways (Castles 1993; Miles 1993). In the late 1980s,

Italy was still being defined as 'pre-racist' (Balbo and Manconi 1992) despite empirical evidence to the contrary (Balbi 1989). In the Netherlands, Wekker (1995: 71) argued that there was 'a general cloak of silence around the topic of racism' and that the term was only seen to be applicable to extremist organisations and working-class Dutch people. In Britain, the debate has more recently focused on the existence of institutional racism, defined in the Macpherson Report[3] as (1999, point 6.34): '. . . processes, attitudes and behaviour which amount to discrimination through unwitting prejudice, ignorance, thoughtlessness and racist stereotyping which disadvantage minority ethnic people'.

In the opening presentation to the two-day seminar on gender and ethnicity held at the University of Bath in 1997, Avtar Brah addressed the significance of confronting racism in her paper on the British Broadcasting Corporation (BBC) Reith Lectures of 1997. In that year, the lectures had been presented by the African-American law professor Patricia J. Williams. Williams spoke about various aspects of the 'race' polemic (1997a, 1997b, 1997c, 1997d, 1997e). Highly critical of the 'liberal ideal of colourblindness' (1997a: 1), she argued that the very subject of 'race' was being 'closeted': 'race matters are resented and repressed in much the same way as matters of sex and scandal: the subject is considered a rude and transgressive one in mixed company, a matter whose observation is sometimes inevitable, but about which, once seen, little should be heard nonetheless' (1997a: 4). For Williams, the phenomenon of closeting race derived in part from a desire 'to conform our surroundings to whatever we know as "normal"' (1997a: 3) and a 'collective aversion to confronting . . . social tensions' (1997a: 2). Research conducted with white women in London found that they preferred to leave the 'unspeakable unspoken' in terms of making connections between 'whiteness, racism and personal responsibility' (Lewis and Ramazanoglu 1999: 40). Indeed, what might be considered as the backlash of 'race' issues has meant that, in some cases, the white majority resents the issue of racism being raised (Essed 1996; Van Dijk 1993). These apparent difficulties in discussing issues of 'race' and racism, particularly in ethnically mixed company, does not signify that race matters are not spoken about. Rather, we need to ask why conversations about 'race' and racism are differently articulated depending on whether they occur within private or public spaces (Aymer 1997). This can lead to only the ethnically segregated few getting to hear the conversation. Racial denial on the part of some ethnic majorities has been described both as 'an innocence that amounts to the transgressive refusal to know' (Williams 1997b: 8) and as a form of power evasion (Frankenberg 1993). In the British context, the negative response to the Macpherson (1999) report is suggestive of this. Macpherson's account of the Metropolitan Police as institutionally racist was seen to be excessive by the Conservative Party leadership and police officers argued that the real problem lay in their apprehension at being accused of racism rather than racism within the force (Bourne 2001).

Research has highlighted the denial of racism at elite levels, used both as a defensive strategy and as a strategy of 'positive self representation' (Van Dijk 1993: 179). The propensity for black professionals to speak more about race matters than their white colleagues even within the same institutional setting (Gillborn 2002) suggests that much greater open dialogue is necessary to confront popular and institutional racism. Such racism contributes to different layers of discrimination in a wide range of social, economic and political spheres. In its most vicious formulation, it culminates in forms of racist violence that have led to the deaths of innocent people throughout Europe.

Immigration and Ethnicity in Europe

Understanding European approaches to immigration in the postwar period is essential for contextualizing the relationship between gender and ethnicity in Europe. Despite predictable differences between countries – linked to specific socio-cultural and political traditions – similar trends can be identified at the European level. Sciortino (2000) has identified four temporal phases in the postwar period regarding migration to Europe: the reluctant acceptance of immigration up until 1973; an immigration stop from 1974 to the Single European Act of 1986; the emergence of a co-ordinated European policy between 1987 and 1994; the attempt to control European migration between 1995–2000. The case studies presented in this book span these various migration phases.

In the first important phase of postwar immigration to Europe, migration was linked to postwar reconstruction. This involved both migration from outside of Europe and migration within Europe. Migration from outside of Europe was typically a form of labour migration linked to existing or former colonial ties. Thus, Algerians moved to France (MacMaster 1997) and Caribbean people to Britain, the Netherlands and France (Chamberlain 1998; Condon and Ogden 1991). Migration within Europe was driven by similar needs and involved for example, Italian migration to Germany and Switzerland (Gabaccia 2000) and Portuguese migration to France (Condon 2000).

In countries such as Britain and France, it soon became apparent that some groups were more desirable than others. In Britain, immigration legislation was subsequently designed in such a way to facilitate the arrival of white Commonwealth migrants while excluding black Commonwealth migrants (Solomos 1989). In France, incentives for the voluntary repatriation of migrants were introduced, but these did not meet their intended North African targets but rather Spanish and Portuguese migrants (Hargreaves 1995). Post 1973, the principal receiving countries justified new restrictive entry policies by pointing to the oil crisis and the ensuing slump in European economies. New trends were initiated as multinational capital exported production processes to offshore locations, thereby moving capital to labour (Phizacklea 1983). Popular and political hostility to ethnic minorities also contributed to the virtual immigration stop to Western Europe. The consensus appeared clear regarding the undesirability – from a socio-cultural and political perspective – of both the presence of particular ethnic minority groups and any additional primary migration.

This change in strategy by many West European countries, as well as rising levels of wealth in countries like Italy, Spain, Greece and Portugal, contributed to new migratory flows to the southern European countries. Former exporters of labour, these countries all became migration receiving societies in the 1970s and 1980s (King and Andall 1999; Anthias and Lazaridis 2000; King, Lazaridis and Tsardanis 2000). Since the early 1990s, geopolitical factors, such as the demise of the Soviet Union, have also had important implications for migration to the EU countries. Widespread mobility and migration have taken place within and from the former Soviet Union (Pilkingston 1998; Wallace 2001). However, the restrictive stance of the EU towards this migration can be seen in the creation of a 'buffer' zone in the new migration space of central Europe, used to control and restrict migration from the East (Wallace 2001). These later migratory movements to Europe need to be understood in relation to global migration trends. There has not only been a widespread increase in the volume of migration, with all corners of the globe implicated, but a more diversified range of immigration typologies (labour migrants, temporary migrants, refugees) (Castles and Miller 1993). Nevertheless, the focus on South-North and East-West migratory flows should be conceptualized alongside extensive South-South migratory flows. As Pugliese (1995: 56) reminds us 'The new arrivals in Europe are only a small part of the enormous population movement originating in the Third World.'

Today, the difficulty encountered in developing a European immigration policy is attributed to uncritical support for a restrictive migration regime amongst European decision makers (Sciortino 2000). This position is based on the unrealistic view that there is no real structural demand for labour in the EU countries. As Vitorino has argued (2000: 17–18): 'It is time to face the fact that the zero immigration policies of the past 25 years are not working but in addition they are no longer relevant to the economic and demographic situation in which the Union now finds itself.' Indeed, the political 'language of crisis and threat' in relation to immigration tends to obscure the important future role that migration will have in relation to many European countries (Geddes 2000: 1). More recently, greater flexibility regarding the primary migration of skilled professionals to Europe has not been accompanied by openness towards unskilled migration (Findlay 2001).[4] At the EU level, then, the issue of migration has been driven by a restrictive agenda and the image of a 'fortress Europe' has been regularly invoked to convey the manner in which EU countries have attempted to put in place impenetrable borders

(Morokvasic 1991; Pugliese 1995; Lutz 1997). These measures have not deterred migrants from seeking entry to Europe but the borders are such that we now routinely witness the deaths of individuals and groups attempting to enter Europe. The 58 Chinese immigrants who suffocated to death in a lorry to Dover, Britain, in the year 2000 is but one of countless horrendous examples. Moreover these deaths are undoubtedly a consequence of the 'undeclared and uncontrolled immigration system' (Vitorino 2000: 18) in EU member states that benefits migration traffickers.

European immigration policy and citizenship criteria[5] also have a role to play in wider questions about the inclusion and exclusion of migrants and ethnic minority European citizens. From a political perspective, a range of incorporation approaches can be identified at the European level, including multiculturalist and assimilationist perspectives (Koopmans and Statham 2000). The emergence of political parties with an explicit and prominent anti-immigration agenda in many European countries gives some indication of the current socio-political climate towards both new migrants and settled ethnic minorities.[6] Moreover, within European politics there has been a trend for the existence of such parties to push the centre political ground to adopt an anti-immigration stance to gain political support, rather than to politically oppose the 'populist anti-immigrant vote' (Rex 2000: 69). 'Race' and immigration thus continue to be used as mobilizing issues in European political elections. In Britain, prior to the 2001 general elections, the Commission for Racial Equality unsuccessfully attempted to eliminate the manipulation of 'race' for political ends through the introduction of an anti-racism election pledge.[7]

This general socio-political climate with regard to immigration is important for situating the experiences of ethnic minority women in Europe. Although ethnic minority women in EU countries span the various phases of migration to Europe, they are all affected – albeit to varying degrees – by the contemporary negative climate towards immigration and ethnic minorities in Europe. Generally, it can be argued that the specific implications of ethnic minority women's status as gendered and racialized minorities have not, on the whole, been afforded due consideration. To generalize an argument put by Williams (1997b: 1) how or whether ethnic minority women in Europe 'are seen depends upon a dynamic of display that ricochets between hypervisibility and oblivion'.

Organization of the Book

As discussed above, the book is organized under four themes. The first section of the book addresses the issue of gender, ethnicity and migration. In Chapter 1, Annie Phizacklea sets out a theoretical framework for understanding women's involvement in migration. How, she asks, can we properly distinguish between women who enter receiving immigration countries as labour migrants, refugees or for family reunification? Phizacklea argues that in order to fully understand gendered migration, we need to re-evaluate the notion that women are simply following male migrants and instead consider their gendered position in their original 'home' country as well as acknowledging the gendered implications of migration regulations in the receiving immigration society. Phizacklea focuses particularly on intermediary migration institutions as offering the possibility for a more nuanced, gendered analysis of migration. More specifically, she argues for the gendered 'unpacking' of the household, understood as a central, though not reified part of the migration process.

In Chapter 2, Jacqueline Andall investigates the important position that paid domestic work has assumed in relation to the feminization of migration flows to a wide range of European countries. She focuses on the gender, ethnic and class implications of contemporary domestic work relationships and highlights the hierarchical yet interdependent nature of these relationships. She emphasizes how casually ethnicity is used in a discriminatory fashion within the sector and argues for a re-evaluation of the structural transformations that have occurred within the sector's recent history. She suggests that sectoral organization of the domestic work sphere will be problematic precisely because of the interdependence inscribed within the relationship but also because of the weaker social and political position of the migrant women who perform this type of labour.

In Chapter 3, Carlota Solé and Sònia Parella investigate the gendered and ethnic segmentation of the labour market in Spain. They highlight the dominance of domestic service as an employment sector for migrant women and consider the wider ethnic stratification of the labour market whereby male and female migrants are concentrated in specific employment sectors. They argue that within the Spanish labour market, male migrants have wider, albeit still restricted labour market opportunities whereas migrant women are overwhelmingly concentrated in the domestic work sector, occupying 'the lowest rung of the ladder'. The authors compare the situation of migrant women with both migrant men and Spanish women to demonstrate how both the labour market and immigration legislation discriminate against migrant women.

The second section of this book examines the relationship between gender, ethnicity and political mobilization in Britain and France. In Chapter 4, Ravi Thiara considers the history of South Asian women's collective activism in Britain, contextualizing this to the broader framework of post-1970s anti-racist activity. She argues that racialized identities within gendered social relations pose difficult issues for those women actively seeking to transform social relations. She suggests that not all differences are reconcilable within the ethnic mobilization framework. In her view, this has led to a trend in the 1990s where activists have had to choose 'safe' issues around which to mobilize. Thiara additionally stresses the 'discomfort' South Asian women have faced regarding their implicit critique *and* acceptance of their ethnic heritage.

In Chapter 5, Cathie Lloyd examines the relationship between social movements and women migrants in France. She, too, highlights the ambivalence of migrant women who may, for example, want to oppose a forced marriage but not betray their family. Lloyd deconstructs the concept of equality in France and focuses on the importance of immigration legislation for contributing to migrant women's invisibility and social difficulties in France. Lloyd's chapter illustrates two issues that assumed national political prominence in France – the headscarf affair and the *sanspapiers* movement. Through an analysis of these two issues, she investigates the difficult space that migrant women's political activism has sought to occupy.

The third section of the book addresses the relationship between gender, ethnicity and Islam in three European countries. In Chapter 6, Ruba Salih discusses opposing projects of modernity amongst Muslim women in Italy. Salih challenges assumptions about representations of authenticity for Muslim women. She demonstrates that to be a Muslim in Italy is not simply a shared identity but rather a contested notion for Muslims, who attribute quite different meanings to Islam. She argues that for Muslim women, different constructions of Islam can be presented as modern. For example, knowledge of Islamic texts can be considered as one way of being a modern Muslim. Alternatively, a more secular version of being a modern Muslim is to construct new versions of authenticity by reformulating different religions and practices.

In Chapter 7, Joke van der Zwaard examines how Muslim women are categorized in the Netherlands. She focuses on how these women manipulate dominant constructions of Muslim women in the Dutch context and self-represent themselves in a way that gains them respect in a discourse that renders them inferior. Her case study analyses similarities and differences across different ethnicities regarding child-rearing and domestic work in the home. In her research she found that Moroccan women did not simply express an individual position but simultaneously sought to improve the social reputation of Moroccans as a group. Her research thus presents a more nuanced view of 'community', emphasizing change as a means to improve the social reputation of the group.

In Chapter 8, Umut Erel focuses on new meanings of citizenship for women of Turkish origin in Germany. Concentrating on professional women, she addresses the gender constructions of German and 'foreign' identities. She argues that women of Turkish origin are negatively constructed as 'traditional' in the well-rehearsed tradition/modernity polarity brought into play with regard to ethnic minority women in Europe. She discusses how women of Turkish origin sometimes feel compelled to choose between a German and a Turkish social identity.

Erel concludes that active political citizenship amongst women of Turkish origin is contributing to new forms of citizenship in Germany.

The final section of the book addresses the relationship between gender, ethnicity and identity in Britain and Russia. In Chapter 9, Anne White looks at the complex notion of Russian national identity and ethnicity in the Russian 'depths'. She moves the debate away from a top-down and largely male state understanding of the relationship between citizenship and identity and focuses instead on what 'nation and ethnic identity mean in the micro-worlds of individual Russians'. Her bottom-up account maintains that it is particularly important to analyse the views of women on this issue given their important role in Russia in transmitting ethnic and national identities. She concludes that women identified with the idea of 'Mother Russia' in part to bolster their self-confidence as mothers, in a social and political context where they were both unable to properly educate their children or give them enough access to Russia's national cultural heritage.

In Chapter 10, Raminder Kaur, addresses the experiences of white women living as a minority ethnic group in a predominantly Asian area of west London, Southall. She thus focuses on the dynamics of 'race' and gender in a context whereby Asian ethnicity is normalized and white women living in the area occupy the unusual position of having a minority status in their local area but a majority ethnic status outside of the area. Through an exploration of whiteness and gender, Kaur describes how white women are 'stared' at in a way that marks them as physically and sexually available. She then analyses their everyday strategies for living in the area. Kaur argues that these strategies are premised much more on articulating and negotiating gender identities rather than 'racial' identities.

Notes

1. There is some consensus about the notion of 'race' as a dynamic social construction, despite the fact that in both popular and political discourse it is often considered as a 'fixed' category. For a succinct overview of theoretical reflections on 'race' see Maynard (1994).
2. See Afshar and Maynard (2000) for a critique of the extent to which feminism has become mainstream.
3. This inquiry was set up to investigate the racist murder, in April 1993, of a young black British man, Stephen Lawrence.
4. Germany, which for so many years had shamelessly refused to acknowledge that it was a country of immigration, found itself competing with the United States for skilled IT workers from India (Findlay 2001; Marshall 2000).

5. See Hansen and Weil (2001) for a useful overview of the nationality and citizenship regimes operative in the EU countries.
6. The Northern League in Italy, the Front National in France, the Freedom Party in Austria, the People's Party in Denmark, the Popular Party in Portugal and Pim Fortuyn in the Netherlands.
7. This was an attempt to establish good practice for political activists at local, national and European elections and the principal objective was to ensure 'that all political campaigns are conducted fairly and free from racial hatred and prejudice' (http://www.cre.gov.uk).

Bibliography

Afshar, H. (1998), 'Strategies of Resistance among the Muslim Minority in West Yorkshire: Impact on Women', in N. Charles and H. Hintjens (eds), *Gender, Ethnicity and Political Ideologies*, London: Routledge.

Afshar, H. and Maynard, M. (1994), 'The Dynamics of "Race" and Gender', in H. Afshar and M. Maynard (eds), *The Dynamics of "Race" and Gender*, London: Taylor & Francis.

Afshar, H. and Maynard, M. (2000), 'Gender and Ethnicity at the Millennium: From Margin to Centre', *Ethnic and Racial Studies*, 23, (5): 805–19.

Allen, S. (1994), 'Race, Ethnicity and Nationality: Some Questions of Identity', in H. Afshar and M.Maynard, M (eds), *The Dynamics of 'Race' and Gender*, London: Taylor & Francis.

Amos, V. and Parmar, P. (1984), 'Challenging Imperial Feminsm', *Feminist Review*, 17: 3–19.

Andall, J. (1999), Cape Verdean Women on the Move: 'Immigration Shopping' in Italy and Europe, *Modern Italy*, 4, (2): 241–57.

Andall, J. (2000), *Gender, Migration and Domestic Service. The Politics of Black Women in Italy*, Aldershot: Ashgate.

Andall, J. (2002) 'Second-Generation Attitude?: African-Italians in Milan', *Journal of Ethnic and Migration Studies*, 28, (3): 389–407.

Anthias, F. (2000), 'Metaphors of Home: Gendering New Migrations to Southern Europe', in F. Anthias and G. Lazaridis (eds), *Gender and Migration in Southern Europe*, Oxford: Berg.

Anthias, F. and Lazaridis, G. (eds) (2000), *Gender and Migration in Southern Europe*, Oxford: Berg.

Aymer, C. (1997), 'Black Women Living with Success and Ambivalence', presentation to seminar on Gender and Ethnicity in Contemporary Europe, University of Bath, 7–8 November.

Balbi, R. (1989) *All'erta siam razzisti*, Milan: Mondadori.

Balbo, L. and Manconi, L. (1992), *I razzismi reali*, Milan: Feltrinelli.

Beccalli, B. (1994), The Modern Women's Movement in Italy', *New Left Review*, 204: 86–112.

Bhachu, P. (1993), 'New European Women and New Cultural Forms: Culture, Class, and Consumption among British Asian Women', in H. Rudolph and M. Morokvasic (eds), *Bridging States and Markets. International Migration in the Early 1990s*, Berlin: Edition Sigma.

Bhavnani, K. (1993), 'Talking Racism and the Editing of Women's Studies', in D. Richardson and V. Robinson (eds), *Introducing Women's Studies: Feminist Theory and Practice*, London: Macmillan.

Bhavnani, K. and Coulson, M. (1986), 'Transforming Socialist Feminism: the Challenge of Racism', *Feminist Review*, 23: 81–92.

Birnbaum, L. (1986), *Liberazione della donna*, Connecticut: Wesleyan University Press.

Bourne, J. (1983), 'Towards an Anti-racist Feminism', *Race and Class*, 25, (1): 1–22.

Bourne, J. (2001), 'The Life and Times of Institutional Racism', *Race and Class*, 43, (2), 7–22.

Brah, A. (1991), 'Questions of Difference and International Feminism', in J. Aaron and S. Walby (eds), *Out of the Margins: Women's Studies in the Nineties*, London: The Falmer Press.

Brah, A. (1996), *Cartographies of Diaspora*, London: Routledge.

Brah, A. (1997), 'The Genealogy of Race . . . Towards a Theory of Grace: Engaging with the 1997 Reith Lectures', presentation to seminar on Gender and Ethnicity in Contemporary Europe, University of Bath, 7–8 November.

Braidotti, R. (1992), 'The Exile, the Nomad, and the Migrant. Reflections on International Feminism', *Women's Studies International Forum*, 15, (1): 7–10.

Bridger, S. (2000), '"Something Unnatural": Attitudes to Feminism in Russia', in A. Bull, H. Diamond and R. Marsh (eds), *Feminisms and Women's Movements in Contemporary Europe*, Basingstoke: Macmillan.

Brown, H. (1999), 'Introduction: White?Women: Beginnings and Endings?', in H. Brown; M. Gilkes and A. Kaloski-Naylor (eds), *White?Women. Critical Perspectives on Race and Gender*, York: Raw Nerve Books.

Bulbeck, C. (1998), *Re-orienting Western Feminisms*, Cambridge: CUP.

Bull, A, Diamond, H. and Marsh, R. (eds), (2000) *Feminisms and Women's Movements in Contemporary Europe*, Basingstoke: Macmillan.

Calabrò, A. R. and Grasso, L. (eds) (1985) Dal movimento femminista al femminismo diffuso, Milan: FrancoAngeli.

Castles, S. (1993), 'Migration and Minorities in Europe. Perspectives for the 1990s: Eleven Hypotheses', in J. Solomos and J. Wrench (eds), *Racism and Migration in Western Europe*, Oxford: Berg.

Castles, S. and Miller, M. (1993), *The Age of Migration. International Population Movements in the Modern World*, London: Macmillan.

Chamberlain, M. (ed.) (1998), *Caribbean Migration*, London: Routledge.

Charles, N. and H. Hintjens (eds) (1998), 'Gender, Ethnicity and Cultural Identity: Women's "Places"', in N. Charles and H. Hintjens (eds), *Gender, Ethnicity and Political Ideologies*, London: Routledge.

Condon, S (1995), 'Compromise and Coping Strategies: Gender Issues and Caribbean Migration to France', paper presented to research seminar on 'Caribbean Migration to Europe', Oxford Brookes University, 22–24 September.

Condon, S. (2000), 'L'activité des femmes immigrées du Portugal à l'arrivée en France, reflet d'une diversité de strategies familiales et individuelles', *Population*, 55: 301–30.

Condon, S. and Ogden, P. (1991), 'Afro-Caribbean Migrants in France: Employment, State Policy and the Migration Process', *Transactions of the Institute of British Geographers*, 11: 440–57.

Davis, A. (1982), *Women, Race and Class*, London: The Women's Press.

Duchen, C. (1986), *Feminism in France*, London: Routledge.

Dwyer, C. (1999), 'Veiled Meanings: Young British Muslim Women and the Negotiation of Differences', *Gender, Place and Culture*, 6, 1: 5–26.

Dwyer, C. (2000), 'Negotiating Diasporic Identities: Young British South Asian Muslim Women', *Women's Studies International Forum*, 23, (4): 475–86.

Dyer, R. (1997), *White*, London: Routledge.

Ergas, Y. (1986), *Nelle maglie della politica*. Milan: Franco Angeli.

Essed, P. (1996), *Diversity. Gender, Color and Culture*, Amherst: University of Massachusetts Press.

European Forum of Left Feminists and Others (1993), Confronting the Fortress. Black and Migrant Women in the European Community, A Report to the European Women's Lobby.

Findlay, A. (2001), 'Brain Drain: The Second Wave', paper presented to the conference 'Strangers and Citizens: Challenges for European Governance, Identity and Citizenship', University of Dundee, 17–19 March 2001.

Frankenberg, R. (1993), *White Women, Race Matters. The Social Construction of Whiteness*, Minneapolis: University of Minnesota Press.

Freedman, J. (2000), 'Women and Immigration: Nationality and Citizenship', in J. Freedman and C. Tarr (eds), *Women, Immigration and Identities in France*. Oxford: Berg.

Gabaccia, D. (2000), *Italy's Many Diasporas,* London: UCL Press

Garcia-Ramon, M. and Monk, J. (eds) (1996), *Women of the European Union. The Politics of Work and Daily Life*, London: Routledge.

Geddes, A. (2000), *Immigration and European Integration*. Manchester: MUP.

Gillborn, D. (2002), 'Education and Institutional Racism', inaugural professorial lecture, Institute of Education, University of London.

Hansen, R. and Weil, P. (2001), 'Introduction: Citizenship, Immigration and Nationality: Towards a Convergence in Europe?' in R. Hansen and P. Weil (eds), *Towards a European Nationality*, Basingstoke: Palgrave.

Hargreaves, A. (1995), 'Immigration, 'Race' and Ethnicity in Contemporary France, London: Routledge.

hooks, b. (1981), *Ain't I a Woman: Black Women and Feminism*, London: Pluto Press.

Hume, M. (2000), 'Feminisms and Women's Movements in the 1990s', in A. Bull, H. Diamond and R.Marsh (eds), *Feminisms and Women's Movements in Contemporary Europe*, Basingstoke: Macmillan.

King, R. and Andall, J. (1999), 'The Geography and Economic Sociology of Recent Immigration to Italy', *Modern Italy*, 4, (2): 135–58.

King, R., Lazaridis, G and Tsardanis, C. (eds) (2000), *Eldorado or Fortress?: Migration in Southern Europe*, Basingstoke: Macmillan.

Kofman, E., Phizacklea, A., Raghuran, P. and Sales, R. (2000), *Gender and International Migration in Europe*, London: Routledge.

Koopmans, R. and Statham, P. (2000), 'Migration and Ethnic Relations as a Field of Political Contention: An Opportunity Structure Approach', in R. Koopmans and P. Statham (eds), *Challenging Immigration and Ethnic Relations Politics*, Oxford: OUP.

Lewis, B. and Ramazanoglu, C. (1999), 'Not Guilty, Not Proud, Just White: Women's Accounts of Their Whiteness', in H. Brown; M. Gilkes and A. Kaloski-Naylor (eds), *White?Women. Critical Perspectives on Race and Gender,* York: Raw Nerve Books.

Lloyd, C. (1998), 'Rendez-vous manqués: feminisms and anti-racisms in France', *Association for the Study of Modern and Contemporary France*, 6, (1): 61–73.

Lutz, H. (1997), 'The Limits of European-ness: Immigrant women in Fortress Europe', *Feminist Review*, 57: 93–111.

MacMaster, N. (1997), *Colonial Migrants and Racism*, Basingstoke: Macmillan.

Macpherson, W. (1999), *The Stephen Lawrence Inquiry*, London: The Stationary Office.

Marshall, B. (2000), *The New Germany and Migration in Europe*, Manchester: Manchester University Press.

Maynard, M. (1994), '"Race", Gender and the Concept of "Difference" in Feminist Thought', in H. Afshar and M. Maynard (eds), *The Dynamics of 'Race' and Gender*, London: Taylor & Francis.

Miles, R. (1993), 'The Articulation of Racism and Nationalism: Reflections on European History', in J. Solomos and J. Wrench (eds), *Racism and Migration in Western Europe*, Oxford: Berg.

Mirza, H. (ed) (1997a), *Black British Feminism*, London: Routledge.

Mirza, H. (1997b), 'Black Women in Education. A Collective Movement for Social Change', in H. Mirza (ed.) *Black British Feminism*, London: Routledge.

Morck, Y. (1998), 'Gender and Generation: Young Muslims in Copenhagen', in S. Vertovec and A. Rogers (eds), *Muslim European Youth*, Aldershot: Ashgate.

Morokvasic, M. (1983), 'Women in Migration: Beyond the Reductionist Outlook', in A. Phizacklea (ed.) *One Way Ticket: Migration and Female Labour*, London: Routledge.

Morokvasic, M. (1991), 'Fortress Europe and Migrant Women', *Feminist Review*, 39: 69–84.

Morokvasic, M. (1995), 'In and Out of the Labour Market: Immigrant and Minority Women in Europe', *New Community*, 19, (3): 459–83.

Parmar, P. (1989), 'Other Kinds of Dreams', *Feminist Review*, 31: 55–65.

Patel, P. (1997), 'Third Wave Feminism and Black Women's Activism', in H. Mirza (ed.), *Black British Feminism*, London: Routledge.

Phizacklea, A. (ed) (1983), *One Way Ticket: Migration and Female Labour*, London: Routledge.

Phoenix, A. (1987), 'Theories of Gender and Black Families', in G. Weiner and M. Arnot (eds), *Gender under Scrutiny*, London: Hutchinson/Open University.

Pilkington, H. (1998), *Migration, Displacement, and Identity in Post-Soviet Russia*, London: Routledge.

Pugliese, E. (1995), 'New International Migrations and the "European Fortress"', in C. Hadjimichalis and D. Sadler (eds), *Europe at the Margins*, Chicester: John Wiley.

Randall, V. (2000), 'British Feminism in the 1990s', in A. Bull, H. Diamond and R. Marsh, (eds), *Feminisms and Women's Movements in Contemporary Europe*, Basingstoke: Macmillan.

Rex, J. (2000), 'Multiculturalism and Political Integration in Europe', in R. Koopmans and P. Statham (eds), *Challenging Immigration and Ethnic Relations Politics*, Oxford: OUP.

Rogers, A. (2000), 'A European Space for Transnationalism?' Transnational Communities Programme Working Paper, WPTC-2K-07.

Rubery, J, Smith, M. and Fagan, C. (1999), *Women's Employment in Europe: Trends and Prospects*, London: Routledge.

Rosenberg, D. (1996), 'Distant Relations. Class, "Race," and National Origin in the German Women's Movement', *Women's Studies International Forum*, 19, (1/2): 145–54.

Samad, Y. (1998), 'Imagining a British Muslim Identification', in S. Vertovec and A. Rogers (eds), *Muslim European Youth*, Aldershot: Ashgate.

Sciortino, G. (2000), *L'ambizione della frontiera. Le politiche di controllo migratorio in Europa*, Milan: FrancoAngeli.

Solomos, J. (1989), *Race and Racism in Contemporary Britain*, Basingstoke: Macmillan.

Truong, T. and Del Rosario, V. (1995), 'Captive Outsiders: the Sex Traffick and Mail-order Brides in the European Union', in J. Wiersma (ed.) *Insiders and Outsiders*, Kampen: Kok Pharos.

Van Dijk, T. A. (1993), 'Denying Racism: Elite Discourse and Racism', in J. Solomos and J. Wrench (eds), *Racism and Migration in Western Europe*, Oxford: Berg.

Vertovec, S. and Rogers, A. (eds) (1998), *Muslim European Youth*, Aldershot: Ashgate.

Vitorino, A. (2000), 'Towards a Common Migration Policy for the European Union', *Migrations, Scenarios for the 21ˢᵗ Century*, International Conference, 12–14 July 2000, Rome, Agenzia romana per la preparazione del giubileo.

Wallace, C. (2001), 'The New Migration Space as a Buffer Zone', in C. Wallace and D. Stola (eds), *Patterns of Migration in Central Europe*, Basingstoke: Palgrave.

Watson, P. (2000), 'Theorizing Feminism in Postcommunism', in A. Bull, H. Diamond and R. Marsh (eds), *Feminisms and Women's Movements in Contemporary Europe*, Basingstoke: Macmillan.

Wekker, G. (1995), '"After the last Sky, Where do the Birds Fly?" What can European Women learn from Anti-Racist Struggles in the United States', in H. Lutz, A. Phoenix and N. Yuval-Davis (eds), *Crossfires. Nationalism, Racism and Gender in Europe*, London: Pluto Press.

Williams, P. J. (1997a), 'The Emperor's New Clothes', The 1997 Reith Lectures, 'The Genealogy of Race . . . Towards a theory of Grace', broadcast on BBC Radio 4, 25 February.

Williams, P. J. (1997b), 'The Pantomime of Race', The 1997 Reith Lectures, 'The Genealogy of Race . . . Towards a theory of Grace', broadcast on BBC Radio 4, 4 March.

Williams, P. J. (1997c), 'The Distribution of Distress', The 1997 Reith Lectures, 'The Genealogy of Race . . . Towards a theory of Grace', broadcast on BBC Radio 4, 11 March.

Williams, P. J. (1997d), 'The War Between the Worlds', The 1997 Reith Lectures, 'The Genealogy of Race . . . Towards a theory of Grace', broadcast on BBC Radio 4, 18 March.

Williams, P. J. (1997e), 'An Ordinary Brilliance: Parting the Waters, Closing the Wounds', The 1997 Reith Lectures, 'The Genealogy of Race . . . Towards a theory of Grace', broadcast on BBC Radio 4, 25 March.

Yuval-Davis, N. (1997), *Gender and Nation*, London: Sage.

Part I
Gender, Ethnicity and Migration

–1–

Gendered Actors in Migration
Annie Phizacklea

The basic question that this chapter seeks to answer is whether conceptually we can move towards a model of migration that avoids casting migrant women as victims of globalizing forces without denying the impact of those same forces on the daily lives of the women in question. As a starting point it is useful to examine what Castles and Miller (1998) argue are the main tendencies that characterize contemporary migratory processes. The first tendency that they refer to is the globalization of migration, the way in which most countries are now affected by migratory movements that are increasingly diverse. The second tendency that they list is the acceleration of migration or the real growth in movements. The third tendency is the differentiation of migration or the way in which many different types of migration are occurring at the same time. The fourth tendency is the increased feminization of migration and the fifth, the growing politicization of migration (Castles and Miller, 1998: 8–9). I would want to add a sixth tendency here, the increased institutionalisation of migration. In what follows we will touch on each of these tendencies from a gendered perspective, though not in the above order.

Globalization: who Benefits?

There are a number of ways in which we can approach the question of globalization. Kevin Robins (1997: 2) has argued that: 'Globalisation is about the dissolution of the old structures and boundaries of national states and communities. It is about the increasing transnationalisation of economic and cultural life, frequently imagined in terms of the creation of a global space and community in which we shall all be global citizens and neighbours.' At an economic level globalization represents the continuation and acceleration of a process that began many centuries ago as Western merchants set out to trade and plunder worldwide. The old colonial division of labour that this gave rise to may have been superseded by the exploits of the transnational company but the beneficiaries are not equally distributed world-wide. Kevin Watkins, senior policy advisor at the British based charity Oxfam notes:

Technological change and the increased flows of trade and investment underpinning globalisation are making the world richer but more unequal. In the mid-1980s, the income ratio of the poorest to richest 5% of the world's population was 1:78. To-day it is 1:123. Average global incomes are rising, but income per person has hardly changed in Africa. Only east Asia has increased its share of global wealth. (*Guardian*, 10 April 2000)

These inequalities have exacerbated the pressures on residents of poor countries to migrate. Much is made of the mobility of cosmopolitan elites and those who possess skills that are in short supply in the affluent world. Far less is said about a major counter-globalization tendency, which is the unwillingness of affluent states to share some of the benefits of globalization with those who just happen to be born at the wrong geographical address. The latter, according to this alternative globalization scenario, must be kept out, or only allowed in to do the jobs that nationals have shunned. Despite an increasing awareness that low birth rates and an increasingly ageing population in affluent countries necessitates some slackening of the stringent immigration controls that govern entry, the increased politicization of migration operates as a powerful counter force to this happening. The political Right throughout the world has always and continues to milk the issue of immigration for every drop it can squeeze out. Feeding on cultural racism, the Right's essentialist and populist charges set liberal forces down a route of demonstrating 'toughness' on issues of immigration. Just as Right-wing politicians and the National Front in Britain in the 1970s shifted the terms of debate to the Right, so did Le Pen's National Front in 1980s France (Lloyd and Walters 1991). Even the rhetoric of Le Pen came to pervade political discourse around immigration and settlement in France, the Pasqua Law of 1986 claiming to be a measure against 'clandestine immigration and imported delinquency' (Lloyd and Walters 1991: 26). This reactionary slide results in, for instance, all asylum seekers being cast as 'phoney' or 'bogus' (as opposed to 'genuine') in popular consciousness and a struggle between nations as to who can appear to be the least attractive to the seekers of asylum (Kaye 1997; Koser 1997). In April 2000 a member of the Liberal Democrat opposition party in the UK lodged a formal complaint with the Commission for Racial Equality condemning both the governing Labour Party and the Conservative opposition for using inflammatory language to whip up hostility to asylum seekers. The Liberal Democrat home affairs spokesman is quoted as saying: 'There is growing concern that the struggle by the Conservative and Labour parties to be seen to be tough on asylum and immigration issues is motivated by short-term party political advantage. We pander to hostility to immigrants at our peril' (*Guardian*, 10 April 2000).

The acceleration and differentiation of migration flows needs to be viewed within the context of what is said above. There is little doubt that in the contemporary phase of global migratory movements that we are witnessing larger numbers of people migrating and a greater differentiation of their 'status'. Countries such as Italy, Spain, the Republic of Ireland, which in the past have been huge exporters of labour, are now labour deficit countries, their economic growth outstripping their ability to 'match people with jobs'. Other regions such as South-East Asia have witnessed a massive increase in internal migrations reflecting regional inequalities in economic growth (Skeldon 1999). The collapse of the old 'communist' bloc has also led to a large East-West exodus, much of which goes unrecorded in official figures, as do the highly organized movements of young trafficked men and women from China to the United States and Europe or Mexico and South American countries to the United States. In 1999 alone, 1,579,010 people were intercepted trying to cross from Mexico into the United States (*Guardian 2*, 17 October 2000). These are the cross-border migrants that hit the media headlines. Far less is written of the increasing numbers of wealthy transnational elites who move smoothly across borders doing business on their way, a topic that has become increasingly 'trendy' amongst academic specialists of migratory processes.[1]

Whether we analyse the media preoccupation with migration or the academic concern, there continues to be (with some notable exceptions) a continuing lack of gender transparency about the substantive and conceptual analysis of past and present migratory processes. In what follows I argue the following: that the 'feminization' of migration is not a recent phenomenon – from the West African slave trade to the neo-liberal retreat from state provision of reproductive services there has always and continues to be a gendered demand for migrant labour; that an often static and essentialist conceptualization of migrant women that reflects the old binaries of 'First' and 'Third' World, 'host society' and 'sending country', ignores changes in gender roles and expectations worldwide; that accounts of contemporary processes of migration and their conceptualization need to ditch the old theoretical divide between structure and agency, only then do gendered actors in the migratory process become active, resourceful agents, not simply victims of a very unequal globalizing world.

How 'New' is the Feminization of Migration?

It is not always clear how the notion of 'feminization' is being used in the literature, most commonly it is used to describe a situation where the actual number of migrants worldwide who are female has rapidly escalated (for instance, Castles and Miller 1998). In other cases the interest is focused on labour migration, as opposed to an aggregated total made up of labour migrants, women entering countries under provisions allowing for family union as well as refugees. While accepting that women constituted 48 per cent of all persons enumerated outside their country of birth at some point during 1970–87, (according to the 1999 edition of SOPEMI, this percentage has remained fairly stable (OECD, 1999)) Zlotnik argues that if we unpack these figures the majority of women who migrate internationally do not do so for work purposes (1995: 229). She goes on to argue that this is especially the case for women migrating legally from developing to developed countries. In contrast, Skrobanek, Boonpakdi and Janthakeroo (1997: 13) argue that in the global flow from South to North 'there are as many women migrants as men'. The question of numbers is fraught for a number of reasons, perhaps most importantly that commentators can only speculate about the numbers of undocumented migrants in the world to-day. As far as contemporary women's labour migration within and from South-East Asia is concerned Lim and Oishi (1996: 87) have this to say:

> The important point concerning the above data is that they refer to legal labour migration and only to that part which is officially recorded as overseas employment migration. They do not cover women who leave a country for reasons other than work (most commonly tourism and education) but in fact end up working at the destination nor women who leave or enter a country illegally, not going through border check points also to work as migrants. When undocumented or illegal flows are also considered, both the numbers and proportions of women are likely to be much higher. For example, illegal Indonesian overseas contract workers are estimated to outnumber their legal counterparts by as many as 7 to 1.

There does appear to be a belated recognition of the importance of women's presence in migration in the mainstream literature, but this recognition has to build on an extant literature which has ostensibly been gender neutral when in fact it has actually been gender blind or simply assumed that women are wives or dependants who are 'following men'. As Skrobanek et al. (1997: 13) argue: 'Independent female migration has escaped accurate documentation: perhaps because women have always appeared less threatening than men to the receiving country.'

These points can be illustrated with reference to migration from Jamaica to the UK prior to the introduction of immigration controls on New Commonwealth migrants in 1962. Davison's analysis of a sample survey carried out in Jamaica in 1961 shows the number of women and men migrating to be equal. He concludes from this that women were 'following' men who had begun to settle down in Britain (Davison 1962: 16). The data reveal a more complex picture: 78 per cent of the women were single (24 per cent classified themselves as living in a stable union) and when asked why they were migrating to Britain, the almost unanimous response was 'to seek employment' (Davison 1962: 36). There was a short time lag in the equalisation of sex ratios in the migration flow from Jamaica to the UK. Foner argues that this may be due to the greater difficulties that women had in raising the considerable funds necessary to pay for their fare (Foner 1979: 57). Certainly, if we look at the economic circumstances of men and women in Jamaica in the 1950s, there is evidence to support this. Access to regular paid employment was even more limited and sporadic for women than it was for men because they were confined to sector's of 'women's work' such as domestic service and small-scale trading, work that rarely allowed women to achieve real financial independence (Smith 1956: 42). Marriage in 1950s Jamaica had a high cultural value but it was assumed that a couple would only enter into marriage when the husband could offer a degree of financial security (the male breadwinner). Any children born into extra-marital relationships were usually incorporated into the mother's household with their grandmother becoming their 'social' mother and their biological mother assuming a parental role that included the provision of financial support for her children. In these circumstances migration offers the opportunity of better job opportunities and the possibility of supporting children left behind through remittances. Brian, Dadzie and Scafe (1985: 32) cite evidence from a 1965 survey of African Caribbean women in the UK which indicated that 85 per cent continued to remit money to financially support families at home. The 1968 Commonwealth Immigrants Act in the UK decreed that where only one parent lived in the UK, dependent children under 18 could only join that parent if he or she could demonstrate that he or she had had 'sole responsibility for the child's upbringing'. Even though legislators knew at the time that this would have a serious impact on women from the Caribbean who had left children at home in the care of their mothers, the rule was introduced and harshly applied by Immigration Appeals Tribunals (Hewitt 1976; Bhabha and Shutter 1994).

This example illustrates a number of points. First is the assumption that women were following men in the migration process. Second is that we need to unpack gender roles in the 'home' country and their social and economic implications if we are to properly analyse the migratory decision-making process. Third, that the regulation of migration is saturated with gendered implications. Moving beyond the Jamaican example we know that throughout Europe regulations permitting the entry of spouses and dependents is only allowed if a sponsor can provide evidence that he or she can support and accommodate them without recourse to 'public funds'. The family thus settles without state support and a 'waiting time' for labour market entry still applies in many European countries. These factors have pushed many 'spouses' into a situation where, whether or not they intended to seek employment, they are forced into seeking some form of 'off the books' paid work out of financial necessity (Phizacklea 1994).

Have we Progressed in Gendering Migration Theory?

To reiterate, most extant accounts of migration have either ignored the gendered dimension or assumed that women simply 'tag' along with husbands or fathers who are the initiators of migratory projects. Thus, although there was some recognition in the 1970s that women were also independent migrants, these accounts often fell into a 'needs of capitalism' trap. I include my own research here, which along with others of the time, subscribed to a political economy of migration approach. That approach basically emphasized the unequal distribution of economic and political power on a global basis and viewed migration as a major mechanism by which capital mobilized cheap labour. Given that capital was mobilizing labour, sometimes in a highly organized way, for instance the guest-worker system in Europe, gendered accounts of migrant labour in the late 1970s and early 1980s reflected this. For instance following the 1966–7 economic recession in what was then West Germany, the new round of recruitment gave preference to women workers (Abadan-Unit 1977). Commentators at the time argued that the 'priority given to female immigrants stemmed from the advantages employers perceived in maintaining large female workforces . . . Employers thus viewed migrant women workers as a reliable source of cheap female labour' (Kudat and Sabancuoglu 1980: 14–15). There is a tendency here to view the gend-ered actor as merely responding to the beck and call of capitalist employers rather than considering the 'bigger' picture, which includes a gendered analysis of the economic, social and political nature of the migrant's home country. None of these spheres are static or unchanging but they may impose certain economic and non-economic pressures as well as opportunities that are gender specific. Individual men and women, in turn, react to these circumstances in very different ways. In the final section of this chapter I will consider some of the explanations that migrant workers themselves give as reasons for migrating.[2] All of the workers in question are what would usually be termed 'independent' migrant workers; they have not migrated under regulations permitting family reunion, few even knew anyone in London. All argue that they migrated for financial reasons and that they responded to opportunities to work abroad, but all of the workers also list other reasons for migration, which are bound up with less obvious 'push' and 'pull' factors. For instance, migration may present itself as the only mechanism for escaping the 'shame' that is heaped on women if they admit to a 'failed' or failing marriage. The structures here are not just the obvious ones such as grinding poverty or structural unemployment. Whatever the reason, we are witnessing a very proactive stance to structural or external constraint by gendered actors in the migratory process.

In an attempt to reinsert agency into the migration theory debate, some have followed Giddens down the structuration route. Anthony Richmond argues: 'Gidden's concept of "structuration", however replaces a static view of social structures as completely external to the individual, with one which emphasises the process by which social structures are created and changed through the exercise of "freedom of action"' (Richmond 1988: 16). Obviously the degree of 'freedom of action' any individual can exercise will be influenced in turn by their access to power and knowledge that are unequally distributed. Nevertheless, Giddens (1984) argues that even the seemingly powerless have the capacity to mobilize and secure 'spaces of control'. This more fluid and dynamic approach to the individual within the migration process is particularly helpful in moving us away from the more mechanical accounts of migration which have often pervaded the literature.

We have seen above how the political economy accounts of the 1970s and early 1980s erred in the direction of giving primacy to structural factors. But if these structuralist political economy accounts of migration erred in the direction of an 'oversocialized' view of migration then they did so in reaction to the neo-classical economic accounts which preceded them and which cast the migrant as a rational decision maker setting off with his or her suitcase to the country best suited to the maximization of their human capital.

The work of Todaro (1969: 1976) is representative of the neo-classical economic approach and can be summed up as a prediction that the volume of transnational migration is significantly related to the real or expected international earnings gap (Massey et al. 1993: 455). Thus at a macro level we are analysing a situation where the 'push' factors determining outward migration are low wages and living standards, and probably structural unemployment, whereas the 'pull' factors are migration destinations which offer employment and higher wages. At a micro level the model assumes that individuals make rational choices about migration, that they weigh up the costs and benefits and will move to the destination that maximizes the net return on migration. Part of this equation will be individual human capital characteristics, such as education and training, which increase the individual's likelihood of gaining employment or higher wages in the migration setting (Borjas 1990). By the early 1980s certain economists moved beyond models of migration predicated on individual rational choice to one where the 'family' was recognized as the effective decision making unit.[3] In the next section of this chapter I will critique these treatments of the family and the household in the migration process. Suffice it to say here that by the early 1980s not only had migration theory fallen into a kind of theoretical impasse between structural accounts and rational decision making accounts – it remained largely gender blind as well.

Some saw the solution to this impasse in the development of migration systems theory.[4] Migration systems theory may be regarded as an improvement in that it 'connects' the different 'levels' of the migratory process but it does not necessarily provide us with an account that is less mechanical. Thus this approach suggests that an understanding of any migratory movement necessitates our incorporation of macro-structural factors with micro-level structures, such as the family, social networks, the huge number of intermediaries now involved in the 'business' of migration and the individual migrant's motivations and understandings. At the macro level we would want to look at the processes of globalization, the free movement of capital, the revolution in communication technologies and the link-ages between sending and receiving societies at a time of increasingly restrictionist attitudes towards the entry of labour, refugees and asylum seekers in states at the 'core'. These macro factors will influence and interact with intermediary instit-utions such as informal social networks and more institutionalized agents such as recruiters, brokers and 'fixers'. They in turn interact with households and the individuals who make up that household.

Others simply turned to the intermediary institutions themselves. Writing in 1989, Monica Boyd argued that 'current migration patterns and new concept-ualisations of migration underlie more recent interest in the role of family, friendship and community based networks' (Boyd 1989: 641). We will consider in some detail this level of analysis because it has become one of the most fruitful areas for the development of genuinely gendered analysis in the migration literature.

Happy Families and Other Myths

Thus, during the 1980s, the study of migration began to shift attention to the role of intermediary institutions in the migratory process, particularly the role of house-holds and social networks. Initially these accounts simply shifted the household into a position of effective decision making unit rather than the individual (see Stark 1984; 1999).

Certainly households are an important unit of analysis in mediating between individual migrants and the larger structural context but we also need an analytical shift that recognizes that households are deeply implicated in gendered ideologies and practices. That recognition is missing in accounts such as Stark's. Rather it is assumed that households represent shared income, resources and goals and that household-wide decisions are made about migration (see for instance Wood 1982; Selby and Murphy 1982).

Empirical work carried out from a gendered perspective during the 1980s and early 1990s explored decision making within households regarding migration and pointed to the hollowness of the assumption that households make collective decisions. In her research on Mexican migration, Hondagneu-Sotelo shows that men who migrated ahead of wives and children did so quite autonomously with little regard for the rest of the family's views on this decision. Rather than the women who were left behind viewing this decision as based on a recognition of family need, they were in fact fearful that they might be abandoned altogether. As male remittances rarely met household consumption expenditure in Mexico, many women effectively became sole heads of households. The result was an increased desire by women to move north in order that husbands resume at least partial social and economic responsibility for family welfare. Hondagneu-Sotelo (1995: 95) concludes; 'Opening the household "black box" exposes a highly charged political arena where husbands and wives and parents and children may simultaneously express and pursue divergent interests and competing agendas'. Hondagneu-Sotelo's detailed research on Mexican families indicates clearly that households are not the cosy rational decision-making units that some accounts would lead us to believe. It is possible that the number of households who sit down around the kitchen table and discuss in a rational way who it is that will make the most money if they migrate, is very small indeed. Goss and Lindquist (1995: 328) have pointed out that this conception of the household is:

> unlikely to be applied uncritically to Western societies and is consistent with the ideological tendency in social sciences to romanticise peasant and community in the Third World. Somehow, members of Third World households, not burdened by the individualism of Western societies, resolve to cooperate willingly and completely, each according to their capacities, to collectively lift the burden of their poverty.

What is interesting is that the type of research carried out by Hondagneu-Sotelo, which opens the household 'black box' to reveal a can of worms, is criticized along the following lines: 'A cautionary note must be introduced here about analyses that concentrate exclusively on the individual motivations of household members and the conflict of interests between them. This has often become the centre of gender-focused research' (Portes 1997: 816). Portes goes on to warn against: 'making respondents' definitions of the situation the ultimate test for theoretical propositions' (Portes 1997: 816). Portes does not make reference to the reason why a growing number of scholars have been keen to give women a voice, a voice that was never heard before and which is often at odds with the overriding assumption in much of the literature, that women simply follow men in an uncomplicated way in the migration process and who belong to benign households where both power and resources are equally distributed.

Thus some of the more recent gendered accounts acknowledge for instance that: 'The household, as we conceive it, has its own political economy, in which access to power and other valued resources is distributed along gender and generational lines' (Grasmuck and Pessar 1991: 202). It is important that we think about the household in these ways rather than the conventional, one-dimensional view of wives entering under regulations permitting family reunion and the subsequent reconstitution of households in the migration setting. The latter is important, but it is only one way in which we can consider households in the migration process. In short, the 'household' is a crucial concept in any account of migration but in very diverse ways and it is only one piece in a very complex jigsaw. For instance, the household cannot be analysed in isolation from other intermediaries such as social networks and other migrant institutions that support transnational migration (Boyd 1989; Hondagneu-Sotelo 1995).

The role of social networks are also central to Hondagneu-Sotelo's (1994: 96) analysis of Mexican migration where she concludes that: 'Traditionally, gender relations in the networks have facilitated men's and constrained women's migration, but this is changing. While patriarchal practices and rules in families and social networks have persisted, through migration women and men reinterpret normative standards and creatively manipulate the rules of gender.' Others have commented on the fact that women have less access than men to the social networks that facilitate migration and that if we are to explain the huge growth of female migration within and from South-East Asia in the last decade we must look elsewhere.

Goss and Lindquist (1995: 335) argue that 'the key component of recent large-scale international migration, largely neglected in the literature, is the complex of international and national institutions that transcend the boundaries of states and locales, linking employers in the developed or rapidly developing economies with individuals in the furthest peripheries of the Third World.' These intermediaries are the employment agencies, the fixers, the brokers and the traffickers who increasingly dominate the migration 'business'; they are central to the way in which migration has become institutionalized from the state down in many countries. For instance nine out of ten foreign placements for Asian workers are handled by recruiters in some form or another. Fieldwork conducted by Goss and Lindquist (1995: 340) in provincial Malinaw, the Philippines, indicates that: 'although 18 per cent of returning migrants claim to have obtained overseas employment without employing brokers, none managed without at least informal assistance of this nature'. Skeldon (1999: 10) cites a study conducted in 1991 that reports that two-thirds of domestic workers in Hong Kong had been hired though a recruitment agency.

Goss and Lindquist (1995: 345) label the complex of intermediaries as 'migrant institutions' and use structuration theory as a way of analysing the interplay between them and the individual: 'Individuals act strategically within the institution to further their interests, but the capacity for such action is differentially distributed according to knowledge or rules and access to resources, which in turn may be partially determined by their position within other social institutions.' They go on to argue that the more institutionalized migration becomes the more fraudulent and corrupt the system becomes. Despite this individuals still seek employment abroad. The authors conclude that: 'Of course this is an indication of relative deprivation in the country but it is also the result of the selective flow of information through the migrant institution. Institutional agents control knowledge about the risks and disappointments of international migration, but it is obviously in their interest to hide these and to promote the advantages of overseas labour' (p. 344).

Elsewhere I have analysed in some depth the role these institutions play in two global industries, the sex industry and the maid's industry (Westwood and Phizacklea 2000). Suffice it to say here that we cannot explain the growth in the feminization of migration, nor the acceleration and differentiation of contemporary migratory movements without reference to this institutionalisation. For instance women may have less access than men to the social networks that facilitate chain migration and employment opportunities, though in the Mexican case Hondagneu-Sotelo argues that this is changing (Hondagneu-Sotelo 1995: 96).

Packing my Bags

In this final section I want to illustrate in the words of women migrant workers themselves the major points of critique that we have touched on in this chapter. We have suggested that the political economy accounts of the 1970s erred in the direction of an oversocialized view of migration. While there is not the space here to discuss yet another theoretical development in the field, transnationalism (basically the way in which migrants forge and sustain complex social, economic and cultural relations between 'home' and the migration setting) it is useful to quote the views of Roberts et al. in explaining its emergence. They argue that this development emerged in large part as a critique of:

> overly structural approaches, and attempted to introduce the actor back into theoretical migration discussions. Countering a tendency to see migration as created by the push and pull of economic factors with migrants conceived as mainly as passive subjects, coerced by states and marginalised by markets, work on transnational migration attempts to impute migrants with decision-making capabilities influencing their outcomes. (Roberts 1999: 253)

This criticism echoes the standpoint of virtually all currently working in the field of migration who are keen to restore a more dynamic, pro-active view of migration.

I have also pointed to some of the problems encountered at an intermediate level of analysis if we fail to unpack institutions such as the household in a gendered way. Finally I have drawn attention to the role that other intermediaries play in the migration process, which has led to the increased institutionalisation of migration, to its differentiation and feminization. In what follows I illustrate some of these points with a few quotations from in-depth interviews carried out with migrant domestic workers in London:

> I left school at sixteen and went to live with my aunt who was working in the Bataan Free Trade Zone. I joined her working in a clothing factory, thousands of people worked

there making clothes for US firms. It was very long hours, but it was sociable, there were other people from my village and the surrounding area. I worked there for three years it wasn't bad, the pay wasn't brilliant, but that's what everyone got and it was better than nothing, there was no work at home. But it was very monotonous as I only sewed one piece of the garment. Then a friend suggested that I went to the agency with him in Manila to find work abroad. My mother didn't want me to go, my supervisor in the factory didn't want me to go, but I borrowed money from my grandmother to buy the plane ticket. I used to send all my money home when I worked in the factory. I knew nothing about Kuwait and I was apprehensive, but I still wanted to go. In Kuwait there were three other Filipinas in the house so that helped with adjustment a lot. (Filipina, in London since 1989, now married with one son)

I left school at fifteen and I worked as a domestic worker before I got married. My husband had no work, he beat me, he's no use, he drinks. A friend found a family who needed a domestic and I came with them to England. I did discuss it with my parents and sister, I just wanted to contribute financially and my employers paid for the ticket. (Indian, 12 years in London, two children in India cared for by sister)

My husband was a truck driver and a womanizer, he contributed little to the family and I decided that I'd be better off on my own, if I went to work abroad I could support my children. My mother-in-law lived close by and cousins as well, my mother in law was prepared to take responsibility for the care of the children. I attended high school until I was fourteen years of age.

Having made up my mind to leave I went to an employment agency which was used by many others to find work in the Gulf. I had to pay 500,000 rupees to the agency to arrange the job and I sold my sewing machine to help finance my trip, I financed my trip myself. My youngest child was only six months old when I left for Saudi Arabia. The agency insisted that my husband signed a document saying that he was prepared for me to go abroad but he was more than happy to do that because my leaving gave him even greater freedom. My main reason for leaving to work abroad was financial, I could provide my children with better opportunities but I also knew that I was better off alone, so the decision was for me as well as the children. My mother did not want me to go but my mother-in-law had agreed to take responsibility for the children.

I went to work for a Prince in Saudi Arabia and I looked after the children from birth. It hurt me so much that as they grew up they showed me no respect, they even spat at me. (Indonesian, left thirteen years ago, two years in London, two children in Indonesia)

Thus, relieving poverty at home, building a better future for their children and escaping from unsatisfactory marriages are just some of the motivational factors for migrating. The key role that employment agencies play is significant amongst the workers from Asia and underlines the extent to which migration has become a business.

Most of the domestic workers interviewed in London fitted the classic model of the 'target' worker when they left their home country. The idea is to make as much money as possible to send home and to return home eventually. However, migratory projects are often not that simple. Those workers who left failing marriages know that their future is uncertain and, not surprisingly they talk only of being able to go and visit home for holidays. Others meet new partners, have children and their financial links with the 'family at home' begin to be eroded. Few of them fit cosily into the classic household strategy of migration model, which assumes that households make rational decisions about who should migrate in order to maximize household returns. Most informed other members of households of their plans only after detailed arrangements had been made, (usually through a recruitment agency for work in the Gulf States if they come from Asia) because, for a range of reasons, they knew there was no alternative but to migrate. Bringing a better life to their families is pre-eminent, sending home money to their families is their priority, but their own aspirations for the future are not just a better paying, legal job but the prospect of moving out of domestic work altogether.

Conclusion

In this chapter I have critiqued the gender blindness of much extant literature in the field of migration. I have focused attention on the role of those institutions and practices that link migrants and non-migrants across space and time and looked critically at the way in which the household is reified in many accounts of migration. A gendered 'unpacking' of the household allows us to retain it as a central unit in the migration process without its reification. In addition, while social networks may be critical for an understanding of some migrations they play a less central role for women in certain parts of the world, for instance Asia, where migration has become institutionalized from the state down. While there is a history of migration within and from Asia there is now considerable evidence to show that, for women at least, intermediaries such as employment agencies and brokers may be of more critical significance in facilitating, even institutionalizing transnational migration. Finally, at the risk of falling foul of Portes' (1997) 'cautionary' note, we can learn from migrant women workers' own accounts about the complexity of the migration process and their own efforts to 'better' themselves and their families.

Notes

1. See special issue of the journal *Ethnic and Racial Studies*, 1999, 22 (2).
2. This research is part of the ESRC Transnational Communities Initiative. Eighty migrant domestic workers in London who were undergoing a process of

regularization of their visa status were interviewed in 1998–9. The author wishes to acknowledge the financial support of the ESRC for this research.
3. Stark's (1984) work is an example of this. See also his Morgenstein Memorial Lectures, 1999.
4. See Castles and Miller (1998) for a summary of this approach and literature.

Bibliography

Abadan-Unat, N. (1977), 'Implications of Migration on Emancipation and Pseudo-Emancipation of Turkish women', *International Migration Review*, 1: 31–57.

Bhaba, J. and Shutter, S. (1994), *Women's Movement: Women under Immigration, Nationality and Refugee Law*, London: Trentham Books.

Borjas, G. (1990), *Friends or Strangers: The Impact of Immigrants on the US Economy*, New York: Basic Books.

Boyd, M. (1989), 'Family and Personal Networks in International Migration: Recent Developments and New Agendas', *International Migration Review*, 3: 638–70.

Brian, B., Dadzie, S. and Scafe, S. (1985), *The Heart of the Race*, London, Virago.

Castles, S. and Miller, M. (1998), *The Age of Migration*, Basingstoke: Macmillan.

Davison, B. (1962), *West Indian Migrants*, Oxford: Oxford University Press.

Foner, N. (1979), *Jamaica Farewell*, London: Routledge.

Giddens, A. (1984), *The Constitution of Society*, Cambridge, Polity Press.

Goss, J. and Lindquist, B. (1995), 'Conceptualising International Migration: A Structuration Perspective', *International Migration Review,* 2: 317–51.

Grasmuck, S. and Pessar, P. (1991), *Between Two Islands: Dominican International Migration*, California: University of California Press.

Hewitt, P. (1976), 'Women's Rights in Law and Practice', *New Community,* Vol.V, Vol.1–2

Hondagneu-Sotelo, P. (1994), *Gendered Transitions*, California: University of California Press.

Kaye, R. (1997), 'Redefining the Refugee: The UK Media Portrayal of Asylum Seekers' in Koser, K. and Lutz, H (eds) *The New Migration in Europe*, Basingstoke, Macmillan.

Koser, K. (1997), 'Out of the Frying Pan and Into the Fire: A case study of illegality amongst asylum seekers', in Koser, K and Lutz, H. (eds) *The New Migration in Europe*, Basingstoke, Macmillan.

Kudat, A. and Sabuncuoglu, M. (1980), 'The Changing Composition of Europe's Guestworker Population', *Monthly Labour Review*, 103, (10): 10–17.

Lim, L.L and Oishi, N. (1996), 'International Labour Migration of Asian Women: Distinctive Characteristics and Policy Concerns', *Asian and Pacific Migration Journal*, 5, (1): 85–116.

Lloyd, C. and Waters, H. (1991), 'France: One Culture and One People?' *Race and Class*, 32, (3): 49–66.

Massey, D., Arango, J., Hugo, g., Kouaci, A., Pelligrino, A. and Taylor, E. (1993), 'Theories of International Migration: A Review and Appraisal', *Population and Development Review*, 19, (3): 432–66.

OECD (Organisation for Economic Cooperation and Development) (1999), *SOPEMI, Trends in International Migration*, Paris: OECD.

Phizacklea, A. (1994), 'A Single or Segregated Market?' in Afshar, H. and Maynard, M (eds) *The Dynamics of 'Race' and Gender*, London: Taylor & Francis.

Portes, A. (1997), 'Immigration Theory for a New Century: Some Problems and Opportunities', *International Migration Review*, 31, (4): 799–825.

Richmond, A. (1988), 'Sociological Theories of International Migration: The Case of Refugees', *Current Sociology*, 36, (2): 7–25.

Roberts, B., Frank, R. and Lozano-Ascensio, F. (1999), 'Transnational Migrant Communities and Mexican Migration to the US', *Ethnic and Racial Studies*, 22, (2): 238–66.

Robins, K. (1997), 'What is Globalisation?', *Sociology Review*, 16, (3): 2–9.

Selby, H. and Murphy, A. (1982), *The Mexican Urban Household and the Decision to Migrate to the US*, ISHI Occasional Papers in Social Change, No.4, Philadelphia: Institute for the Study of Human Issues.

Skeldon, R. (1999), *Migration of Women in the Context of Globalisation in the Asian and Pacific Region*, Women in Development Discussion Paper Series No. 2, Social Development Division of the ESCAP Secretariat, United Nations.

Skrobanek, S., Boonpakdi, N. and Janthakeero, C. (1997), *The Traffic in Women*, London: Zed Books.

Smith, R.T. (1956), *The Negro Family in Guiana*, London: Routledge.

Stark, O. (1984), 'Migration Decision-making: A Review Article', *Journal of Development Economics*, 14: 251–9.

Stark, O. (1999), *Altruism and Beyond*, Cambridge: Cambridge University Press.

Todaro, M. (1969), 'A Model of Labour Migration and Urban Unemployment in Less Developed Countries', *American Economic Review*, 59: 138–48.

Todaro, M. (1976), *Internal Migration in Developing Countries*, Geneva: ILO.

Westwood, S. and Phizacklea, A. (2000), *Trans-Nationalism and the Politics of Belonging*, London: Routledge.

Wood, C.H. (1982), 'Equilibrium and Historical Structural Perspectives on Migration', *International Migration Review*, 16, (2): 298–319.

Zlotnik, H. (1995), 'The South-to-North Migration of Women', *International Migration Review*, 1: 229–54.

2

Hierarchy and Interdependence: The Emergence of a Service Caste in Europe
Jacqueline Andall

Domestic service is generally viewed as a pre-modern employment sector. Its continued presence in twenty-first century Europe is thus both intriguing and perplexing. The current demand for domestic workers in Europe should not, however, simply be considered as a continuation of the past. Rather, the new structural permutations of the sector warrant further investigation. In some European countries one can detect a certain ambivalence regarding the employment of domestic workers. This is largely because old-fashioned 'domestic service' is perceived as historically centred in a pre-modern time marked by feudal relations and unfree bonded labour (Coser 1973). At the same time, the demise of the European welfare state (Cochrane 1993), combined with changing patterns of family organization within Europe, encourages both governments and individuals to consider domestic workers as both useful and necessary. How are we to explain the resurgence of paid domestic work in Europe and what can this tell us about gender relations in European countries and class and ethnic stratification within the broad category of gender? European societies organize social reproduction in a variety of ways – unpaid reproductive labour, paid labour within the home and paid labour external to the home. Why is paid domestic work an attractive option to European families and is this leading to the emergence of a 'service caste' in Europe? [1]

One of the problems implicit within any study of domestic work relates to the impossibility of ascertaining the extent of such work. Domestic work is intrinsically a 'hidden affair', executed within the privacy of the employers' home. The invisibility of paid domestic workers can be likened to the invisibility of unpaid housework performed by women (Oakley 1974) but reproductive labour tasks are not attributed on the basis of gender alone (Glenn 1992). In other words, women's relationship to domestic work is not universal. Rather, reproductive labour must be understood as divided along gender, ethnic and class lines. It is this internal differentiation within the category of gender, and the competing tensions that it engenders, which account for the inscription of 'hierarchy and interdependence' (Glenn 1992: 3) within the domestic work relationship. In this chapter, I shall be arguing for more explicit recognition of new trends within an old employment sphere, which takes into account organizational distinctions between live-in and live-out work, and relates these distinctions to ethnicity and racialization processes. I also want to refute Momsen's (1999: 14) assertion that domestic work for contemporary migrants in Europe is 'work for a short period in a foreign country'.[2] In fact, it is the long-term, rather than the earlier short-term nature of live-in domestic work that needs to be highlighted as an important new trend. To my mind, this transformation is problematic for female employers and employees alike and raises difficult issues regarding the legal regulation of the sector.

The Domestic Work Sector

Domestic work covers a multitude of household tasks. These include cleaning, shopping, cooking, serving food, caring for children, the elderly and the infirm. Domestic workers can be employed to cover one, several or all of these tasks. The usage that European countries may make of domestic workers can differ. In Britain, for example, both academic research and the media have recently highlighted a resurgence in domestic work. Part-time cleaning, nannies, live-in au pairs and mother's helps are the main forms of domestic work activity in Britain (Cox 1999). Academic research has emphasized the new needs of the British middle classes, which include their desire for quality leisure time. Gregson and Lowe (1994), for example, indicated a growing trend by dual income professional couples with young children to employ nannies and cleaners. The British Media has similarly addressed the rise of the 'new servant class'.[3] Writing in the *Guardian*, Henry Porter suggested that domestic service did not necessarily facilitate leisure but rather enabled the middle classes to work longer hours. His emphasis in fact underscores his subsequent pronouncement regarding middle-class employers' liberal attachment to the idea that 'it is old-fashioned or somehow unacceptable to use people in your home as servants' (*Guardian*, 30 May 1996: 2). In other words, middle class employers may feel uncomfortable and ambiguous about employing 'help' in Britain, but their doing so can be rationalized more easily if it is seen as relating to their working commitments rather than to their leisure.

Other European countries have a less ambiguous relationship to the employment of domestic workers. This can be partially attributed to the different historical development of the sector in various countries. The traditional coterie of servants that had existed in Britain had virtually disappeared by the end of the Second World War (McBride 1976). Conversely, in some Southern European contexts, the domestic work sector maintained its traditional organizational form as live-in labour into the post-war period. Thus, when migrant women entered the sector in the Southern European countries, the existing structural conditions of the sector remained intact. In this way, for example, live-in domestic service constitutes a labour market *niche* for female migrants (Escrivà 2000; Ribas-Mateos 2000; Solé, this volume). This is in contrast to the British context, where a break in the traditional form of domestic service – despite attempts to retain it through refugee and labour migration[4] – partially explains why its resurgence is occurring in a reformulated fashion. Southern European countries have consequently all preserved a form of domestic work that closely approximates the historical image of the live-in servant. Nevertheless, as the European report on domestic work has clearly demonstrated, Northern European countries are similarly implicated in the growth of this type of domestic work (Anderson and Phizacklea 1997).

A number of structural features have normally been associated with the domestic work sector. These include: migration, the economic system, the gender dimension and domestic work as a transitory employment sector. All of these features can be found within a broad range of historical examples of domestic work, from pre-industrial European societies (see Fauve-Chamois 1998) to twentieth century North America (Katzman 1978). Variations within these traditional structural features of domestic work shed light on the emergence of a new service caste in Europe.

Domestic Work Relationships: Ethnicity and Class

The tendency to obscure differentiation within the domestic work sector has particular implications for the visibility of class and ethnicity issues. The various permutations of paid domestic work entail a range of structural conditions specific to the domestic task undertaken. Thus, the organization of part-time cleaning, live-in domestic work and nannying may involve certain commonalities but these different sectors are equally distinguished by their own internal modes of operation. Furthermore, the workers who execute these differentiated domestic tasks may also be different.[5] In their research on the increase in the employment of nannies and cleaners in contemporary Britain, Gregson and Lowe (1994) found not only two quite different typologies of employees, but also diverse ideologies underpinning the employment of domestic workers. In relation to nannying, they found that it was 'the ideological construction of childcare as something which should be home-based, child-centred and performed by the child's natural mother' that was the main push for a nanny-form of childcare provision in 1980s Britain (Gregson and Lowe 1994: 180). The nannies employed by the new middle classes of the 1980s and 1990s, particularly outside London, were young, unmarried, from 'white-collar, intermediate status households' (p. 124) and did not live in. Cleaners, on the other hand, were more consistently married, older and from working-class backgrounds. [6]

In most contexts, ethnicity or the negative racialization of specific groups has additionally constituted an integral feature of the domestic work sector. In 1930s Britain, for example, the limited local employment available to women in depressed areas such as Wales meant that domestic service in London was frequently the only option available to them. However, the Welsh were negatively racialized and stereotyped as dirty and breeding like rabbits (Glucksmann 1991). This connection between depressed economic regions, migration and domestic service is an enduring one if we consider contemporary examples of domestic work. Nevertheless, the migration of African and Asian female migrants from depressed economic regions to Europe presents a slightly modified framework. In these cases, a visible racialized differentiation and, more significantly, often an absence of citizenship rights, has perpetuated, if not exacerbated the already poor working conditions of live-in domestic workers. This is partly because some employers exploit the weakened bargaining position of undocumented migrants (see Chang 1994).[7]

Research demonstrates that employers construct and adhere to racialized hierarchies of employees (Andall 2000a; Anderson and Phizacklea 1997; De Filippo 2001). This can affect a worker's pay, working conditions and general treatment. It can mean that women belonging to a particular ethnicity, often regardless of other factors, such as education, will be predominantly employed to do cleaning, whereas a different ethnic group will be employed more readily to care for children or the elderly. One area of racialized difference concerns the distinction between au pairs, nannies and domestic workers. According to Enloe's (1989: 180) model, located at the apex of the hierarchy are 'professional nannies, usually white . . . [with] formal qualifications and organizational support'. A second tier is inhabited by young female au pairs, also normally white. Au pairs generally seek employment for a limited period of time, in some cases prior to university. Finally, one finds the domestic workers, 'women of color from less privileged communities within their employers' country or from abroad' (p. 180). Clearly employment as a live-in au pair for one year is quite different to live-in employment as a domestic worker for many years. Significantly, au pairs are generally young women with no formal training in child-care, however, they continue to be hierarchically positioned above domestic workers who are associated with the historical stigma of emanating from the uneducated working classes. In point of fact, within some ethnic groups currently working in Europe as domestic workers, educational attainment levels can be high (Ribas-Mateos 2000). Nevertheless, this does not necessarily reposition them within the hierarchy, indicating the importance of racialization processes in structuring the domestic work relationship.

Historically, where women from a range of ethnicities have been employed in domestic service, ethnicity has been a significant factor, suggesting that wider considerations relating to discrimination and exclusion are important. Thus, at the turn of the twentieth century in the United States, domestic work frequently functioned as an interlude prior to a late marriage for European women migrants. For African-Americans, on the other hand, it represented a more permanent occupational status (Gross 1991). Furthermore, unlike second-generation European-Americans who were able to move into white collar sectors, second-generation Japanese-American women were still largely concentrated in the domestic work sector (Glenn 1990).[8] Writers commentating on the contemporary Canadian situation have demonstrated the significance of ethnicity and stereotyping for influencing both migratory trends and the placing of domestic workers (Baken and Stasiulis 1995; Stiell and England 2000). In Britain, the nationality of the potential employee was cited by recruitment agencies as the 'most important consideration' (Cox 1999: 141). Racialization processes are not simply related to colour but also to other issues such as perceived proximity of culture and religion. In the Greek case for example, Catholic Filipina domestic workers are privileged over Muslim Albanian domestic workers (Lazaridis 2000). These examples suggest that in order to investigate the changes to the demand and supply of paid domestic work in Europe fully, it is important that ethnicity is incorporated more fully into analyses of the sector. In several European countries a wide range of different ethnicities are currently employed as domestic workers (see Friese 1995; Anderson and Phizacklea 1997; Anthias and Lazaridis 2000). What differences might we expect to find amongst East European, African, Asian or South American domestic workers? Will domestic work constitute a temporary interlude for some of these women or will it emerge as a transgenerational permanent occupational niche for specific groups?

Woman to Woman: Female Strategies for which Women?

Contemporary perspectives on domestic work have been influenced by a range of different literatures, including feminist theorization on unpaid domestic work, the literature on ethnic diversity and class analyses of labour. The issue of paid housework and unpaid housework have, however, tended to develop their own separate literatures, leading also to a separation of the principal protagonists of these literatures – white middle-class women and black, migrant or working-class women (Glenn 1992). Unpaid household labour and domestic service are in fact closely linked and efforts need to be made to connect these literatures more closely. Moreover, the current nature of migratory trends to Europe also means that class differences between women overlap, in that middle-class female migrants from the developing world are to be found in working-class occupations in Europe.[9]

Domestic work has historically been constructed as a relationship between women but it is important not to lose sight of the wider patriarchal framework that structures this relationship. Nevertheless, in a number of instances, the demand for and employment of domestic workers has been used to demarcate boundaries of womanhood and femininity. Moving beyond status boundary demarcators, however, changes in women's lives have undoubtedly affected the characteristics of domestic work. In relation to contemporary Europe, it is middle-class women's desire to combine family work and employment that stands at the core of trans-formations within the domestic work sector. The different welfare and employment regimes operative throughout Europe condition the choices employed women make in relation to family work (Rubery et al. 1999; Garcia-Ramon and Monk 1996). Hantrais and Letablier (1996) have identified three broad models for Europe. The first model allows for the juxtaposition of family and employment via state support. This can either be premised on objectives of equality (Denmark, Sweden) or to support the well-being of the family (France, Belgium). The second group exhibits a sequential ordering of work and the family. Within this model states are supportive of the family as an important social institution but the care of young children is deemed to be the duty of families, but particularly mothers. States categorized under this model (Austria, Germany, Luxembourg, Netherlands and Italy) tend to adopt a redistributive approach whereby the mother normally reduces employment to care for children. The final group consists of those states that have very low levels of state intervention to assist parents in combining employment with family life. Countries placed in this category were either ideo-logically opposed to state intervention, viewing the family-employment relation-ship as a matter for individuals to resolve (Britain, Ireland) or may have been committed to supporting women's involvement in paid employment but were not in a financial position to do so (Portugal, Spain and Greece). Models such as these however, are never water-tight categories and there are differences in the way other scholars group or categorize specific countries.[10] Indeed, as García-Ramon and Monk (1996) have noted in their comparison of women in the European Union, a major problem of such comparative research is the lack of entirely comparable data. It is therefore important to consider individual countries in depth.

In the following section, I will look specifically at the Italian case. It can be broadly asserted that, in the Southern European states, it is the family or community networks that provide the most support for women seeking to reconcile family and employment obligations, but there are still considerable differences between these countries. A number of factors indicate that Italy is indeed a very useful case to study. Firstly, from a high birth rate in the early postwar period, it now has one of the lowest birth rates in the world (Livi-Bacci 2001). Secondly, one of the most significant features of the Italian labour market since the 1970s has been its femin-ization, in terms of both demand and supply (De Luca and Bruni 1993). Thirdly, from the 1970s onwards, there was a very direct correlation between changes in Italian women's employment and the commencement of single sex female migration from Africa and Asia to Italy exclusively for the live-in domestic sphere (Andall 2000a). These three factors are not only interlinked but they also exemplify the hierarchy and interdependence that inscribe existing private employment relationships between different strata of women in Italy and, to different degrees, in Europe.

The Italian Case: The New Employers

It is in relation to a 'Mediterranean welfare regime model' (Trifiletti 1999: 76) that most Italian scholars interpret the presence of migrant women in the domestic work sphere in Italy (Ambrosini 1999; De Filippo 2001; Caritas 2001; Reyneri 2001).[11] This perspective is also echoed by one of the main Italian trade-union union bodies (Meschieri 2000). The argument is that the use of migrant domestic workers in Italy is a consequence both of Italian women's increased presence on the labour market and the absence of an Italian welfare model to accommodate this fact by the universal provision of state support services. A book presenting a global overview of domestic workers went so far as to suggest that, in Europe, 'migrant women domestic workers . . . are thought to be more prevalent in Italy than in other countries' (Momsen 1999: 7).

Italian women's labour market presence has frequently been described as atypical in comparison to women in other European countries. This is mainly because of their lower employment rates. In 1996, for example, the Italian employment rate for women was 36.1 per cent against a European Union average of 50.2 per cent (Rubery et al. 1999). The Italian situation is also seen to be atypical because of the comparatively low number of female part-time workers, 6.2 per cent in 1994 (Del Boca 1998). In addition, the existence of protective policies only for secure jobs leads to Italy being located within a 'difficult participation' model (Trifiletti 1999: 81). Official data on women's employment in Italy however masks the extent of the informal economy, estimated as between 20 per cent and 30 per cent of GDP (Del Boca 1998). Moreover, diffused forms of economic production lead to 'atypical' employment for Italian women, such as small family businesses or in the informal labour market (Vaiou 1996).

Nevertheless, Italian women's greater presence on the labour market runs parallel to the existence of strong kinship ties in Italy. A range of factors, including, residential proximity, the length at which young people co-reside with their parents, the frequency of face to face interaction among family members suggest that in comparison with most other Western European countries 'the strength of kin relations in Italy is greater than elsewhere' (Barbagli 1997: 34). Italy's population is also ageing at a faster rate than the European Union average and is moreover, particularly marked in specific regions (Golini, cited in Barbagli 1997). Set against a backdrop of reciprocal family obligations, this raises an important issue of care for Italy's elderly population. Research in Bologna showed a reduction in the number of elderly people living in extended families between 1981 and 1991. However, the fact that there had been no parallel rise in the number of elderly people living in institutions suggests that Italian families, including groups of siblings, rather than following strategies adopted in some other European Union countries, may prefer to employ a (migrant) domestic worker to live in with elderly relatives. In the 1996 employment contract for the sector, provision was made for a new type of domestic worker whose job it was to 'be present' at night (from 9.00 pm to 8.00 am) (Il Sole 24 Ore). It is probable that such employees will be increasingly used by Italian families to care for elderly relatives.

In the 1980s, the sociologist Dalla Costa (1988: 28) suggested that while Italian women sought paid employment outside the home, if there were no available female relatives prepared to perform domestic labour on their behalf, Italian women would be reluctant to use 'a good part' of their wage paying 'a coloured [sic] or white domestic help'. As a consequence, she argued, some of these women chose to reject marriage and maternity. Del Re (2000) has echoed this argument by attributing the extremely low fertility rate in Italy to Italian women's desire to be present on the labour market. Other studies note that the past Italian practice of withdrawing from the labour market after motherhood (Balbo and May 1975) has been replaced by a withdrawal from motherhood in order to be present on the labour market (Trifiletti 1999). The high percentage of grandmothers who perform child-care duties for their working daughters should be noted.[12] Implicitly supporting Dalla Costa's contention, Ambrosini (2000) has argued that given that the costs of employing a domestic worker legally can be as much as the average salary of an Italian woman, this problem is circumvented by employing migrant women illegally at less than half the 'legal' rate. These arguments suggest that there is still some way to go for Italian women to achieve greater balance between their productive and reproductive roles. However, *which* Italian women are able to achieve greater balance through the use of paid domestic labour remains an important question.

The increase in women's supply on the Italian labour market is not in dispute. Nonetheless, the high correlation in Italy between women's increased presence on the labour market and an advanced educational level (De Luca and Bruni 1993) needs more emphasis. This suggests that Italian women with low educational levels not only find it difficult to find work in the formal sector but are also unlikely to be financially able to employ domestic workers. Dalla Costa's (1988) argument that maternity was becoming a luxury for women with high levels of income continues to be of some relevance for the debate on domestic work.

Ultimately, it is only families located within higher income groups who have access to this particular strategy of family care (Vaiou 1996). To reiterate, the use of migrant domestic workers as one strategy for reconciling paid employment with reproductive labour is of benefit for a particular class of women. Women from less privileged backgrounds, who nonetheless need to reconcile the same family and child-care needs, are reliant on family members and the future development of accessible social infrastructures by governments. Such a perspective belies the 'need versus luxury' argument commonly found in debates about migrant domestic workers in Europe. It could be argued that there is a 'need' for migrant domestic workers, given the absence of alternative options, but it is simultaneously a luxury for employers and should be recognized as such. Furthermore, the acceptance of live-in domestic workers as an ideal solution to a general lack of welfare infrastructure may harm the development of different, universal and accessible solutions for a wider range of women.

Migrant Women as Domestic Workers in Italy

The presence of migrant women in Italy has entailed some modification to the domestic work sphere. Numerical quantification, however, remains difficult, as statistical information about women legally employed in this sphere fails to give an accurate picture of the real situation, given that irregular employment is an intrinsic feature of the domestic work sector. Indeed, it has been estimated that one in four of migrant domestic workers are employed irregularly (Caritas 2001). Nonetheless, even working with figures for legally employed migrant domestic workers, a number of important trends can be highlighted. By 1996, migrant domestic workers represented 46.3 per cent of all domestic workers in Italy. This national figure, however, masked regional differentiation whereby in the major cities migrant domestic workers constituted the majority in the sector (70.5 per cent in Rome and 72.7 per cent in Milan) (Caritas 1999). In 1999, there were 114,182 migrant domestic workers paying social security payments within the domestic work sector (Caritas 2001). The presence of male migrants within the sector is notable. For example, there are virtually no Italian men legally employed in the domestic work sector – 3 per cent of the total in 1998 – but this figure rises to 24.3 per cent for male migrants (Caritas 1999).

Within the wider Italian migration scenario, domestic work has represented something of an anomaly. For example, after the promulgation of the 1990 immigration law, which attempted to control the entry of foreign migrants, special provisions were enacted to ensure that channels were left open for domestic workers (see Andall 2000a). For the regularization programme introduced for undocumented migrants in 1996, housekeeping was the largest sector regularized

(40 per cent) and in cities such as Milan the figure went up to 48 per cent (Reyneri 2001).[13] More recently, under the new highly restrictive immigration law currently being proposed by Italy's Centre-Right government,[14] domestic workers will be the only sector whereby undocumented workers will have access to an amnesty.[15]

An important consideration when addressing how transformations in the domestic work sector affect Italian women and migrant women is the extent to which there is widespread support for the presence of migrant women as family carers. However, the validation of their presence and the support they give to Italian families has also led to a tendency to avoid some of the more problematic aspects of domestic work for migrant workers. In his discussion of the informal economy, Ambrosini (1999: 90) for example, has argued that the live-in relationship between employer and employee involves a kind of patronage, whereby employers pay their employee less than they should and do not pay their social security insurance but 'at the same time they welcome and often . . . protect and help domestic workers, for example by helping to find employment for their relatives'. Although he maintains that such families tend to eventually regularize the situation of their employees, this 'gap' has severe consequences for migrant workers in the long term. Indeed they may find they need to work several years past the normal retirement age to compensate for the lack of insurance contributions paid in early years. Some domestic workers, even after forty years of employment, are not eligible for the minimum pension (Solinas 1999). Moroever, little is being done to counteract the vast salary differentials between different ethnic groups in the same region (De Filippo 2001). Huge regional salary differentials indicate the difficulty of moving to other cities where higher wages can be procured. This is not simply a result of the manner in which employment is obtained in the domestic work sphere, but given the extremely limited free time that live-in domestic workers enjoy, the close vicinity of other family members is an important factor for many workers (Andall 2000a).

This latter point relates to further important structural modifications to the domestic work sector in Italy and that is the transformation of the live-in sector from a transitory employment sector for Italian women prior to marriage to a long-term employment sector for migrant women, with or without families. The African women who migrated to Italy in the 1960s and 1970s generally found it impossible to move out of the domestic work sector and the most that they could aspire to, regardless of their individual experiences and education, was movement from the live-in sector to live-out work (Andall 2000a). This has meant that the domestic work sector constituted a permanent employment sector for migrant women, and it is only in recent years, that there has been some limited movement out of this sector (De Filippo 2001). This is despite the fact that migrant domestic workers are more highly qualified than their Italian counterparts. A survey carried out by the domestic workers association ACLI found that whilst Italian domestic workers had low levels of education (83.3 per cent of their sample group had a below average level of education, against a comparable figure of 47 per cent for migrant domestic workers), one in ten migrant domestic workers had attended university or had a degree (Solinas 1999).

From a European perspective, however, migrant women's interdependence rests on the fact that it is indigenous European women's reluctance or inability to perform domestic tasks that facilitates migrant women's migration to Europe. In the Italian context, Filipina women are numerically, the largest group of migrant domestic workers (23,591 in Lazio, 19,717 in Lombardy) (Caritas 2001). As has been shown, even professional women from the Philippines working as domestic workers abroad can earn up to six times their earning capacity as a professional in the Philippines (Eviota, cited in Chang and Groves 2000).

The demand for domestic workers in the Italian context has indeed led some to see the sector as rather privileged in the wider migration context, given that in some regions their employment has been less precarious. The importance of this should not be underestimated, given long-standing restrictive attitudes to incoming migration in most European countries (see introductory chapter).[16] This runs parallel to a very recent phenomenon whereby European governments have begun actively to recruit highly skilled professionals (Findlay 2001). The domestic work sector is unmistakably categorized as an unskilled sector of the economy. Nonetheless, despite the stringent measures adopted by many European governments to keep unskilled migrants out, governments have shown themselves remarkably willing to make provisions for the domestic work sector.[17] However, the demand in this sector contributes to the difficulties that migrant women in Italy face in trying to move out of the sector. In this regard, economic regional differentiation in Italy is certainly significant. Further migration to more economically dynamic areas, with more diversified economic sectors, is frequently the only way out of the live-in domestic sphere for migrant domestic workers in the more economically depressed south of the country (De Filippo 2001).

An important issue for those migrant women in Italy who find themselves restricted to the live-in sector of domestic work concerns their performance of motherhood. The social and economic 'invisibility' of domestic workers is often extended to the invisibility of their children. Migrant mothers choose a private solution, from within a very limited range of (unpalatable) options, as a means of reconciling their *own* family and work responsibilities. In the 1970s and 1980s, migrant women generally had little option but to send or leave their children with relatives in the country of origin or place them in residential homes in Italy (Andall 2000a). In some cases, more convoluted arrangements were made drawing on diasporic networks across several countries (Andall 1999). In the 1990s, although child-care was also being provided within community networks by recently arrived migrants in Italy, this was still problematic (Favaro and Napoli 1998).[18] Momsen

(1999: 12) argues that the nature of maid and mistress hybrid identities can lead to 'similarities of femininity and motherhood sometimes overcoming differences of race and class'. To my mind, this is rather dangerous slippage. 'Maid and mistress' may have similar responsibilities of motherhood, but the live-in domestic worker's ability to perform these responsibilities are severely *curtailed* by the domestic work relationship whereas those of the employer are *facilitated*. Indeed, most studies of domestic work demonstrate that quite different notions of femininity apply to the female employer and the female employee and that domestic workers are sometimes employed to enhance the class-based femininity of the female employer (Cock 1980; Romero 1992; Andall 2000a). From a feminist perspective, it is perhaps more palatable to stress the interdependent nature of the domestic work relationship, but marginalizing its hierarchical nature offers a false picture of the contemporary domestic relationship and the manner in which class and ethnicity operate within it.[19]

Sectoral Organization in Europe and Italy

It is the structural organization of the live-in sector of domestic work which creates a rigid template against which migrant women carve out some degree of personal autonomy. While this suggests that greater political mobilization and trade union activity is required in this sphere, the nature of that mobilization and who is effectively protected by the gains of such mobilization is equally of paramount importance.[20]

The personal and individual nature of the domestic work relationship renders it notoriously difficult to organize. In some European countries, female migrant domestic workers have very little, if any labour market protection. For example, from a legislative perspective, domestic workers in Greece have been described as being treated as 'disposable nappies', leaving them open to excessive work hours with no paid sick leave or pensions (Lazaridis 2000: 66).[21] Greater attention thus needs to be paid to sectoral organization, with due consideration of organizations' representatives and whose interests they are in a position to represent. Furthermore, the transformations that the sector is undergoing in contemporary Europe should be reflected in new and responsive legislation.

At the European level, a number of initiatives have begun to emerge. For example, RESPECT, a European network of domestic workers organizations has been established to defend the rights of domestic workers. It calls for the recognition of the importance of domestic work and the protection of domestic workers' rights (RESPECT 1999). At the institutional European level, the focus has been on regulating domestic work in the informal sector. To this end, a report was tabled to the European Parliament by the Committee on Women's Rights and

Equal Opportunities in October 2000.[22] The motion for a resolution once again revealed a vision of the domestic work relationship as an interdependent gendered relationship. Thus, changes in indigenous women's lives in Europe were seen as creating the demand for female migrant workers in the sector. The motion noted that indigenous European women's paid employment was increasing, that both parents in families were increasingly working full time and that this change in family and work circumstances, as well as the importance of leisure time had fuelled the demand for domestic help. The large numbers of female migrant workers in the sector was similarly noted and calls were made for a specific legal framework for the sector.

Once again, the propensity to view domestic work as primarily an interdependent relationship between women tends to negate the hierarchical nature of the relationship. A more explicit recognition of this fact is important if legislation is to protect the weaker party fully. Indeed, how this inherently conflictual, competitive and unequal relationship is reconciled should lie at the heart of legislative negotiations. Employers and employees have different but equally important needs. However, is it really possible to claim, as has been argued in relation to the Portuguese case, that the change in legal status for the domestic work sector in Portugal has made provision 'to ensure that neither side is placed at a disadvantage' (European Parliament 2000: 15)? Legislation drawn up for the Italian sector espoused similar objectives; nonetheless, a close reading of such legislation reveals an unequal structural relationship for domestic workers, *even when properly and legally employed*. Within the legislative framework, where the issue of competing tensions is most acute, the issue is normally resolved to the benefit of the employer (Andall 2000a). Moreover, organizations such as the ACLI-COLF in Italy,[23] which have played a critical role in the development of the sector, have struggled to deal with the complexity of the gender, class and ethnic dimensions of domestic work (Andall 2000b). Indeed, research undertaken in the northern Italy city of Bologna, suggests that independent political mobilization by a group of Filipina domestic workers was not welcomed by the local ACLI branch and other charities working within the sector as they felt that the demands of these organized women were becoming excessive (Zontini 2000). The main trade union body in Italy, on the other hand, is campaigning against the informal employment of domestic workers and promoting tax breaks for employing families. It is also promoting a change in the law to accommodate new forms of employment relationships (Meschieri 2000a).

It is clear that the historical presence of an association such as the ACLI-COLF in Italy has facilitated legislative improvements. Nevertheless, these attainments simultaneously confirm the difficult conditions for domestic workers. In the most recent legislation, the working week for live-in domestic workers was only reduced by one hour from 55 hours to 54 hours, still far exceeding the working week established for other employment sectors (Il Sole 24 Ore). Moreover, domestic workers continue to be excluded from legislative measures enacted to facilitate women's maternity, such as that on parental leave (law 53/2000).

One of the strategies proposed in the report to the European Parliament to reduce the incidence of employment in the informal economy was that of simplifying administrative procedures to enable employers to declare their workers. The new Italian legislation conforms to this by offering employers the opportunity to register their employees on the Internet, but also by offering tax breaks (Il Sole, 24 Ore). Similar fiscal provisions have been introduced in other European countries, such as France and Germany (European Parliament 2000).

An important factor guiding the approach of both Italian voluntary sector activism and trade-union activism is the unchallenged consensus that domestic workers are a necessity for Italian families. In a hearing to the European Parliament, the trade-unionist responsible for the domestic work sector within the CGIL trade union body ended her speech by stating 'it is no longer a luxury to have a domestic worker, but a necessity' (Meschieri 2000b). This view is in part due to modifications within the sector, where a shift from care for the home to care for people has been observed (De Filippo 2001). But it also relates to the immediate postwar history of Italy, whereby live-in domestic work for poor Italian women was widespread and was seen as a luxury for their wealthy employers. This idea of domestic workers as a necessity is also evident in the strategy and ideology of the ACLI-COLF (Andall 2000b). It could however, be argued that the propensity to view domestic workers as a necessity rather than a luxury evades the true power hierarchy implicit in this interdependent relationship between employer and employee. If the domestic worker is seen as a necessity for the implicit and explicit support of the Italian family then we might expect that any sacrifices that have to be made will be made by the employee. Thus, although most commentators acknowledge the long-term difficulties of live-in domestic work for migrant women, its advantages for migrant women are always stressed. Ultimately, however, better working and social conditions for domestic workers throughout Europe will be determined not only by their own ability to organize and protect their rights but also by the strategy and objectives of institutional bodies operative in individual countries. In the mid 1990s, the outgoing President of the clerical voluntary sector organization API-COLF,[24] admitted to finding it almost impossible to respond to the needs of migrant domestic workers (Faccincani 1995). Moreover, whilst conceding differences between the circumstances of migrant women domestic workers and Italian domestic workers, they erroneously interpreted migrant women's presence in the sector as competitive rather than complementary (API-COLF di Torino 1995).

In Italy, the role of religious organizations and voluntary sector associations has been particularly influential in the field of immigration and specifically for the domestic work sector. Such organizations continue to have an important function in placing migrant domestic workers with Italian families. Nonetheless, as Ambrosini (1999: 177) notes, rather than representing a path to social integration in Italy, they are firstly 'willing and efficient support bodies and secondly, logistical and organisational spaces for migrant initiatives'. To what extent such organizations implicitly condone the racial stereotyping pervasive within the sector, for example, is a question that has yet to be answered. Given existing regional disparities within Italy, we might expect wage differentials within the domestic work sphere to differ substantially across the regions, but significant differences within a given region should be attributed principally to the racist categorizations applied to domestic workers in addition to their immigration status. Research undertaken in the northern city of Turin, for example, showed that salaries for live-in workers ranged from 1,300,000 lire to 3,000,000 monthly (Cardenas and Franzinetti 1998, cited in De Filippo 2001).

As the management and activist profile of national domestic workers associations begin to change we may see some change in the agenda of these organisations. In 1999, Lidia Obando, a Nicaraguan woman, was the first migrant woman to be elected as head of the ACLI-COLF organization in Italy. As she noted, migrant women have been voluntarily active in the organization for many years, but not as employees (interview, Rome, April 2001). Migrant women's involvement in existing associative structures throughout Europe is likely to grow and should contribute new perspectives to the current strategies of a range of organizations. The atypical nature of the sector signifies that greater sectoral organization at local, national and European levels will be necessary to provide more humane working conditions for migrant domestic workers in Europe.

Conclusions

Migrant women from Africa, Asia and Eastern Europe are currently performing the function of a service caste in a wide range of European countries. They are gradually replacing the indigenous working class women who previously performed this type of work. It might be premature to claim that migrant women represent the beginning of a new transgenerational service caste, however, we cannot rule out that this may indeed become the case for some ethnic groups.

Migrant women are present in the domestic work sector in structurally different ways from their former indigenous counterparts. Firstly and most significantly, these women have migrant status. This means that their very presence in Europe is often conditional on an employment contract and this weakens their bargaining position in terms of employment conditions with their employers. Secondly, the domestic work sector is internally segmented and migrant women are frequently employed in its most problematic working arena – the live-in sphere. Live-in work is not only challenging because it is difficult to monitor working conditions and because there is a lack of separation between work space and private space but it is especially problematic because it is no longer performed principally by young single women without families of their own. Migrant women in the live-in sphere frequently *do* have their own families. While their families must become 'invisible', this does not erase their empirical reality. Migrant women's ability to perform their mothering roles is further damaged by the long-term nature of their employment within the live-in domestic work sphere, again, an important new transformation within the sector.

It is undoubtedly true that the domestic work relationship between women is an interdependent one, reflecting patriarchal frameworks and a lack of accessible welfare structures that enable all women to reconcile their reproductive and productive roles. However, the domestic work relationship is also implicitly hierarchical and, in the European context, increasingly racialized. These facts need to inform the work of those organizations striving to improve the sector's working conditions. Indeed, acknowledging and responding to the structural modifications that have occurred within the domestic work sphere in Europe, in terms of both service user and provider, is essential for dragging this employment sector into the twenty-first century.

Notes

1. The term is from Katzman's (1978: 273) study of black domestic workers in the United States (1870–1920) where he argued that they formed a 'service caste' in the American South.
2. This was undoubtedly true of earlier forms of migration for domestic servants. In the interwar years, for example, mobility within Europe of German women to the Netherlands for domestic work was a temporary strategy for approximately two years prior to marriage or another job. See Henkes (2001).
3. In 1998, the *Express* newspaper headlined with the story 'Can't Do It, Won't Do It', reporting the £4 billion a year spent on a variety of domestic help (*Express*, 25 September 1998). In the same year, the property page of the *Sunday Times* featured an article noting that building developers were beginning to incorporate staff quarters into their designs to reflect the demand for domestic help. See 'servants make an entrance', *Sunday Times*, Property, 1 November 1998).

4. Between 1933–9 Britain accepted 20,000 refugees for domestic service only (Kushner 1990). See also McDowell (2001) regarding the recruitment of Latvian women for domestic service in the 1950s.

5. The Female Middle Class Emigration Society is a historical example of such differentiation. In 1862, it was established in the UK to procure 'respectable' work for single middle-class women in colonial settler societies. Domestic service, seen as suitable for working-class women was rejected by middle-class women who felt it would diminish their higher social status. Employment as a governess or nanny was perceived to be acceptable and moreover facilitated the retention of social distinction between the classes. For more on this type of migration, see Swaisland (1993) on the emigration of single British women to South Africa. See also Henkes (2001) regarding class differences between German domestic workers in the Netherlands in the interwar years.

6. Gregson and Lowe (1994) also noted the rise in the number of benefit dependent younger women, who had begun to engage in part-time cleaning.

7. This was globally apparent when Zoe Baird, the nominee for United States Attorney General in 1993, was found to be employing two undocumented immigrants.

8. For more on the experiences of European women migrants as domestic workers in the United States see Harzig (1997).

9. See Kushner's (1990: 55) historical parallel with Jewish refugee domestic workers in 1930s Britain. He recounts the activism of a woman in Cambridge who was shocked to find that 'dons' wives could treat somebody who was in every way as good as them in an absolutely terrible manner'.

10. For example, with regard to the Italian case, Trifiletti (1995) argues that the Italian welfare system should be seen as fragmentary and inconsistent as opposed to rudimentary.

11. Similar analyses can be found in relation to other Southern European countries (see Lazaridis 2000; Ribas-Mateos 2000; Escrivà 2000).

12. One study showed that grandparents provided the care for working parents for 46.1 per cent of the three- to five-year-old age group and 45.5 per cent of the under-two age group (Menniti et al. 1997).

13. Although an estimated 15 per cent of the labour contracts required for regularisation were false and many of these false contracts were in the housekeeping sector, this would still make the domestic work sector an important labour market activity in the Italian context (see Reyneri 2001).

14. *Disegno di Legge*, n.795, March 2002.

15. Currently, there is widespread political manipulation of the issue of undocumented migrants in Italy. While the stereotype presented is that of a dangerous individual involved in illegal activities, it has been argued that many are in

fact 'young Asian and Latin-American women employed irregularly and living in middle class families' (Ambrosini 1999: 175).

16. See also Kushner (1990) for historical parallels of flexibility towards domestic workers within a generalized context of restriction.

17. See Escrivá (2000) regarding Spanish provisions.

18. See Ribas-Mateos (2000) regarding the separation of married Filipina domestic workers from their children for over 10 years in Spain. See also Romero (1997) on the implications of domestic work from the children's perspective.

19. Thus, Anderson (1999) notes in her comparison of domestic workers in the EU that employers' perception of themselves as benevolent and helping poor female migrants even meant that food and board *without* payment could be offered to employees.

20. In the late 1930s, under the aegis of the Trade Union Council's women's department, the newly established National Union of Domestic workers excluded thousands of refugee women (Kushner 1990).

21. For more on the general and legislative situation of domestic workers in other European countries see Anderson and Phizacklea (1997) and European Parliament (2000).

22. European Parliament (2000) Final Report on 'Regulating domestic help in the informal sector', Committee on Women's Rights and Equal Opportunities. Rapporteur: Miet Smet. 17 October 2000.

23. Italian Christian Workers' Association. COLF is an abbreviation for 'family collaborator'.

24. For more on this organization see Andall (2000a).

Bibliography

Ambrosini, M. (1999), *Utili Invasori. L'inserimento degli immigrati nel mercato del lavoro italiano*, Milan: FrancoAngeli.

Andall, J. (1999), 'Cape Verdean Women on the Move: "Immigration Shopping" in Italy and Europe', *Modern Italy*, 4, (2): 241–57.

Andall, J. (2000a), *Gender, Migration and Domestic Service. The Politics of Black Women in Italy*, Aldershot: Ashgate.

Andall, J. (2000b), 'Organising Domestic Workers in Italy: The Challenge of Gender, Class and Ethnicity', in F. Anthias and G. Lazaridis (eds) *Gender and Migration in Southern Europe*, Oxford: Berg.

Anderson, B. (1999), 'Overseas Domestic Workers in the European Union, in J. Momsen (ed.) *Gender, Migration and Domestic Service*, London: Routledge.

Anderson, B. and Phizacklea, A. (1997), Migrant Domestic Workers: A European Perspective, Department of Sociology, University of Leicester.

Anthias, F. and Lazaridis, G. (eds) (2000), *Gender and Migration in Southern Europe*, Oxford: Berg.

API-COLF (1995), *Immigrazione e disoccupazione*, API-COLF XV Congresso Nazionale, API-COLF: Rome.

Aymer, P. (1997), *Uprooted Women. Migrant Domestics in the Caribbean*, Westport: Praeger.

Bakan, A. and Stasiulis, D.K. (1995), 'Making the Match: Domestic Placement Agencies and the Racialization of Women's Household Work', *Signs*, 20, 21: 303–35.

Balbo, L. and May, M.P. (1975), 'Woman's Condition: The Case of Post-War Italy', *International Journal of Sociology*, 5: 79–102.

Barbagli, M. (1997), 'Family and Kinship in Italy', in M. Gullestad and M. Segalen (eds) *Family and Kinship in Europe*, London: Pinter.

Caritas di Roma (1999), *Immigrazione. Dossier statistico 1999*, Rome: Anterem.

Caritas di Roma (2001), *Immigrazione. Dossier statistico 2001*, Rome: Anterem.

Chang, G. (1994), 'Undocumented Latinas: The New "Employable" Mothers', in E. Glenn, G. Chang and L. Forcey (eds) *Mothering: Ideology, Experience and Agency*, London: Routledge.

Chang, K. and Groves, J. (2000), 'Neither "Saints" Nor "Prostitutes": Sexual Discourse in the Filipina Domestic Worker Community in Hong Kong. *Women's Studies International Forum*, 23, 1: 73–87.

Cochrane, A. (1993), 'Looking for a European Welfare State', in A. Cochrane and J. Clarke (eds), *Comparing Welfare States. Britain in International Context*, London: Sage.

Cock, J. (1980), *Maids and Madams: A Study in the Politics of Exploitation*, Johannesburg: Raven Press.

Coser, L. (1973), 'Servants: The Obsolescence of an Occupational Role', *Social Forces*, 52: 31–40.

Cox, R. (1999), 'The Role of Ethnicity in Shaping the Domestic Employment Sector in Britain', in J. Momsen (ed.) *Gender, Migration and Domestic*, London: Routledge.

Dalla Costa, M. (1988), 'Domestic Labour and the Feminist Movement in Italy since the 1970s', *International Sociology*, 3, (1): 23–34.

De Filippo, E. (2001), 'La componente femminile dell'immigrazione', in E. Pugliese (ed.) *Rapporto Immigrazione. Lavoro, sindacato, società*, Roma: Ediesse.

Del Boca, D. (1998), 'Labour Policies, Economic Flexibility and Women's Work: The Italian Experience, in E. Drew, R. Emerek and E. Mahon (eds), *Women, Work and the Family in Europe*, London: Routledge.

Del Re, A. (2000), 'The Paradoxes of Italian Law and Practice', in L. Hantrais (ed.), *Gendered Policies in Europe*, Basingstoke: Macmillan.

De Luca, L. and Bruni, M. (1993), *Unemployment and Labour Market Flexibility: Italy*, Geneva: International Labour Office.

Enloe, C. (1989), *Bananas, Beaches and Bases: Making Feminist Sense of International Politics*, London: Pandora.

Escrivà, A. (2000), 'The Position and Status of Migrant Women in Spain', in F. Anthias and G. Lazaridis (eds), *Gender and Migration in Southern Europe*, Oxford: Berg.

European Parliament (2000), Final Report on 'Regulating Domestic Help in the Informal Sector', Committee on Women's Rights and Equal Opportunities, Rapporteur: Miet Smet, 17 October 2000.

Faccincani, C. (1995), *Relazione di apertura del XV Congresso Nazionale*, API-COLF XV Congresso Nazionale.

Fauve-Chamois, A. (1998), 'Servants in Preindustrial Europe: Gender Differences', *Historical Social Research*, 23, (1/2): 112–29.

Favaro, G. and Napoli, M. (1998), *Bambini 'Senza'. Madri filippine e peruviane e problemi di cura dei loro figli*, Milano: Centro Come.

Findlay, A. (2001), 'Brain Drain: The Second Wave', presented to conference on 'Strangers and Citizens: Challenges for European Governance', University of Dundee, 17–19 March 2001.

Friese, M. (1995), 'East European Women as Domestics in Western Europe: New Social Inequality and Division of Labour Among Women', *Journal of Area Studies*, 6: 194–202.

García-Ramon M.D. and Monk, J. (eds) (1996), *Women of the European Union: The Politics of Work and Daily Life*, London: Routledge.

Glenn, E.N. (1990), 'The Dialectics of Wage Work: Japanese American women and Domestic service, 1905–1940', in E.C. DuBois and V.L. Ruiz (eds), *Unequal Sisters: A Multicultural Reader in US Women's History*, New York: Routledge.

Glenn, E.N. (1992), 'From Servitude to Service Work: Historical Continuities in the Racial Division of Paid Reproductive Labor', *Signs*, 18, (1): 1–43.

Glucksmann, M. (1990), *Women Assemble. Women Workers and the New Industries in Interwar Britain*, London: Routledge.

Gross, S. (1991), 'Domestic Labor as a Life-Course Event: the Effects of Ethnicity in Turn-of-the-Century America', *Social Science History*, 15, (3): 397–416.

Gregson, N. and Lowe, M. (1994), *Servicing the Middle Classes*, London: Routledge.

Hantrais, L. and Letablier, M. (eds) (1996), *Families and Family Policies in Europe*, London: Longman.

Harzig, C. (ed.) (1997), *Peasant Maids – City Women*, Ithaca: Cornell University Press.

Henkes, B. (2001), 'Maids on the Move: Images of Femininity and European Women's Labour Migration duirng the Interwar Years', in P. Sharpe (ed.) *Women, Gender and Labour Migration*, London: Routledge.

Il Sole 24 Ore (2001) *Collaborazioni Domestiche. Guida al trattamento delle colf dall'assunzione a fine rapporto*, Norme e Tributi, 9 aprile 2001.

Katzman, D. (1978), *Seven Day a Week. Women and Domestic Service in Industrializing America*, Oxford: OUP.

Kushner, T. (1990), 'Politics and Race, Gender and Class: Refugees, Fascists and Domestic Service in Britain, 1933–1940', in T. Kushner and L. Lunn (eds), *The Politics of Marginality*, London: Frank Cass.

Lazaridis, G. (2000), 'Filipino and Albanian Women Migrant Workers in Greece: Multiple Layers of Oppression', in F. Anthias and G. Lazaridis (eds), *Gender and Migration in Southern Europe*, Oxford: Berg.

McBride, T. (1976), *The Domestic Revolution*, London: Croom Helm.

McDowell, L. (2001), 'Out of place? Feminine domesticity, geographies of difference and the working lives of women European Volunteer Workers in Britain, 1946–1960', unpublished paper.

Menniti, A., Palomba, R. and Sabbadini, L. (1997), 'Italy: Changing the Family from Within', in F. Kaufman, A. Kuijsten, H. Schulze and K. Strohmeier (eds), *Family Life and Family Policies in Europe*, Oxford: Clarendon Press.

Meschieri, M. (2000a), 'Italia: I negoziati del contratto nazionale per il lavoro domestico', *Respect*, maggio–giugno.

Meschieri, M. (2000b), 'Intervento di Meschieri Marinella', Audizione Parlamento Europeo 19 September 2000.

Momsen, J. (1999), 'Maids on the Move', in J. Momsen (ed.), *Gender, Migration and Domestic Service*, London: Routledge.

Oakley, A. (1974), *The Sociology of Housework*, London: Martin Robertson.

RESPECT (1999), *Lavoratori e lavoratrici domestiche immigrate in Europa compartono i loro consigli e le loro esperienze*, Brussels.

RESPECT (2000) *Il cartellone di RESPECT*.

Reyneri, E. (2001), 'Migrants in Irregular Employment in the Mediterranean Countries of the European Union', *International Migration Papers 41*. Geneva: International Labour Office.

Ribas-Mateos, N. (2000), 'Female Birds of Passage: Leaving and Settling in Spain' in F. Anthias and G. Lazaridis (eds), *Gender and Migration in Southern Europe*, Oxford: Berg.

Romero, M. (1992), *Maid in the USA*, London: Routledge.

Romero, M. (1997), 'Who Takes Care of the Maid's Children? Exploring the Costs of Domestic Service', in H. L. Nelson (ed.) *Feminism and Families*, London: Routledge.

Rubery, J. Smith, M. and Fagan, C. (1999), *Women's Employment in Europe*, London: Routledge.

Solinas, A. (1999), *Costruire una società multietnica: le ACLI-COLF tra impegno sociale e lavoro di cura*, XV Assemblea Nazionale ACLI-COLF.

Stiell, B. and England, K. (1999), 'Jamaican Domestics, Filipina Housekeepers and English Nannies: Representations of Toronto's Foreign Domestic Workers', in J. Momsen (ed.), *Gender, Migration and Domestic Service*, London: Routledge.

Swaisland, C. (1993), *Servants and Gentlewomen to the Golden Land*, Oxford: Berg.

Tobío, C. (1997), 'Women's Strategies and the Family-Employment Relationship in Spain', paper presented to ESRC Seminar on Women's Search for Identity in Contemporary Europe, University of Bath, November 1997.

Trifiletti, R. (1995), 'Family Obligations in Italy', in J. Millar and A. Warman (eds), *Defining Family Obligations in Europe*, Bath Social policy Papers, University of Bath.

Trifiletti, R. (1999), 'Women's Labour Market Participation and the Reconciliation of Work and Family Life in Italy', in L. den Dulk, A. van Doorne-Huiskes and J. Schippers (eds), *Work-Family Arrangements in Europe*, Amsterdam: Thela-Thesis.

Vaiou, D. (1996), 'Women's Work and Everyday Life in Southern Europe in the Context of European Integration', in M.D García-Ramon and J. Monk (eds), *Women of the European Union: The Politics of Work and Daily Life*, London: Routledge.

Zontini, E. (2000), 'Invisible but not Helpless: Third World Women's 'Everyday Politics' in an Italian City', presented to ASMI City and Identity conference, November, London.

3

Migrant Women in Spain: Class, Gender and Ethnicity

Carlota Solé and *Sònia Parella*

Introduction

This chapter aims to study female migration in Spanish society from the perspective of the discrimination that women face in the receiving society in terms of the dimensions of class, gender and ethnicity. Discriminated against in their society of origin and with fewer possibilities to accumulate capital and labour skills, migrant women find themselves in a society totally fragmented along the lines of class and ethnicity. Gender adds another dimension to the stratification of the job market that migrants are condemned to bear. In addition to her condition as a migrant, the female migrant also encounters difficulties on the basis of gender. All of these factors would appear to fully justify the need to study in detail the process of the labour migration of women.

In Spain, since the mid-1980s, migratory flows have become increasingly female. The proportion of women varies according to the country of origin but by 1991 women represented 47 per cent of the total of migrants in Spain, rising to 48·2 per cent in 1998. Non-European Union (EU) female migration is mainly composed of women from Morocco (26.1 per cent), Peru (9.7 per cent), Dominican Republic (9.6 per cent), China (5.5 per cent) and the Philippines (5.2 per cent) (OPI 1998, 1999). Nearly 42 per cent of non-EU migrant women have a working permit – data are not available for migrant women working without an employment contract – although we can differentiate between groups of migrant women according to their labour incorporation: while African and Asian women are less economically active and usually married, Latin American and Filipina women are economically active and it is not common for them to migrate on their own while maintaining family responsibilities in the country of origin (Solé 1994).

So the 'feminization' of migratory flows and the increase in the labour-market activity of women migrants from the Third World indicate that this is not dependent immigration, rather many of these women emigrate for basic economic reasons. Migrant women, due to the convergence of the three-dimensional process of discrimination, are placed at the very bottom of the labour-market structure in the receiving society. Men are employed in a range of activities – such as agriculture and construction – women are employed mainly in domestic service (cooking, cleaning, caring for children and the elderly). Domestic service, characterized by its invisibility, vulnerability and insecurity, has become practically their only opportunity for work, regardless of their level of education and previous work experience.

The massive incorporation of Spanish women into the labour market in recent years, added to the phenomenon of the ageing population and the lack of social policies to assist families, have all meant that the demand by urban, middle-class Spanish women for home help has increased. Spanish women are unable to combine their presence in the productive and the reproductive spheres and thus choose to delegate responsibility for domestic chores to other women. This process points to inequalities of class and ethnicity between women.

Here, we understand the socio-cultural integration of migrants as the process by which the latter are incorporated into the occupational and social structure and progressively accept the institutions, beliefs, values and symbols of the receiving society without renouncing their own (Solé 1981). This chapter will focus on the first level of socio-cultural integration – the legal and occupational level – without which the process of integration into the receiving society and culture by migrant groups would be incomplete. The situation of outright subordination at both the legal and occupational level of the migrant population has been the object of many studies (Solé 1995; Martínez Veiga, 1997). However, the situation of women warrants a different analysis, given that the idea is to incorporate a gender perspective and to explore the specific types of subordination to which these women find themselves exposed in Spain as a result of a three-dimensional process of discrimination.

In the following section, theoretical reflections will be offered on the approach and the framework of analysis that allow us to highlight the subordination of migrant women and their consequent social marginalization. We will then apply a gender perspective to two areas. Firstly, we will consider legislation and migration policies in Spain – the institutional factors – focusing above all on their effects on women as the subjects of rights and on their position in the occupational and social structure. Secondly, the position of the female migrant worker will be analysed in the Spanish labour market in relation to both male migrant workers and Spanish female workers, taking into account the influence of socio-economic factors and their specific consequences for women migrants considered as a group.

Female Migrants: Analytical Approaches

The starting point for our analysis is that traditionally the issue of female labour migration has been studied from the perspective of the receiving country. Thus the problem of female migrants has usually been defined – as indeed has socio-cultural integration and immigration in general – in terms of the receiving society and the socio-economic situation and position that these women find themselves in compared to Spanish women. This assumption leads to comparisons between migrant women, their male counterparts and Spanish women. Thus, one speaks of the subordination or marginalization of migrant women and migrants in general, taking as a reference point the social standing of those with access to jobs, status, and economic, political and ideological power.

Labour migrants (and consequently women) find themselves in a position of subordination due to the fact that they come from a different place of origin, in terms of both geography (they come from the so-called Third World) and ethno-culture (their cultures of origin are non-Western and thus, in terms of Western ethnocentrism, are considered inferior). The result is that subordination takes place along ethnic lines. At this point we should distinguish between ethnic and racial lines, in that it is not so much racial differences that determine migrant women's subordination in occupational terms and marginalization in social ones when compared to male migrants and Spanish women; it is rather cultural differences and the implicit consideration that Western civilization and culture are superior to others.

Despite the major contribution of feminist approaches to power relations in society, the problem of female migrants for academics perhaps lies in an absence of epistemological distance, and may fall into the trap of cultural ethnocentrism, which considers that Western women's problems are shared by women migrants from the Third World. Women do not form a homogeneous category; rather, gender inequalities take on different forms, depending on the society in question, and these inequalities interact with the dimensions of social class and ethnicity. In this sense, the major mistake of the middle-class feminist is to take for granted that, independent of social class and ethnicity, sexism is experienced in the same way by all women, as if there existed a 'generic woman'. In any case, the racial oppression suffered by black women in a racist and sexist society is presented as if it were an additional factor of discrimination, when in reality it represents a different one altogether (Spelman 1988).

Racist prejudices and stereotypes are present in everyday life and in the relationship between migrant women and the institutions. Thus, two features form the framework for analysing the problems of migrant women. Firstly, the nature of their paid work is conditioned by their subordination in a segmented labour market. Secondly, migrant women endure marginalization and invisibility both in the labour hierarchy and in social life. These are the structural conditions that are the source of problems for migrant women.

Male migrant workers are also incorporated into a segmented labour market and thus relegated to the lower echelons of the Spanish labour market. This process of 'ethno-stratification' or the 'ethnicization of the labour market' takes on two distinct forms. In the first place, migrants are forced to accept those jobs rejected by increasingly skilled Spanish workers, who are more choosy and less willing to accept non-skilled manual jobs that are risky, dirty and poorly paid. The increase in the educational level of the Spanish population, accompanied by the consequent increase in occupational expectations, together with the rapid development of the welfare state and the maintenance of family networks, has greatly increased the level of the 'threshold of acceptability' on the part of male and female Spanish workers, despite long-term unemployment and increasing levels of job insecurity (Villa 1990). Secondly, the migrant labour force has access to those jobs for which Spanish workers also apply, but migrants suffer 'positive discrimination' due to the fact that they accept worse working conditions. This is often related to the informal economy, which allows for cost reductions, greater flexibility and the reduction of inflation (Solé 1995). This is the case in certain labour-intensive activities, such as personal services or agricultural harvesting. This 'positive discrimination' with regards to access to certain kinds of jobs is complimented by negative discrimination in the job itself, particularly in terms of wages, the nature of the task performed and working conditions. On the basis of a labour market which is highly segmented along ethnic lines, and in which women are additionally confined to certain employment sectors (horizontal and vertical segregation), migrant women suffer from three-fold discrimination (Morokvasic 1984; Boyd 1984; Sassen 1984). This discrimination is the result of the convergence of processes of discrimination on the grounds of gender and 'race', to which we should add their exploitation on the grounds of class.

In terms of segmentation along gender lines, 'positive discrimination' favours female labour in terms of access to jobs that have traditionally been considered to be 'female'. This type of horizontal segregation relegates women to those activities that are an extension of their skills as mothers, wives and carers (teaching, health, cleaning, sewing, the care of children and the elderly) all learned during gender socialization processes (Torns and Carrasquer 1987: 239). Thus, the collective patriarchal mindset attributes certain qualities and skills to women that make them especially suitable for certain occupations. Women also face discrimination in terms of worse pay, greater job insecurity, and vertical occupational segregation.

Given that the interrelationship between the categories of gender, class and ethnicity or 'race' is the basis of this analysis, the link between gender and ethnicity is easier to validate empirically. Traditionally women are associated with shouldering domestic responsibilities that are reproduced in two spheres. Firstly, in their participation on a part-time basis in the labour market, in working conditions generally unacceptable to other male workers, both Spanish and migrant, and secondly in the productive tasks of the various economic sectors where they are most highly concentrated. In the light of this sectoral or sub-sectoral concentration, the relationship between gender and ethnicity demonstrates forms of discrim-ination associated with stratified inequalities. Thus, in those occupations in which women are most highly concentrated or that are almost exclusively reserved for men, very few women are employed in managerial or senior positions (Fenton, 1999: 54–5).

Through immigration legislation, the state exploits the insecurities associated with being a woman and being a migrant. This leads to an inferior social status for migrant women, due both to their gender and to the fact that they are not consid-ered citizens. In this way, the correlation between the kind of activities considered the preserve of women and unacceptable for the Spanish labour force is both controlled and legitimated. The jobs are dirty, routine, insecure and they situate migrant women in the most economically vulnerable and socially defenceless segment of the working class. This three-fold discrimination is what situates migrant women in those 'labour-market niches' that are rejected by Spanish women. Consequently, the invisibility of migrant women increases further due to the kind of jobs that they mainly undertake (such as domestic service, cleaning services, caring for the sick). These jobs are considered to be marginal activities in the occupational structure of Spain. However, these three dimensions of dis-crimination also place migrant women in positions of extreme subordination in terms of power relations within society. In the context of an advanced industrial society, competition to reach the higher positions of status and power automatically relegate migrant women, unfamiliar with the workings of power in the receiving society, to a situation of subordination in the labour market. With regard to social marginalization, the image and social construction of migrant women as being responsible for their marginal situation in both the labour market and in society at large reflects and reinforces the dominant stereotypes and prejudices of the receiving society. Thus, this invisibility does not only mean that migrant women seek to go unnoticed in order to avoid rejection, but also that they are not taken into consideration in parliamentary debates, nor in the media. Overall, they do not form part, or at least they do not appear to form part, of the society in which they are working and/or living.

Many of the stereotypes that have been associated with migrant women are easily exposed as such. Migrant women are active in the labour market. The value they give to jobs outside the ambit of the home is based not only on the wages they can earn but also on the opportunities for social interaction with people in their socio-economic environment, both migrant and authoctonous. This is despite the linguistic and cultural difficulties that they seek to overcome and the fact that, in the majority of cases, their paid work, domestic service, continues to restrict them to the private sphere of the home. In some circumstances, knowledge of the language of the receiving country is vital to carry out certain activities that involve contact with people, for instance, in institutions or commercial agencies. In this case, there are clear-cut examples of discrimination against migrant women compared with their Spanish counterparts.[1]

Overall then, labour market conditions and the dominant value system in Spain are the structural factors that determine the situation of migrant women. It is also important to note the social construction of migrant women in Spain, whereby they are considered to be responsible for their marginal situation. This social construction derives from stereotypes and prejudices that are dominant in Spain. However, our research (Solé 1994) shows that migrant women are capable of challenging their situation and are just as capable as their male counterparts of seeking employment in a highly segmented labour market. In other words, their segregation, subordination and marginalization cannot be considered to be the result of a predisposition to accept a situation as given, but rather is the outcome of structural factors within Spain.

An additional stereotype in Spain is that of migrant women as victims or somehow fortunate, given that they have been able to escape from poverty and misery. This social projection should be re-examined, if not rejected altogether. In many cases, women who emigrate from their native countries to the West, including Spain, do not do so because they suffer from a situation of chronic economic insecurity. Many have access to resources, such as a relatively high level of education, which generate expectations for better life, not only in purely monetary terms, but also in terms of higher levels of personal freedom.

Overall, the position of migrants in the labour market and in society as a whole is conditioned by socio-economic factors, the content of immigration policies, the attitudes and prejudices of the native population, without forgetting the strategies of the migrants themselves (Colectivo IOÉ 1999). The first two factors will be considered in the following two sections.

Legislation and Immigration Policy

It is the legal framework that defines the 'range of opportunities' for the integration of migrants, by a process known as 'institutional discrimination' (Cachón 1995). The key that opens the door to a situation of legality for migrants is the possession of an employment contract that proves that an employment relationship exists. Thus, migrants' presence is legitimized by their productive capacity, with immigration policies seeking cheap labour according to labour demand (Mestre 1999). By placing the emphasis on an employment contract, reducing the link with society to wage labour, migrants have very limited possibilities for social integration. Legal status does not mean that they enjoy the status of citizens – rather, migrants are converted into the holders of a series of obligations and of very few rights in the receiving society for a set period of time, thus creating 'second-class citizens'. Migrants must obey laws over whose design and control they have no say, and are only allowed a certain degree of autonomy, and even then it is limited to the sphere of the market (Zapata 1996).

Another effect of immigration policies is the tendency to favour the concentration of migrants in certain sectors of activity, characterized by the worst working conditions, which contributes to the 'ethno-stratification' or 'ethnicization of the labour market' (Wallerstein 1991). On the one hand, the state limits the circulation of migrants by always taking into account the 'national employment situation' when granting work permits. On the other hand, the state ratifies what the market has already laid down as the range of labour opportunities for migrants, by means of an annual quota policy that represents those job offers not taken up by Spanish workers.

However, the 'institutional framework of discrimination' affects male and female migrants differently. In this sense, we can observe the legal construction of migrant women as a subordinated subject, or even as a non-subject (Mestre 1999). As we shall see below, immigration policy either condemns migrant women to depend on their husbands, through family reunification policies, or it forces them to work in those female activities that are shunned by women in the receiving society (domestic service).[2]

From the outset, the fact that immigration policy is clearly based on labour market activity – in that legal stays are based on the possession of a work permit – especially affects migrant women. For women who work in domestic service with no employment contract it is much more difficult than for their male counterparts to prove that they are active in the labour market and thus they are often forced to take measures that lead to an irregular situation or to family reunion. Given that the right to family reunion is very restrictive in Spanish legislation, this becomes a very costly option.[3] In addition, the status of women present through reunification policies generates a situation of legal dependency on the husband. It also prevents them from having access to a work permit. If one reads the way the laws that govern these rights have been drawn up, it is difficult to conclude that they are openly discriminatory against women. However, by examining those who are most affected and who are implicitly referred to, it seems clear that such laws are aimed at women. According to Mestre (1999), family reunion is based on the idea of the stabilizing influence of the woman, and on her 'character of mediation', as key to the process of the settlement of groups, given that in the private sphere the woman guarantees order, socialization and the maintenance of the family unit. Once more, the demand is made that 'the woman remains in the private sphere and that the man goes out into the public one' (Mestre 1999: 29).

Leaving aside the case of women present under family reunification policies, Spanish immigration policy also clearly encourages female labour migration as a response to the demands of the Spanish labour market for workers in the domestic service sector. The establishment of the quota system in 1993 – with an annual average of 60 per cent of work permits for domestic service – gave the state a new role in the recruitment of migrant women in the light of the shortage of Spanish labour. Thus, the policy of quotas not only selects migrants according to nationality, the activity which they are to carry out and the geographic destination, but also – albeit indirectly – according to gender. This situation clearly affects the composition of migratory flows and migratory strategies, given that they produce a 'pull' effect that encourages women migrants to be at the head of the migratory chain in the knowledge that Spanish immigration policy offers them more possibilities to normalize their legal situation than their male counterparts.

Thus, the state clearly contributes to the construction of a labour market segmented along gender lines, in which domestic service becomes *the* sector of activity for migrant women, and, as we shall see in the next section, this sector is characterized by its invisibility, insecurity and exploitation. The special labour regime of domestic service establishes labour relations that are very different from the general regime applied to the 'male' labour market, and which fail to provide meaningful protection for the female worker (Quesada 1991). In addition, it is very often the case that in the ambit of domestic service there are no written employment contracts and that the jobs form part of the 'hidden economy', leaving the nature of the relationship to be established by the individuals involved. Given that one of the individuals is often a migrant woman in an irregular legal situation – but seeking a labour contract to obtain a work permit and thus avoid deportation – it is not surprising that many cases of exploitation arise.

To sum up, following on from the conclusions of Solé (1994), it is more likely that women migrants only enjoy rights derived from others, due to the fact that family reunion predominates in which women are inactive and that women are often employed in the hidden economy or in family businesses where they do not receive remuneration. This situation means that migrant women are unprotected and reinforces gender inequalities in both the public and the private sphere.

Migrant Women in a Segmented Labour Market

The analysis of the main economic sectors in which the migrant population is employed in Spain leads to the conclusion that 76·3 per cent of the 197,074 migrant workers with a valid work permit were concentrated in five sectors at the end of 1998: domestic service (30·7 per cent), agriculture (18·6 per cent), unskilled jobs in hotels and catering (11·4 per cent), unskilled jobs in construction (8 per cent) and the retail sector (7·6 per cent) (Ministerio de Trabajo y Asuntos Sociales 1999). These are jobs where general working conditions are worst in terms of human capital, atypical work, labour relations, working conditions in the strict meaning of the term, and wages (Cachón 1997). These five sectors, however, only represent 36·7 per cent of total employment among the Spanish population in work, which is clear evidence of the ethno-stratification of the job market, given that migrants occupy the lower echelons of the job market, not because of their lack of qualifications, but rather because of other factors such as the discriminatory practices of employers and of the state itself.

While the non-EU foreign labour force as a whole, both men and women, are affected by the processes of ethno-stratification, the distribution of foreign workers by gender according to occupation allows us to identify the existence of very different levels of job opportunities for men and women. According to 1998 figures, 67 per cent of female migrant workers are household employees, followed by 10·3 per cent who work in the hotel and catering sector. However, the real figure of migrant women who work as domestic employees is difficult to estimate using the number of work permits, because approximately 80 per cent of female migrants that work in domestic service do so without an employment contract (Marodán et al. 1991). In terms of male workers, there exists a more balanced distribution, with 27·5 per cent working in agriculture, 12·1 per cent in construction and 10·2 per cent in hotels and catering, and thus the range of options open is much wider.

If we incorporate the perspective of gender into the analysis, we can see that while the migrant population as a whole is forced into jobs that have lower levels of social status and remuneration, it is the female migrant population that occupies the lowest rung of the ladder: domestic service. Thus, a double stratification of the labour market can be perceived, on the basis of gender and ethnicity. Consequently, even though we start from the assumption that both groups, male and female migrants, suffer from a situation of subordination when compared with the Spanish population, migrant women come below their male counterparts, given that in addition to their status as 'economic migrants' we must add that of being 'women'. Both dimensions constitute the key lines of stratification of the labour market which interact and reinforce each other.

The confinement of migrant women to domestic service is based on the combination of inequalities associated with gender, class and ethnicity, all of which are responsible for the fact that Spain receives them with the prejudice that they are only capable of carrying out 'female' tasks. Their status as women favours this kind of implicit or informal labelling process, regardless of their level of education and previous professional experience. As they are not only migrants from poorer countries, but women, too, they are assigned the corresponding cultural background, which provides a contrast between their 'traditional' and 'underdeveloped' nature – deeply devalued – and that of Western women, considered more modern and emancipated (Oso 1998). Such stereotypes and prejudices, forming part of the dominant belief system, reinforce to an even greater degree the discrimination against migrant women, turning them into ideal candidates for carrying out tasks related to social reproduction, due to their 'docile' nature, their 'patience' and their submissiveness.

Certainly it is true that a fuller analysis should be made of the working conditions of men and women in order to obtain more reliable results regarding which of the two occupies a lower position in the labour market. However, despite the difference in situations, the mere fact that domestic service is regulated by a very weak and often informal contractual relation, that it is accompanied by the idea of servitude, and that it takes place within the private sphere of the home, all provide sufficient reason for us to be able to conclude that domestic service facilitates invisibility and defencelessness on the part of those employed in it, and as such the employer enjoys a wide margin of discretion.

Domestic/family work now enjoys the officially-recognized status of salaried work since its regulation in 1985, the conditions laid down in this special regime are discriminatory compared to other sectors, placing it very firmly in the secondary segment of the labour market. It can be argued that seasonal agricultural workers, basically men, are also victims of exploitation and job insecurity; but by merely using quantitative criteria we see that domestic service involves up to 70 per cent of migrant women workers. From the above it may be concluded that, even though the labour market is perceived as being dual in nature, this duality takes on many different forms and has highly differentiated dimensions that coincide with ethnic and gender lines of division (Martínez Veiga 1997).

Migrant women in Spain present many distinct personal histories, circumstances and geographical, economic, social and cultural backgrounds. In addition they have a very great variety of working careers. Despite all of these differences, it would appear to make sense to study migrant women as a group, given that there exist structural factors that have a great influence over them and that relegate them to a very specific 'niche' in the job market: domestic service.

Migrant women accept this place in the occupational structure due to the fact that their 'threshold of acceptance' of working conditions is lower than that of Spanish woman. This level is basically defined by the position occupied by workers in the system of social reproduction, in both the family and the class structure (Villa 1990). In the case of migrant women workers, the pressing need for income in order to accumulate savings and maintain dependent family members, the lack of networks that provide economic aid in Spain – unlike Spanish women – a migratory project of return, the influence of ethnic recruitment networks and the perception of a labour market segmented along the lines of gender and ethnicity, all lead them to lower the threshold below which job opportunities would be considered 'socially unacceptable', regardless of qualifications. Logically, the 'level of acceptance' of these women in Spanish society is below that which they would employ in their country of origin, especially in the case of qualified and/or middle-class women. Domestic service represents a profoundly devalued occupation in the mind's eye of their sending societies, often not considered to be an occupation, and thus many of these women would reject it.[4] For all of these reasons, employment in domestic service in Spain brings with it, in certain cases, problems associated with self-esteem and the gap between social and occupational status. This is especially the case of migrant women who, according to the Colectivo IOÉ (1998: 24), 'experience downward mobility' in that they are women who go from performing a function that requires qualifications in their country of origin (such as teachers, nurses) to finding themselves confined to the private sphere of domestic service, regardless of their level of qualifications, and to being 'bossed by everyone' in the receiving society. In the case of women who are inactive in the labour market in their country of origin, as happens with many Moroccan migrant women, work in domestic service provides them with a 'relative promotion', in that it offers an opportunity to embark upon an economic trajectory outside the family. In addition, the weakness of control mechanisms and social prestige considerations allows them to accept jobs that in their country of origin they would never accept given their low levels of social status (Colectivo IOÉ 1998).

However, independently of the social devaluation that domestic service suffers from in Spain, as Catarino and Oso (2000) point out, it is the occupation with most advantages for migrant women in terms of the accumulation of savings, given that those that work on a live-in basis are provided with board and lodging and thus are able to save virtually all of their earnings. In addition to the accumulation of savings, domestic service facilitates the arrival and entrance into Spain of new migrants, to such a degree that migrant women find it easier to obtain work than their male counterparts. The stratification of the labour market along the lines of gender and ethnicity has meant that, for migrant women, the decision to migrate, far from bringing considerable improvements in their situation compared with that experienced in the country of origin, has produced the opposite effect: downward mobility, with the exception of the economic aspect. This arises due to the fact that the patriarchal structures are transferred from the country of origin to the receiving country and, as such, gender relations remain essentially unaltered.

The comparison between the labour situation of migrant women and Spanish women leads to the conclusion that, although both groups are victims of sex discrimination, such discrimination takes on different forms as a result of the process whereby, for migrant women, class and ethnic inequalities are super-imposed onto each other. Thus, Spanish working women are victims of a different kind of occupational segregation compared to migrant women. Firstly, despite the fact that both groups are relegated to occupations generally considered to be 'female', Spanish women, unlike migrants, enjoy a wider range of choice and are present in sectors that require secondary or higher education. This is the case in certain social services and in education although these activities are less well paid and are held in less social esteem than those professional activities that are performed by their male counterparts. Secondly, only 6·7 per cent of Spanish women are employed in domestic service, compared with a figure of 70 per cent for migrant women. Thus, domestic service is no longer the main occupation for Spanish women, and comes low down in the list of occupations held by them. This is vital to understanding the recruitment of migrant women as domestic employees.

In the above section, we have seen how institutional actions, using immigration policy as an instrument, play a key role not only in regulating the entry of migrant women, but also in their entry into the labour market as domestic employees. Another key aspect in understanding the integration of migrant women into the labour market is the rising demand for domestic help. This is a consequence of the process of externalization of part of the job of reproduction by the urban middle classes. Domestic service satisfies a series of necessities that have arisen due to changes in Western societies, including Spain, such as the increasing levels of female participation in the labour market, the ageing of the population and the insufficient development of policies designed to help families. Given this situation, Spanish women have great difficulties reconciling their dual role in the repro-ductive and the productive sphere, whereas Spanish men continue to avoid sharing domestic and family-related tasks. This is the context for the emergence of the process of commodification of what has, until now, been unpaid work performed by women. However, this process retains traditional patterns of gender behaviour, given that women continue to perform such tasks. In the face of demands for professional skills and given the lack of value assigned to domestic and family-related work, some reproductive tasks are rejected by those Spanish women with sufficient levels of income. Instead, such tasks are delegated to other women. This is where 'new' occupational spaces appear for migrant women, given the lack of Spanish women willing to be employed in domestic service due to an increase in levels of education and job expectations over recent years. In this way, a transfer of the burden of reproduction can be witnessed between women of different social class and ethnic origin, while patriarchal relations are perpetuated and men continue with their one-dimensional participation in the labour market.

The majority of working migrant women are employed in domestic service, but it must also be pointed out that this is also an occupation that employs those Spanish women with few economic means at their disposal. However, the two groups of women do not carry out the same tasks, rather a process of ethno-stratification emerges within domestic service, in that tasks related to social reproduction are divided along ethnic lines. This leads to the ethnicization of the least-valued tasks and of the least-desired working conditions by Spanish women. Thus, migrant women are to be mainly found in live-in domestic service, which is rejected by their Spanish counterparts due to its low social prestige, the strong connotations of servitude that accompany it, and the lack of personal autonomy that it implies. Foreign workers emerge as a means of filling this gap in the labour market, until recently filled by Spanish workers from a rural background, not only because the job market fails to offer them other possibilities, but also because it represents an opportunity to save on those expenses associated with housing and food. Consequently, in the case of live-in domestic service, a process of substitution has occurred, with migrant women substituting Spanish women. In contrast, such a process of substitution does not occur in live-out domestic service; rather both groups compete for the same jobs, with the proportion of migrant women being much lower. In this kind of work, migrant women are much more likely to be working without an employment contract, to suffer exploitation, and to carry out the least-valued tasks, such as attending to the sick and the elderly.

In the hotel and catering sector, the second most important sector for non-EU migrant women, the jobs generally performed are related to cleaning and cooking, with very few working as waitresses. This is in contrast to the situation for Spanish workers. Despite the fact that in this industry the connotations of arbitrariness and servitude related to domestic service do not exist, in practice, according to the Colectivo IOÉ (2000), conditions of job insecurity and abuse by superiors do exist. However, the fact that the work is carried out in a public space means that it is easier to defend women workers than if they were in the private space of the home.

Conclusions

Migrant women from the Third World face discrimination based on 'race' in addition to that based on social class and gender. Ethnicity and gender determine the place of women workers in the system of production, in the occupational structure, and, consequently, in the social structure. These are not additional factors to the actual situation of sexual and racial discrimination; rather they act as elements that constitute and define their working and social experience (Anthias and Yuval-Davis 1992, quoted in Fenton 1999: 165).

The comparison of the situation of migrant women with Spanish women and with their male counterparts, demonstrates a process of threefold discrimination. This discrimination on the grounds of ethnicity, social class and gender results in the subordination of migrant women in occupational and ethno-cultural terms. As a consequence, the ethnicization of the concept of subordination, linked to gender inequalities, leads to social marginalization. Social marginalization of migrant women involves their invisibility, both in the work sphere (given the kind of job carried out and the conditions accepted) and in the socio-economic sphere (they are not considered as social actors or agents who decide and/or participate in public life).

The circle closes with the migrant women suffering from personal marginalization as a result of social marginalization. They are relegated to the role of substitutes for labour market activities, while they suffer from a form of 'positive discrimination' that condemns them to carrying out reproductive tasks rejected by

Spanish women. The ideological legitimization of subordination in the job market, social marginalization and political subordination, all rest on the prejudices and stereotypes present in Spain towards migrant women. Thus, the social construction of migrant women as victims or as women who were somehow fortunate to have entered the Spanish labour market, and as submissive women, dependent on their husbands or fathers, with no will of their own, is not questioned. This is despite the evidence that they possess educational levels above those necessary to carry out the jobs for which they are employed, and that they themselves have embarked upon the migratory trajectory, attracted by demand in Spain.

The structural factors that convert migrant women into 'second-class citizens', and the demand for female labour are promoted by a state that seeks to avoid racial conflict, while maintaining a labour market that is segmented along gender and ethnic lines. Within migrant groups, such structural factors affect women much more than men, since economic migration is not only conditioned by ethnicity and social class, but also by gender. Thus, migrant women occupy positions in the occupational structure below their male counterparts and are doubly marginalized in social terms. In addition, they are deemed to comply with and accept the twin situation of subordination at work and social marginalization compared to their male counterparts, and threefold discrimination when compared to workers in general, given that their 'natural' submission to the element of discretion in their working contracts is taken for granted. The prejudices and stereotypes that encourage this portrayal are reinforced by the fact that these women suffer from a process of downward occupational mobility in terms of both the occupation and its assigned social value compared with the externalized labour market activity carried out in their countries of origin.

A non-ethnocentric approach to the problem of migrant women reveals the threefold discrimination that they face in Spain. In addition, it allows us to under-line social and occupational competition between migrant women and their male counterparts and those Spanish women in the same situation of inferiority and subordination in the productive process and occupational structure. It also shows the difficulties faced and the enormous efforts needed to overcome the defence-lessness and invisibility in which migrant women's employment subordination and marginalization in Spain are perpetuated. Understanding this situation is the first step on the road to taking political decisions and to putting into practice immig-ration policies based on integration rather than exclusion.

Notes

1. For example, the political need by certain regional and local administrations and governments in Spain to use Basque, Galician or Catalan as a main language

of communication in their political, social and cultural institutions (parliament, ministries, institutes, and so forth).

2. These jobs are shunned by local women because they are at the bottom of the occupational hierarchy and they offer low rewards, inferior working conditions, limited job prospects and security and women are subjected to implicit and explicit exploitation by their employers. Besides, these jobs are the greatest example of gender discrimination for Spanish women, because they are associated with characteristics traditionally ascribed to women – docility, obedience and 'caring'. But this situation does not mean that Spanish women who work outside their home and who must pay for external domestic work, do not realize how important the contribution of domestic service is to maintain family cohesiveness.

3. These are the main requirements for the applicant: possession of a residence permit; regular and sufficient income to support family members; suitable housing provision. Family reunion is limited to parents and children, according to EU legislation (Ezquerra 1997).

4. The wage disparities are clearly observable in the case of Filipina women: the salary of a domestic employee in Catalonia is 23 times that which would be earned in the Philippines for the same job. The only reason for accepting such a job is the difference in salary. Despite the fact that it is socially acceptable for young educated women to emigrate to work in domestic service, these women would not work as such in their country of origin, given that the occupation is associated with poverty and a lack of education (Ribas 1994).

Bibliography

Anthias, F. and Yuval-Davis, N. (1992), *Racialized Boundaries. Race, Nation, Gender, Colour and Class and the Anti-racist Struggle,* London: Routledge.

Boyd, M. (1984), 'At a Disadvantage: The Occupational Attainments of Foreign born Women in Canada', *International Migration Review,* 18, (4): 1091–119.

Cachón, L. (1995), 'Marco institucional de la discriminación y tipos de inmigrantes en el mercado de trabajo en España', *REIS,* 69: 105–24.

Cachón, L. (1997), 'Notas sobre la segmentación del mercado de trabajo y la segregación sectorial de los inmigrantes en España', paper presented to the conference *La inmigración en España,* Madrid, 16–18 October.

Catarino, C. and Oso, L. (2000), 'Servicio doméstico y empresas de limpieza. Hacia una "etnización" de los servicios de reproducción social en la Península Ibérica', *Papers. Revista de Sociologia,* 61: 187–207.

Colectivo IOÉ (1998), 'Mujeres inmigrantes en España. Proyectos migratorios y trayectorias de género', *Ofrim Suplementos,* diciembre, 11–38.

Colectivo IOÉ (1999), *Inmigrantes, Trabajadores, Ciudadanos,* València: Universitat de València.

Colectivo IOÉ (2000), *Inmigración y trabajo en España. Trabajadores inmigrantes en el sector de la hostelería,* Madrid: IMSERSO.

Ezquerra, J. J. (1997), 'El derecho a vivir en familia de los extranjeros en España', *Migraciones,*1: 177–215.

Fenton, S. (1999), *Ethnicity. Racism, Class and Culture,* London: Macmillan.

Marodán, MªD. (ed.) (1991), *Mujeres del Tercer Mundo en España. Modelo migratorio y caracterización sociodemográfica,* Madrid: Fundación CIPIE.

Martínez Veiga, U. (1997), *La integración social de los inmigrantes en España,* Madrid: Trotta.

Mestre, R. (1999), 'Por qué las inmigrantes no trabajan. Breve crítica feminista al derecho de extranjería', *Jueces para la Democracia*, 33: 22–33.

Ministerio de Trabajo y Asuntos Sociales (1999), *Estadísticas de permisos de trabajo a extranjeros 1998,* Madrid: Ministerio de Trabajo y Asuntos Sociales (MTAS).

Morokvasic, M. (1984), 'Birds of Passage are also Women', *International Migration Review,* 18, (4): 886–907.

Observatorio permanente de la Inmigración (OPI) (1998–1999), *Indicadores de la inmigración y el asilo en España,* n. 4, n. 5.

Oso, L. (1998), *La migración hacia España de las mujeres jefas de hogar,* Madrid: IMU.

Quesada, R. (1991), *El contrato del servicio doméstico,* Madrid: La Ley.

Ribas, N. (1994), 'Origen del proceso migratorio de la mujer filipina en Cataluña', *Papers. Revista de Sociologia*, 43: 101–14.

Sassen, S. (1984), 'Notes on the Incorporation of Third World Women into Wage-Labour Through Immigration and Off-Shore Production', *International Migration Review,* 18, (4): 1144–65.

Solé, C.(1981), *La integración sociocultural de los inmigrantes en Cataluña,* Madrid: CIS.

Solé, C. (1994), *La mujer inmigrante,* Madrid: Instituto de la Mujer.

Solé, C. (1995), *La discriminación racial de los inmigrantes en el Mercado de trabajo,* Madrid: CES.

Spelman, E. (1988), *Inessential Women,* London: Verso.

Torns, T. and Carrasquer, P. (1987), 'Entorn dels conceptes de dona i treball a Catalunya', in J.Mª Rotger (ed.) *Visió de Catalunya,* Barcelona: Diputació de Barcelona.

Villa, P. (1990), *La estructuración de los mercados de trabajo,* Madrid: MTSS.

Wallerstein, I. (1991), 'Universalismo, racismo y sexismo, tensiones ideológicas del capitalismo', in E. Balibar and I. Wallerstein (eds) *Raza, nación y clase,* Madrid: IEPALA.

Zapata, R. (1996), 'Ciudadanía y estados de bienestar', *Sistema*, 130: 17–34.

Part II
Gender, Ethnicity and
Political Mobilization

−4−

South Asian Women and Collective Action in Britain
Ravi K. Thiara

Introduction

This chapter is located within the wider project of deconstruction, initiated in the 1970s and 1980s, by black[1] feminists when they began to challenge not only the practice of white feminism but also some of its central categories and theories. This resulted in new discourses challenging earlier invisibilities and represent-ations of black women. More recently poststructuralism and postmodernist deconstructionism has created a space for discourse about difference, subjectivity and agency, also allowing black women to be foregrounded. What has this meant for South Asian[2] women? How does it relate to the broader goal of transforming social relations grounded in power and privilege, subordination and exclusion at both discursive and material levels? These are some of the questions/issues examined in relation to the history of collective action by South Asian women.

The location of South Asian women in post-war Britain, as both racialized and gendered subjects, is determined by a complex matrix of 'race', class, gender and ethnicity. Rather than looking at how certain categories have become racialized or gendered, the focus of my discussion is on the role of a racialized category, South Asian women, in determining and constructing gendered action. In partic-ular, the chapter seeks to provide an overview of the forms of collective action taken by South Asian women, by locating them within the broader canvas of anti-racist struggles since the 1970s. In so doing, it seeks to demonstrate the multiple, complex and contradictory locations of South Asian women in resistance politics in Britain.

It is argued that the search for the 'real' or 'authentic' South Asian woman is misguided, as it homogenizes and naturalizes this category, especially as the term 'Asian', itself constructed in the West, encompasses diverse groups with differ-ing histories, interests and experiences. While problematizing the notion of a unitary South Asian woman's experience, my intention is to present a generalized picture while also highlighting the complex and multidimensional nature of their knowledge, experiences and narratives critical to any deconstruction. In setting this out, I want to look at how South Asian women have attempted to create a 'third space' in an attempt to challenge racialized exclusions as well as to transform social relations within families and communities as gendered subjects. By pointing to the rich history of organization, I not only challenge the commonly accepted unidimensional view of South Asian women as passive objects but also hope to problematize some central categories within the ethnic mobilization discourse. My purpose in this chapter then, is to explore, share and develop some ideas, many of which draw on existing work on which my research seeks to build.

Postwar Migration

South Asian migration to Britain was part of the larger postwar migration flow when, at a time of economic expansion, black labour was recruited to meet widespread labour shortages caused by the reluctance of indigenous workers to take up undesirable employment. Consequently, South Asian migrants found themselves concentrated in low-paid, unskilled or semi-skilled work especially in the textile, manufacturing and transport industries. Both the political and public responses to black migration, and the historical racialization of immigration as a political issue in Britain has been insightfully documented by a number of scholars (Solomos 1989; Anwar 1986; Layton-Henry 1984).

Black migrants themselves were a highly diverse group, not only in terms of racial and ethnic origin but also in terms of history, class and geographical origin, with the majority coming from the Indian subcontinent and the West Indies. In Britain, they were unevenly distributed though the majority settled in inner-city and industrial areas, mainly in London and the South-East, Midlands, the North and North-East, and the South West and Wales. According to the 1991 census, the estimated minority ethnic population constitutes 5.5 per cent of the total population of Britain; almost 50 per cent are British born, clearly undermining the assumption that minority groups are 'immigrants'. Of the total, those of South Asian origin (2.7 per cent) comprise the largest grouping (with 1.5 per cent Indian, 0.9 per cent Pakistani and 0.3 per cent Bangladeshi), followed by those categorized as black groups (1.6 per cent) with 0.9 per cent Black-Caribbean, 0.4 per cent Black-African and 0.3 per cent Black-Other (Owen 1994: 15).

The migration of South Asian women, as dependants of men, was generally later than that of men, with the exception of East African Asians who migrated as family units. Amongst factors impacting on the timing of women's migration has been government legislation aimed at reducing black migration generally. Indeed, many Bangladeshi and Pakistani families remain divided even today; this is reflected in the ratio of women to men which is lower among minority ethnic groups than that of the wider population but is especially the case among South Asians where Bangladeshis have 89 fewer women for every 1,000 men (Owen 1994: 28–9).

Within the migration flow, Indian women generally arrived in Britain before those from Pakistan and Bangladesh[3] and were drawn into the labour market, often in low-paid unskilled and semi-skilled work or as homeworkers, as their incomes became crucial to the financial survival of their families. The shift from manufact- uring to the service industry, from manual to non-manual jobs, and from full-time to part-time work, resulting in higher unemployment rates for men, has made the participation of South Asian women in the labour market even more critical to their families.[4] This is reflected in figures from the 1991 census that show the percent- age of Indian women to be the highest among those economically active minority groups (30 per cent) as compared with 7 per cent of Pakistani and 2 per cent of Bangladeshi women. This compares with 25 per cent of economically active Black-Caribbean women, the other group whose migration took place at a similar time to the Indian group and who have been subjected to similar labour market changes (Owen 1994: 30). In part, these differences are explained by the age structure of the three South Asian groups where those aged under 16 are higher among Pakistani and Bangladeshi groups.[5] Generally, the South Asian group is younger in make-up than white and other minority women (Owen 1994: 30). Today, South Asian women are mainly concentrated in the West Midlands, Greater London and West Yorkshire; Indian women constitute the largest group in Greater London and West Midlands whereas Pakistani women predominate in West Yorkshire, while the largest percentage of Bangladeshi women is to be found in Greater London (Owen 1994: 34).

As pointed out by Brah, South Asian women's reality is 'constituted around a complex articulation of the economic, political and ideological structures that underpin the interrelationship between race, class and gender' (Brah 1992: 64). Consequently, this complexity further necessitates the deconstruction of the category 'South Asian women' as it encompasses a highly heterogeneous group marked by differences of geographical origin, language, class, religion and caste. As discussed by Brah, the accompanying cultural and gender systems are equally different (Brah 1992: 64).

Their structural location results in much commonality, but the timing of mig- ration has led to differing issues and concerns for the different categories of South Asian women. Given that Sikh women are among the earlier migrants, prominent issues for them relate to redundancies and unemployment at a time of radical change in the nature of employment. Indeed, they have been involved in numerous industrial disputes since the 1970s that raised various issues including low wages, differential rates for the same job, racial and sexual harassment and the endemic racism among white workers and trade unions. As relative newcomers, on the other hand, Bangladeshi women have been excluded from the labour market and housed in some of the worst accommodation in Britain (Brah 1992: 65) but are also organizing around issues of racist attacks and inadequate housing for their families.

Given the existence of other insightful examinations of the position of South Asian women in relation to areas such as education, family and waged work, my focus here is specifically on their role in collective action. In so doing, I hope to highlight how gendered and racialized social relations, in articulation with state policies and discursive practices, impact on the formation of their subjectivity. Implicit to this is a rejection of 'European orientalist ideologies which construct Asian women as "passive"' (Brah 1992: 65).

As convincingly argued by Brah, state racism in Britain targeted at South Asians has been legitimized through a particular ideological construction of Asian marriage and family systems, as seen in the debates around immigration controls. Indeed, contemporary racialized discourse around the position of South Asian women continues to be informed by that of colonial times (Brah 1992: 68). Much of the contemporary popular, academic and political discourse continues to represent South Asian women as the passive victims of out-of-date male-dominated traditions and practices, as witnessed in recurrent press reports of arranged marriages[6] that have often been the only means of giving visibility to Asian women. Removed of their agency/subjectivity, women are depicted as the done to rather than the doers and a pathologized Asian family and outmoded cultural practices seen as the only culprits rather than race, class and gender systems of domination. Furthermore, Asian culture is presented as an unchanging pure essence instead of being understood as a continuously constituting and contested dynamic that presents a possible site of resistance for minority communities.

Thus, despite the white feminist attack on the family as a primary site of women's oppression, for South Asian women, it remains an important site of support in a hostile society. This is not to overlook the forces of male power, which maintain unequal social relations within the family and household. A study carried out as early as 1979 shows that the ideology of domesticity was equally accepted among both white and Asian girls, revealing a complexity of collusion, resistance and opposition (Brah 1979). Indeed, South Asian women's organizations have systematically sought to challenge not only the exercise of male violence, discussed later in the paper, but also articulated the need for Asian women to make their own choices about how and why they challenge their marriage systems within a context where Asian marriages have become so deeply ingrained within racialized discourses (Trivedi 1984). While an important site of tension, negotiation and challenge, the issue of marriage is not the only significant factor for South Asian women, as amply demonstrated by the challenges they have posed both at discursive and practical levels.

Black 'Community' Action

The existence of ethnic mobilization as a salient feature of modern societies is widely accepted. In Britain, attempts have been made to distinguish ethnic from other forms of mobilization as well as to examine the conditions under which it occurs and the processes that give rise to ethnic leaders (Rex and Tomlinson 1979; Werbner and Anwar 1991; Rex 1991; Rex and Drury 1994). Many of these earlier attempts have come under scrutiny recently and though acknowledged for providing some useful insights, they have been criticized for remaining at the level of generality with limited applicability for contemporary developments. More importantly, much of this work has been highlighted as retaining a stereotypically essentialist unitary view of culture.

Poststructuralism and postmodernism have warned against unitary homogeneous categories; thus the notion of a unitary racism has been replaced by that which sees it as changing and historically situated within particular contexts. Consequently, questions of cultural production and politics of identity have been foregrounded in recent times as distinct from culturalist explanations of the 1970s, which emphasised the cultures, and traditions of the 'victims' (Hall 1988). Indeed, the contemporary period is marked by the emergence of new ethnicities and a complexity of racisms on the one hand and a fragmentation of 'blackness' as a political identity, with a foregrounding of ethnic and cultural difference on the other (Solomos and Back 1995: 36).

The reality of racism and exclusion and ideas about 'race' and ethnicity have been among the most powerful factors in determining the extent and nature of minority ethnic mobilization in Britain. Marginalized in major sectors of British society, such as employment, housing and education, and the overt racism of the British state, as reflected in immigration legislation, for instance, along with its failure to acknowledge and effectively meet the needs of black groups, was a major motivating factor in generating self-organization. Community mobilization and self-organization were a strong feature of migrant reality from the early days. From the late 1960s and 1970s, a multitude of organizations were established, both formal and informal, to organize around a range of welfare, cultural, religious and political objectives in their bid to increase the cultural autonomy, political influence and economic independence of migrant groups. These began to shape political debate and policy agendas and later 'community leaders' began to represent their 'communities' in political bodies that saw a need to involve minority organizations as part of broader trend in public policy. It has been estimated that at the beginning of the 1990s, there were approximately 2000 minority ethnic organizations (Werbner and Anwar 1991: 13). This mobilization has been detailed by numerous writers (Rex and Tomlinson 1979; Werbner and Anwar 1991; Solomos and Back 1995) while there have been fewer attempts to look beyond the organizations to the individuals themselves (Werbner and Anwar 1991). My intention here is not to rehearse such historical detail but to problematize some of the main categories within the discourse, namely community, identity and representation especially when applied to South Asian women.

In the 1980s and 1990s, the contours of black resistance politics have changed dramatically resulting in new forms of minority mobilization as evident in the complexity of ways that racialized political identities have been constructed and reconstructed in recent times. According to Solomos and Back (1995), the trans-formation of minority ethnic political mobilization has often been determined by a mixture of local, national and global forces. In their study they demonstrate the ways in which black political mobilization in the 1990s is marked by heightened attempts by minorities to compete for state-allocated resources as well as to penetrate mainstream political and policy agendas. This period has also signalled a time when black mobilization has itself become more fragmented and less cohesive.

Much of the debate within black organization and politics has focused on the issue of 'black' and its applicability to both African-Caribbean and South Asian groups. Black groups migrating to Britain were differentially racialized but their structural location within major areas of life exposed them to similar processes of racism. Influenced by the Black Power movement in the United States where 'black' became a label of pride, the term was increasingly used by both South Asian and African-Caribbean organizations and activists in the 1970s in an attempt to foster solidarity. Debate about the applicability of 'black' has been prolific since the late 1980s and amply aired elsewhere (Brah 1992; Modood 1994). What it sought to do was emphasize cultural difference at the expense of a politics of unity against racism; in the process it failed to recognize that political and cultural meanings could differ across contexts. As convincingly argued by Brah (1992), this critique overlooked the fact that rather than seeking to deny other major factors which shape and define identities of black groups in Britain, 'black' was used to mobilize collective action and foster solidarity against racism at a particular historical moment. According to Solomos and Back, 'while it is necessary to question essentialist and simplistic notions of blackness, it is important to retain a political and analytical notion of blackness as a way of describing points of convergence and volatile alliances' (1995: 213).

In the 1990s, this critique was reflected in the development towards the ethnicization and depoliticization of community politics resulting often in a greater emphasis on acceptable and safe issues. There is greater engagement with the state as many organizations are dependent on state funding. The term/concept of 'black' has been replaced by other definitions of difference such as 'Asian/Muslim/ Indian', labels that seek to mobilize different cultural, religious and political identities for differing political purposes and outcomes.

Collective action by South Asian women remains an anomaly within the writing on ethnic mobilization as existing frameworks and categories deployed are unable to speak effectively to organized action by women. For instance, a key characteristic of ethnic mobilization is seen to be the 'development of a dramatic and heightened sense of identity/group consciousness' (Rex and Drury 1994: 15). Indeed, Rex has argued that an ethnic group, more than a class, has the ability/advantage of appealing to strong ethnic bonds/ties. However, this cannot be uncritically applied to mobilization by South Asian women, which often involved an implicit critique of the ethnic heritage along with its acceptance; it does not take sufficient account of the sense of discomfort women have and mobilize against. This oversight reinforces the widely accepted notion that ethnic leaders are always men. Indeed, women have often been seen as damaging the interests of the ethnic group because they engage in an internal critique that is seen to be detrimental to the group project, as reflected in the promulgation of leaders that violence against women is not a problem within South Asian communities. Moreover, discussions about ethnic mobilization always focuses on benefiting the group, rather than also contesting and attempting to transform inequalities within as well as without.

Given the marginalization and negation of self that results from racism and sexism, notions of empowerment, community and identity have been central to the agendas of all resistance movements since the 1960s (Yuval-Davis 1994). While differing definitions of empowerment have been offered by a range of writers, many of whom accord centre stage to autonomous grass roots organization (Hill-Collins 1990), as convincingly argued by Yuval-Davis (1994: 180), it is necessary to be critical of the ideology of empowerment and the accompanying notions of community, identity, culture and ethnicity.

The notion of community is central to that of empowerment, whereby the individual is placed within a larger homogeneous collectivity, the entity that undergoes the process of empowerment by tackling its oppression. Within Britain, independent 'community organizations' or ethnic mobilization are largely viewed as the vehicles that further the cause of marginalized groups. It is critical, however, to problematise the notion of community, which is generally formulated as a bounded natural unit, a given in which an individual is either included or excluded, and which leaves little room for internal differentiation. As Yuval-Davis argues:

the 'naturalness' of the 'community' assumes a given collectivity with given boundaries – it allows for internal growth and probably differentiation but not for ideological and material reconstructions of the boundaries themselves. It does not allow for collectivities to be seen as social constructs whose boundaries, structures and norms are the result of constant processes of struggles and negotiations or more general social developments. (1994: 181)

Just as the existence of black people exposed dominant formulations of the 'English community' as racist and exclusive, South Asian women's organizations posed a challenge to the notion of the 'wholeness' of a 'community' with 'leaders' as a chauvinistically constructed collectivity. Similarly, the empowerment discourse overlooks the existence of conflicting interests (as between men and women; Asian and African-Caribbean) and instead includes an 'automatic assumption of Sa progressive connotation of the 'empowerment of the people', assumes a non-problematic transition from individual to collective power, as well as a pre-given, non-problematic definition of the boundaries of 'the people' (Yuval-Davis 1994: 181).

In her analysis of the processes that underline the emergence of local and national black leaders, 'as historically and situationally located social agents' and their constitutive communities, Werbner differentiates four types of communities – as imagined, interpretive, 'suffering' and 'moral' (1991: 20–34). Her categories are useful, but she fails to further analytically differentiate these so that women are also made visible although she recognizes the salience of class. In this way, much of the scholarship has colluded to perpetuate the invisibility of women, subsuming their interests with those of men and hence failing to recognise that communities are not only racialized but also gendered.

As highlighted by Yuval-Davis, discourse on community reduces ethnicity[7] to culture and/or identity. She argues that ethnic mobilization, which seeks to mobilize relevant cultural resources for different political goals, or indeed where the same categories of people are constructed differently for different political projects (for example, 'Paki' by the far right, 'Black British' by those seeking to unite across difference against racism, and more recently 'Muslim fundamentalist' by those engaged in anti-Islamic discourse), is a clear indication that ethnicity cannot be reduced to culture. For instance, South Asian women's organizations often constructed new boundaries and included those previously defined as outsiders so that 'Asian' included Sikh, Muslim and Hindu. As pointed out by Brah (1992: 58), 'difference is constructed differently within various discourses. These different meanings signal differing political strategies and outcomes.' Important questions are thus posed for minority groups generally and for women in particular. Should differences be overlooked in the interests of the group? Is group solidarity and collective action always desirable? Under what conditions does the ideal of an overarching solidarity become unacceptable? Moreover, culture itself cannot be conceived in fixed, ahistoric, and essentialist ways as is often done in the multi-culturalist discourse (Sahgal and Yuval-Davis 1992).[8]

Differences within groups (gender and class) along with mobilization of ethnicity for differing political purposes further problematizes the notion of 'community representatives/leaders', uncritically accepted in ethnic mobilization discourse. Is mere membership of a group adequate to confer the role of representatives to individuals? It has been suggested that at best such people can be considered to be advocates although multi-culturalist policies have placed the 'burden of representation' on members of subjected groups (Mercer 1988) while at the same time interference in internal community matters has been rejected as part of the continuum of racism. This has meant that male leaders continue to determine policies relating to women. It has also had obvious implications for women who have sought to engage in an internal critique, for instance women who have organized around male violence or fundamentalist politics. It also poses issues for an analysis of the leadership of women's organizations themselves; so to what extent does Werbner and Anwar's (1991: 21) finding that Black leaders are generally all 'elite members of their communities' hold true for South Asian women?

Given that individuals will locate themselves in more than one group at any one time, as seen in the cross-cutting and overlapping alliances built by black women, the question of identity needs to be conceptualized in different ways to that commonly adopted in 'identity politics' discourse. Identity is constantly negotiated, is multifaceted and often within mobilization manipulated and constructed – it is situational. The need to preserve and construct positive collective and personal identities within a racialized context has involved many contradictions for women, who are often accused of divisiveness when emphasizing their specificity. This has often resulted in them being forced to accept a male-defined notion of a collective/community identity. The state itself has played an important role in creating imagined ethnic communities for the purposes of allocation and administration of resources and services. This has had obvious implications for minority groups, as for example when 'Afro-Caribbean' collapses people with different histories, identities and geographies. Moreover, as highlighted by Drury (1994: 20), it serves to create imagined communities within ethnic groups as leaders emerge professing to represent their communities, and is 'likely to obscure and underrepresent the concerns of particular sections of the ethnic group' like women.

South Asian Women and Collective Action

Questions of identity and subjectivity have been central to both black community politics and Black women's politics in 1970s and 1980s Britain. Subjectivity itself, as convincingly argued by Mama, has to be viewed as dynamic, multiple and as socially and historically produced, involving different discursive locations and contradictory experiential incidents and situations. It is organically generated from social, cultural and political conditions that are themselves changing and sometimes contradictory (Mama 1995: 159). This section provides an overview of the types of issues around which South Asian women have sought to organize and the contradictions that emerged, as well as the challenges that were posed for collective action. It also assesses the impact of black feminism with its emphasis on difference and subjectivity on feminist theory and practice.

Collective action by South Asian women has to be located not only within the broader backdrop of anti-racist struggles but also within the development of the black feminist movement. This movement, an organic development in the 1970s and rooted in a period of heightened racism during a deepening economic crisis, was grounded in the everyday material reality and struggles of black women against both the racism of the British state and society and the challenges posed to women by their disempowering location within their own communities. Some parallels existed with the white women's liberation movement (WLM), but the latter was critiqued for its failure to take on the specificity of black women in its universalizing claims. Frustration at the marginalization of gender issues within black organizations as well as the inability of the WLM to give attention to racism and the particularity of black women within feminist theory and practice was the motivating factor in the formation of autonomous black women's organizations in the 1970s. While a range of black self-help groups existed, as already noted, the birth of feminist black women's groups introduced a new dimension onto the political agenda.

The black feminist movement posed a challenge both at the level of feminist theory and its failure to particularize the universal, and launched a critique at the racist, Eurocentric and class biases inherent in white feminist agendas. From the beginning, black feminism emphasized the international context of race, class and imperialism demanding that primacy not be given to one over the other but the intersections of all be examined. Beginning in the 1970s, black feminists stressed the need to take account of the global social relations of power and the ways in which western feminism served to reproduce the categories through which the 'West' constructs itself as superior to 'others' (Carby 1982). Additionally, some of the central categories of feminism were critiqued along with the invisibility and representation of the 'other' in feminist discourse. Contrary to earlier feminist claims, the end of the 1970s and 1980s clearly demonstrated that 'woman' was not a unitary category and could not be a universalizing claim, blind not only to the global relations of power but also to the historically specific processes of racialization of gender, class and sexuality. Emphasis on difference was the main way through which racism in feminist theory and practice was challenged and exposed so that by the 1990s 'woman' as a unitary category no longer had currency both among activists and within feminist theory.

At a practical level, while the priorities of local black women's groups were determined by localized contexts, generally they aimed to challenge the specific oppression resulting out of racism, sexism and class faced by different categories of black women. The tension implicit to early organisation surrounded the need to, on the one hand, form broad-based alliances and, on the other, to assert distinctiveness and specificity. Attempts to retain sensitivity to difference while developing effective political strategies revealed numerous tensions among women on various political issues. These ranged from differences in the analysis of racism vis-à-vis other systems of inequality through to those between feminists and non-feminists, all resulting in different priorities and strategies (Brah 1992: 10). Identity politics and the emphasis on authenticity of personal experience also posed particular tensions for feminism as it opened up the way for women to build hierarchies of oppression, enabling many facing multiple oppressions to carve a higher moral ground.

Given this wider context, collective action by South Asian women has evolved and manifested itself in a number of ways and has been reflected in a range of political opinions and projects that makes the task of categorizing such organizations difficult. It is worth noting that resistance by South Asian women has deep historical roots both in the subcontinent and Britain, although it may have contradicted the conventional wisdom of what was seen as politically relevant for women. Whether as feminist collectives or religious and welfare groups, their central aim has been to create supportive and enabling contexts for women with a broadly shared experience. Activities have generally centred around the need to provide appropriate information, support and advice, challenge injustice and racist practices through campaigning work, organize social and cultural activities, provide education and training, as well as space for women to organize politically around issues defined as relevant to their lives. Irrespective of their own political leanings, groups have also built alliances with other organizations in order to make a statement about their dis/location in British society. As shown by Phizacklea and Brah, among others, Asian women have led a number of industrial disputes as well as being at the forefront of numerous immigration and defence campaigns along with public protests against violence against women (Phizacklea and Miles 1987; Brah 1992).

South Asian women's groups organized around a range of issues including racist abuse and harassment, deportations and immigration laws and violence against women. Immigration has been one of the major areas for Asian women's organizations. State-orchestrated witch hunts against 'arranged marriages' have served to victimize women and frustrated their attempts to establish normal family life through the enforcement of the primary purpose rule,[9] humiliating 'virginity tests' and X-ray examinations. As a response to racist and sexist immigration practices, numerous anti-deportation campaigns have been spearheaded and successfully fought by Asian women's organizations (see Trivedi 1994: 45–6).

Violence against women has been a major issue around which Asian women have organized since the late 1970s, which has resulted in the establishment of numerous Asian women's refuge support services throughout the country. The setting up of separate Asian women's refuges, which created a safe and supportive space for women and children, challenged both the racism within the refuge movement and the largely male assumption that violence was not a problem within Asian communities. Committed organization by Asian women served to raise the public profile of this issue, which was achieved through a combination of public demonstrations, setting up of support services, conferences and campaigns. In so doing, women confronted many challenges, both from vested interests within their own communities and from the local state, and still continue to face many contradictions. Not only has this concerted action around violence against women challenged patriarchal practices within Asian families and communities but also contested the notion that it is a result of 'backward cultural practices'. In recent years, Southall Black Sisters' committed support and campaigning behind Kiran-jeet Ahluwalia[10] (a woman convicted for the murder of her abusive husband and later released after concerted campaigning by Southall Black Sisters) clearly captured the public attention and is one aspect of the range of protest action by South Asian women in Britain.

This dynamic history of collective action by South Asian women, seeking to build unity not only across 'race' but also ethnicity, religion, caste and regional differences, throws up many questions. To what extent were Asian women's organizations attempting to establish distinctive (ethnic) cultural and political institutions in their bid to establish relative autonomy from the wider society? Or were they an implicit rejection of the 'communal option' while attempting to build broader agendas based on commonality of experience in their objective of self-determination, control and recognition? As noted, much of the mobilization by South Asian women, which soon became a public protest movement, was organized around the issue of violence against women. This not only challenged their gendered but also their racialized identities and involved many contradictions and tensions as it became an arena for women not only to expose Western orientalist constructions of them as 'passive' and 'exotic' objects but also a vehicle for challenging those practices that were detrimental to women on their own terms and conditions. It is a challenge that continues as women try to define and foreground their subjectivity as a complex and multiple reality. For many individual women, South Asian women's organizations provided a key site for nurture and development, especially those who sought to find a political home and an alternative site for their committed involvement; the fact that they have also been a platform for the building of individual careers cannot be overlooked. The debate about the extent to which the leadership of women's organizations managed to reflect their constituencies continues even today but the involvement of numerous 'ordinary' women in many key struggles is testimony to the attempts that many organizations have made to ensure that they do not become divorced from those that they seek to represent.

The issue of funding has been critical in the development, survival and agenda setting of organizations. At times it is possible for groups to mobilise internal funding, but this has not been the case with South Asian women. According to Werbner (1991: 33), 'state funding also depends on "fictions" of communal unity; it both divides immigrant communities . . . into discrete ethnic groups, and implies that each such group is an undivided unity . . . It created dependency . . . It divides and rules.' State funding can have a potentially positive role through a regularization of procedures and accountability structures and the appointment of professionals, but it has been argued by many activists and writers that this professionalization led to a depoliticization and bureaucratization of collective action and 'community' protest politics.

The demand for autonomy and self-reliance, on the one hand, and the right to state funds (dependence), on the other, produced critical dilemmas for South Asian women's organizations. Negotiation, reform and protest have tended to mark the numerous localized and national struggles waged by a range of organizations. Generally, there has been a shift from direct action against the state to intraethnic conflict and competition over scarce resources leading to fragmentation within and between ethnic groups, reducing the potential for solidarity. Undoubtedly, as the last two decades illustrates, increased engagement with the state through state funding and resources has generally reduced the ability of organizations to mobilize against the state and defused the potential for direct action. Any engagement that takes place does so on the terms determined by funding bodies. Thus radicalism has been reduced to the level of rhetoric and the reality determined by negotiation and accommodation in contexts where it is difficult for groups to set their own agendas (Eade 1989).

At a theoretical level, poststructuralism with its decentreing of grand theories and narratives has proffered new ways of addressing complex social realities and is important in its insights for feminist thought and practice. Indeed, as noted earlier, discussions of difference have become central to contemporary feminist theory and practice. It is important to examine how 'race' continues to create racialized categories, such as South Asian women, but it is crucial not to reinforce essentialist notions of difference (the idea that there exists a pure essence across cultural and historical barriers). Earlier black feminist discourse stressed the specificity of black women, but recently we have been urged to guard against essentializing this specificity, so that 'black and white feminism should not be seen as essentially fixed oppositional categories but rather as historically contingent fields of contestation within discursive and material practices' (Brah 1992: 1).

Given the poststructuralist, deconstructionist foregrounding of difference, the question facing feminism is to what extent such a discursive position empowers and enables collective political action at a concrete level or indeed to what extent the two are contradictory? How can an analysis that is so flexible and inclusive inform and feed into material politics that is built on contradictions and conflicts? Yuval-Davis (1994: 189) has argued strongly for a 'coalition politics' view of all politics, where the 'differences among women are recognised and given a voice, without fixating the boundaries of this coalition in terms of "who" we are but in terms of what we want to achieve'. Although her 'transversal politics' framework is useful[11] it not only overlooks the fact that coalitions can be built across those differences that are more acceptable, powerful and privileged but also the existence of differences that are not always reconcilable; it also potentially reduces the broader goal of transforming social relations to smaller issue-based struggles and gains.

Furthermore, the importance of considering whether difference has a different-iating role along with questions of who defines difference and the way in which different categories of women are represented has been stressed by Brah. She argues that when talking about difference, it is important to ask whether difference affirms diversity or is used for discriminatory and exclusionary practices. So how are different groups of women represented and how do women construct and represent their specific experiences, as well as the circumstances under which difference is used to assert a collective identity (Brah 1992)?

Conclusion

This chapter has sought to highlight how racialized identities located within gendered social relations pose complex dilemmas for women seeking to challenge and transform social relations. Collective action by South Asian women, marked by tension and contradiction, challenged not only the masculinist 'community' politics but also racist discursive and material practices in postwar Britain. Through a range of strategies, including political and cultural activism, conscious-ness raising and interpersonal relationships, they have sought to cope with and confront this dominant order.

The complex reality of South Asian women, who themselves are active at a number of levels, has been underlined to demonstrate their multidimensionality, which has challenged existing discourse. Furthermore, some central categories deployed in ethnic mobilization discourse, which continues to overlook the dyn-amic history of organization by women, have been shown to be problematic. While warning against promoting an essentialist notion of South Asian women and Asian communities, it has been argued that much of the existing discourse continues to retain 'community' as a universalizing and homogenizing category that subsumes class, gender, age, generation and spatial differences. Moreover, the notion of identity as multiple, complex and situational has been emphasized together with the need to deconstruct the uncritically accepted notion of 'community leaders and representatives'. This leads us to ask a number of questions: what challenges has difference (race, class, religion, caste and generation) posed for South Asian women? What has collective action sought to challenge and assert? What have been the consequences of collective action for women themselves and their 'communities'? What attempts have been made to deal with the inherent contradictions in organization? What responses has women's activism elicited in their families and communities?

Notes

1. Where I use the term 'black' it refers collectively to all minority groups who are subjected to anti-black racism.
2. 'South Asian' refers to people whose origins lie in India, Pakistan, Bangladesh and Sri Lanka. The terms 'South Asian' and 'Asian' are sometimes used interchangeably.
3. While the majority of West Indian migrants arrived between 1948 and 1962, migration from India took place between 1965 and 1974. Migration from Pakistan continued until the late 1970s and early 1980s while over a third of Bangladeshis arrived during the 1980s (Owen 1994: 31).
4. It is evident that the level of self-employment among South Asians is increasing at a faster rate than that for whites (Anwar 1991: 10).
5. According to Brah, culturalist explanations (emphasizing religion and family) which explain the lower levels of economic activity by Muslim women fail to take account of a number of factors, including the later migration of women from Pakistan and Bangladesh; differences in economic activity between Muslims from Africa and those from the sub-continent; regional variations between South-East/West and Yorkshire and West Midlands; women's socio-economic and local labour market location prior to migration; and the structure of localized labour markets in areas of Muslim settlement (Brah 1992: 67).
6. Recent government and activist attention, especially the campaigning by Southall Black Sisters, being given to 'forced marriages' needs to be distinguished from the recurrent discourse around arranged marriages. For more on Southall Black Sisters see Griffin (1995) and Southall Black Sisters (1990).
7. She defines ethnicity as the 'politics of collectivity boundaries around myths of common origin/destiny aimed at promoting the collectivity via access to state and civil society' (Yuval-Davis 1994).
8. According to Yuval-Davis (1994: 85), 'multi-culturalism constructs society as composed from basically internally homogeneous units – an hegemonic

majority, and small unmeltable minorities with their own essentially different communities and cultures which have to be understood, accepted and basically left alone . . . in order for the society to have harmonious relations.'

9. The primary purpose rule sought to prove that a marriage was genuine and not engaged for the purpose of obtaining citizenship in the UK.

10. Kiranjeet's story is documented in the book *The Circle of Light* by Ahluwalia and Gupta (1997).

11. 'In "transversal politics", perceived unity and homogeneity is replaced by dialogues which give recognition to the specific positionings of those who participate in them as well as the "unfinished knowledge" that each such situated positioning can offer' (Yuval-Davis 1994: 194).

Bibliography

Ahluwalia, K. and Gupta, R. (1997), *Circle of Light: The Autobiography of Kiranjeet Ahluwalia*, London: HarperCollins.

Anwar, M. (1986), *Race and Politics*, London: Tavistock.

Brah, A. (1979), *Inter-generational and Inter-ethnic Perceptions: A Comparative Study of South Asian and English Adolescents and their Parents in Southall, West London*, Ph.D. thesis, University of Bristol.

Brah, A. (1992), 'Difference, Diversity, Differentiation', in J. Donald and A. Rattansi (eds) *'Race', Culture and Difference*, London: Sage.

Carby, H. (1982), 'White Woman Listen! Black Feminism and the Boundaries of Sisterhood', in CCCS *The Empire Strikes Back*, London: Hutchinson.

Eade, J. (1989), *The Politics of Community: The Bangladeshi Community in East London*, Aldershot: Gower.

Griffin, G. (1995), 'The Struggles Continue – An Interview with Hanana Siddiqui of Southall Black Sisters', in G. Griffin (ed.) *Feminist Activism in the 1990s*, London: Taylor & Francis.

Hall, S. (1988), 'New Ethnicities', in K. Mercer, *Black Film British Cinema: ICA Documents 7*, London: British Film Institute.

Hill-Collins, P. (1991), *Black Feminist Thought*, London: Routledge.

Layton-Henry, Z. (1984), *The Politics of Race in Britain*, London: Allen & Unwin.

Mama, A. (1995), *Beyond Masks: Race, Gender and Subjectivity*, London: Routledge.

Mercer, K. (1988), *Black Film British Cinema: ICA Documents 7*, London: British Film Institute.

Modood, T. (1994), 'Political Blackness and British Asians', *Sociology*, 28, (4): 859–76.

Owen, D. (1994), *Ethnic Minority Women and the Labour Market: Analysis of the 1991 Census*, Manchester: Equal Opportunities Commission.

Phizacklea, A. and Miles, R. (1978), 'The Strike at Grunwick', *New Community*, IV (3): 268–78.

Rex, J. (1991), *Ethnic Identity and Ethnic Mobilisation in Britain*, Monograph No. 5, Centre for Research in Ethnic Relations, University of Warwick.

Rex, J. and Drury, B. (1994), *Ethnic Mobilisation in a Multi-Cultural Europe*, Aldershot: Avebury.

Rex, J. and Tomlinson, S. (1979), *Colonial Immigrants in a British City*, London: Routledge & Kegan Paul.

Sahgal, G. and Yuval-Davis, N. (1992), *Refusing Holy Orders: Women and Fundamentalism in Britain*, London: Virago Press.

Solomos, J. (1989), *Race and Racism in Contemporary Britain*, London: Macmillan.

Solomos, J. and Back, L. (1995), *Race, Politics and Social Change*, London: Routledge.

Southall Black Sisters (1990), *Against the Grain: A Celebration of Survival and Struggle*, London: SBS.

Trivedi, P. (1984), 'To Deny our Fullness: Asian Women in the Making of History', *Feminist Review*, 17: 37–52.

Werbner, P. (1991) 'Black and Ethnic Leaderships in Britain: A Theoretical Overview', in P. Werbner and M. Anwar (eds), *Black and Ethnic Leadership: The Cultural Dimensions of Political Action*, London: Routledge.

Werbner, P. and Anwar, M. (eds) (1991), *Black and Ethnic Leadership: The Cultural Dimensions of Political Action*, London: Routledge.

Yuval-Davis, N. (1994), 'Women, Ethnicity and Empowerment', in K. K. Bhavnani and A. Phoenix (eds) *Shifting Identities, Shifting Racisms*, London: Sage.

–5–

Women Migrants and Political Activism in France
Cathie Lloyd

This chapter will look at some recent initiatives to improve the position of women migrants that have been taken up by an increasingly diversified social movement. I shall focus on how migration affects women's status and the way in which alternative routes have been found to express and develop their expertise through voluntary associations. I shall show that migrant women are increasingly involved with the broader women's movement in France, which in turn is more aware of their situation than it was 10 years ago. To begin, I set the scene by examining the general position of women migrants from a diversity of communities. The questions of personal status regimes, discriminatory migration legislation, racist discrimination in society and social isolation are central. I then consider three main groups: the well-established migrant community from North Africa, more recent migrants from West Africa, who have been very active in the *sanspapiers* movement,[1] and women from Turkey, some of whom are Kurdish refugees. These three groups have encountered similar problems but within different contexts, depending on the political environment and the availability of support structures such as community associations.

When women come to France as migrants they enter a context of institutions and a discourse that constructs them in a particular way. In the past the revolutionary egalitarian idea of 'fraternity' has reinforced the marginalization of women in France and this fits into more general concerns about the narrowness of the way in which supposedly universalist ideas like equality and liberty have been used to define the position of women. Like the double burden that has been used to refer to women's economic roles, women migrants inhabit a climate that may be hostile to migrants and asylum seekers and also oppressive of women.

The idea of universal 'fraternity' has been used in many different contexts throughout the post-1945 period in France. While it contains a gender-specific statement about 'brotherhood', it also suggests a normative maleness: political man is male (Pateman 1988; Walby 1994). During the French Revolution fraternity was celebrated at the *Fête de la Fédération* on 14 July 1790 to express a quasi-religious mystique of unanimity, expressed in the song 'Il n'est plus de Bastille/ Il n'est qu'une famille' 'No more Bastille/ We're just one family now' (Vovelle 1985: 101). This expression of universal brotherhood through the metaphor of the family was always rather ambiguous; partly because of the way it was developed in terms of practice and popular culture, partly because of the conflictual context in which it was framed. Expressions of universal fraternity were frequently spiced with bloody threats to 'our enemies': there were groups of people who were excluded from fraternal feelings such as the aristocracy and counter-revolutionaries. This ambiguously expansive notion appeared to ignore the position of women and it was articulated through the idea of the family, which related directly to women's role as mothers and daughters. Most accounts of the different formulations of the Declaration of the Rights of Man (sic) omit Olympe de Gouges' *The Universal Declaration of the Rights of Women and the Citizen* in 1791 (de Gouges 1989 (first published in 1791); Vovelle 1985). Condorcet's work was more widely recognised, particularly his *Mémoires sur l'instruction publique* (1790–1) in which he emphasized that universal equality should include African slaves and women because equality could never be achieved if some sections of humanity remained unequal. Women should be educated to develop their powers of reason, which Condorcet thought would be different, based more on their powers of observation than that of men (Lloyd 1998b).

In her theoretical work, which she developed during a long involvement with the antiracist and women's movements,[2] Colette Guillaumin has made an important contribution to our understanding of the relationship between racism and sexism that has informed debates between migrant women and sections of the French women's movement (Guillaumin 1995). She emphasized the way in which sexual and racial categories are constructed in society. Women's unpaid labour and the exploited labour of racialized minorities are indicators of the appropriation of their bodies and labour common to all people in that category, transcending the boundaries of class. So women are constructed as part of an appropriated category. Guillaumin offers important insights into the workings of patriarchy inside and outside the home, helping us to understand that even as women may be developing emancipated lives outside marriage, patriarchal structures continue to oppress them. She also provided an important critique of the essentialist approach to difference, stressing the social basis of the construction of 'difference'. Part of this construction for women is invisibility – and Guillaumin's analysis of the media presentation of women as not fully present or as only present in terms of certain characteristics such as their age or their ethnicity or their status, may also throw light on the way that violence against women can go unremarked and unreported (Guillaumin 1992). Guillaumin did not directly address the paid work of migrant women but her work is highly pertinent. For many years even the *existence* of migrant women was ignored by social scientists concerned with racism.

This theme of the powerful but limited Enlightenment ideas of equality and difference is a problem for migrant organizations, antiracists and activists in the women's movement, as will become clear later when I look at recent debates. Feminist scholars today argue that the self-image of France as the cradle of the Rights of Man may have delayed the recognition of women's rights. Women gained the right to vote in 1944, at the Liberation.[3] By the late 1990s only 5 per cent of deputies in the National Assembly were women (Fraisse 1994; Reynolds 1987). It was only after a sustained campaign for *parité* that legislation was introduced[4] to give women and men equal access to public office and required all political parties to produce electoral lists at all levels (municipal, regional, national, European) containing equal numbers of women and men. The first report of the official body set up to monitor this situation showed that women occupied a marginal place in French politics, comprising only 10 per cent of the Assemblée Nationale, 5.9 per cent of the Senate but represented slightly better in regional and municipal councils (25 per cent and 22 per cent respectively) and making up 40.2 per cent of the French delegation to the European Parliament (Observatoire de la parité entre les femmes et les hommes 2000).

Partly because of France's demographic deficit, women's employment has always been encouraged so that 87 per cent of women with one child work, 80 per cent of part-time workers are women and social service provision for maternity and paternity leave and for unmarried couples are relatively generous (Lloyd 2001).[5] These reforms, like the new measures designed to tackle racial discrimination in employment and housing, only apply in their entirety to French citizens, and therefore only to those migrant women who have taken French nationality. Despite these limitations, the improved context of women's rights in general is important for migrant women living in France.

Central to our understanding of the position of migrant women in France is how they are situated both in terms of wider society and within their own family sphere. A woman entering France through family reunification becomes dependent on her husband like never before, for her residence status and for her ability to engage with wider society. The countries of the Maghreb have legal codes of personal status[6] that are recognized in the bilateral agreements with France. This has led to complex legal cases over the recognition of repudiation and polygamy. In their relations with wider society migrant women are faced with a whole set of attitudes that produce a social construction of their place(s) as women and as migrants. These may vary according to her ethnicity, age, economic and legal status.

The General Legal Position of Women Migrants in France

The situation of women migrants is particularly affected by two main sets of factors: firstly, the general view towards migrants and, secondly, their status as

women. Immigration officials assume (wrongly) that the primary migrant is male
and that women come as part of a family migration. Apart from the obvious problems this may cause to the single female migrant, this throws all women back onto
their status in their family – either their family of birth or of marriage – ignoring
their wider roles and aspirations. They also ignore the position of Portuguese
women who often migrated on their own account to undertake domestic work
(Condon 2000). To unscramble this complex set of issues we will look at general
provisions for migration (including asylum seekers) in France, and then at the way
in which migrants' status as women is affected by migration.

Regulation of Migration

In 1945 a National Office of Immigration (ONI) later re-named the Office of
International Migrations (OMI) was set up to regulate entry, work and residence
of migrants. It was shaped by the idea that the country's demographic deficit could
be made up by encouraging family migration, but which tended to favour Catholic
Europeans rather than Muslim North Africans. However, migration to France
was organized on a very complex basis often with the aim of avoiding the heavy
bureaucracy of the OMI. Some migrants (almost exclusively male) were recruited
directly by their employers by offices set up in the country of origin. The vast
majority entered France without work or residence permits and were subsequently
regularized, which encouraged the development of an exploitative sector of the
labour market (Wihtol de Wenden 1988). A wide variety of different regulations
applied to people of different origins: Algerians and others from French ex-
colonies were largely unregulated until the mid 1970s, then many were covered
by bilateral agreements. The Overseas Departments had their own office, the
BUMIDOM, which recruited people into low-paid public sector jobs in the post
office and hospitals and for domestic labour (Condon and Ogden 1991).

During this period (the 1950s, 1960s and 1970s) it was assumed that integration
of migrants would take place through assimilation – by taking French nationality.
From the 1980s a bewildering number of changes in the law, indicates the presence
of a harsh polemic about the role of immigration in France. In the 1980s, following
considerable pressure from migrant and antiracist groups there were moves
towards the establishment of a 10-year combined residence and employment card
(Lloyd 1998a).[7] Changes of government saw a renewed emphasis on deportation[8]
followed by a relative liberalization.[9] Following a long debate about nationality
(Long 1988), a right-wing government in 1993 introduced a reform of the Nationality Code, increased identity controls and new regulations for entry, reception
and settlement of foreigners in France.[10] The assumption was that foreigners had
no automatic right to enter or stay in France: the official aim was 'zero immigration'.

This law reduced the options for family reunification but went much further, subjecting marriage between French and foreign persons to intrusive scrutiny and limiting the residence right of the spouses of French citizens. Even people who had come to France as children and who had lived there all their lives saw the guarantee of staying in the country withdrawn once they had reached adulthood.

The Position of Migrant Women

The number of migrant women in Europe has increased since the early 1980s but this increase should not distract us from their presence and importance in the past. Researchers have revised their ideas as they became aware of the inadequacy of migration data kept by the ONI, which in the early days did not keep records about spouses or families (which is how women would have been categorized and then made to disappear). Max Silverman points to the large number of Italian and Spanish migrant families living in France in the 1930s (Silverman 1992). We also know that there were substantial numbers of women among Algerian migrants during the 1950s, and that they were active in supporting the national liberation movement. Benjamin Stora has commented on this role of Algerian women who were sometimes able to organize protest when Algerian men were not and Abdelmalek Sayad has documented more than 350,00 Algerians living in France, many of them families who raised funds for the FLN and were systematically harassed by the French police (Sayad 1999; Stora 1991).

There was constant family migration in the 1960s: 41,000 per annum on average, rising to 55,000 between 1965 and 1969 (Tapinos 1992). There was considerable variation between different groups: family migration was high among Italians and Spanish in the 1960s, and towards the end of that decade there was a considerable movement of Portuguese. More than 70,000 people entered as family migrants between 1972 and 1973 (Kofman et al. 2000).

Since 1974 and the formal 'ending' of labour recruitment through immigration, the entry of women through family reunification has been one of the main forms of new immigration.[11] Controversy continued, however, so regulations fluctuated according to changes in government policy, notably in 1976 when the Secretary of State for Foreign Workers, Paul Dijoud wanted to encourage it while a year later Lionel Stoléru halted it for three years. Following intense pressure from activists and a court case brought by the solidarity organization *Groupe d'Information et de Soutien des Immigrés,*[12] the government relaxed the rules, but prevented spouses from seeking employment (Kofman et al. 2000; Silverman 1992). In the period 1976–80 more women than men were granted work permits.

By 1999 women constituted 47 per cent of the general immigrant population. The majority were aged between 20 and 40 years: for the age group up to the age of twenty which included people who have been brought up in France, there were roughly equal numbers of males and females. Since the late 1990s there has been a relaxation of measures facilitating family reunion, but there is also an increased awareness of the migration of single women, who may be seeking professional advancement, a better education or escaping the insecurity of poverty, oppression within the family, perhaps as a result of pregnancy outside marriage, widowhood, divorce or as a result of HIV infection. There is also significant female immigration organized through trafficking networks of prostitution or domestic workers from Eastern Europe and Asia and the Far East.

Migration can be a route to self-improvement, many women are initially thrown back on the resources of their families. The family is for many an essential refuge in a hostile and alien environment, the channel through which contact with the country of origin is maintained and visits are exchanged. In some cases women are more exposed to exploitative situations. As the transmitters of culture, often held responsible for the family honour, they may become dependent on and under the surveillance of their husbands, fathers, brothers or sons. Here we can see the impact of the personal status codes for Muslim women (marriage, divorce, repudiation, domestic violence, contraception and childbirth). Their relationship with their family structure and wider culture may involve them in conflict over polygamy, sequestration, forced marriage or even clitoridectomy. In French law their rights of residence or employment are linked to those of their husband.

Rights of Entry and Independent Status

Under the Right-wing government of 1993–7, very restrictive regulations were imposed on migration, which have been barely altered by Socialist administrations. The Pasqua laws imposed a period of two years before the spouse could gain independent status. This was restored to one year in 1998, but during this period there were numerous cases of women trapped in an unhappy marriage, suffering abuse and violence.

On arrival in France, many women became completely dependent on their husbands for the first time. For instance, West African men had previously been employed on short-term contracts in low-paid, insecure manual occupations, in street or public transport cleaning or in manual jobs in factories. As the tertiary sector became important opportunities opened up for men and women in largely unregulated hotel and catering jobs. While they worked in France, their families had been forced to cope in a variety of ways, including the extensive networks of women market traders (most notably the Yoruba), who in some West African societies have considerable autonomy and authority. In the early months of family reunification there was often great friction as men took charge of the household finances because they had a better grasp of the French language. As several researchers have shown, women from Senegal and Mali were well placed to recapture some of this ground by setting up trading and savings groups (*tontines*), which were also used to develop friendship and community networks (Institut Panos 1993; Nicollet 1994; Quiminal 1991). This was a difficult situation, and many women's groups continue to campaign around these difficult transplanted relationships, which have left many at the mercy of their husbands in a foreign country. Women's groups have campaigned around the key demand for spouses to be given independent status upon entry, and this has been taken up, notably by the Green Party (*Les Verts*) who, at the time of writing, have a voice in government (Comitè de Suivi des Lois sur l'Immigration 2000; RAJFIRE 2000).

Immigration regulations pose problems for women in polygamous marriages. There have been cases where women have not known that their husbands have taken second wives until they returned to France with them. Apart from the difficulties of living in such a situation in cramped, insalubrious accommodation, far from the support of relatives, since 1993 the regulations have changed and only one wife in a polygamous relationship can be admitted to France. This affects the immigration and social rights of the second and subsequent wives. They often live a vulnerable and insecure existence entering France on tourist visas and attempting post hoc regularization. In some cases a man may arrange for his wives to come to France in turn, which means that none of them have residence rights (RAJFIRE 1999), but irregular immigration status also means that these women lack the right to claim social security and health benefits. This has resulted in cases where one wife is forced to borrow another's papers in order to seek medical attention.

L'Affaire du Foulard

The 'affair' of the Islamic headscarf is really a series of disputes about the right of women to cover their heads in schools, colleges and universities rather than one, specific case. In its early phase in 1989 the 'affair' illustrated the lack of power and control of women over matters relating to them. A national debate about whether or not they should be allowed to wear headscarves took place: The extreme-right Front National (FN) used the issue as an excuse to protest against what they depicted as the 'Islamization' of France. Trade unions, freemasons, antiracists, the Arab League, different Muslim organizations all pronounced on the headscarf. The covers of weekly magazines were dominated by pictures of young women wearing the *hijab*. But the debate took place literally over their heads: they were not invited to comment.

The details of the first 'headscarf affair' of 1989 is well documented (Gaspard and Khosrokhavar 1995; Spensky 1990). It began with the suspension from school of two young Moroccan women who wore headscarves in the classroom. This was seen as going against the ideals of secular education whereby pupils and teachers leave religious views and symbols outside the classroom. However, these girls were being treated in an exceptionally confrontational way: it had long been informally accepted that pupils could wear crucifixes to school for instance, and this was not the first time that headscarves had been worn in class. The specific implications of the *affaire* for the status of migrant women in France were submerged by the discussion about the relationship between Muslim culture and state secular education. While acknowledging that there was an issue about women's position, many French women academics such as Dominque Schnapper and Elisabeth Badinter strongly defended the emancipatory work of secular, republican education and upheld the decision to exclude the headscarf-wearers from school or claimed that the ban on headscarves would help women to dispense with the symbols of patriarchal power (Spensky 1990).

The response from antiracist organizations was also ambiguous. *SOS-Racisme* met behind closed doors for a whole day, and then offered support for what they termed 'open secularism'. They focused on the general debate about the integration of young people whose parents had migrated to France but made no reference to women. The vice-president, Gisèle Halimi, resigned arguing that *SOS-Racisme* needed to confront the position of equal rights for women and not just to focus on 'successful integration' (*Libération*, 2 November 1989; *Politis*, 9 December 1989).

One association, Expressions Maghrebines au Feminins (EMAF), opposed the idea that girls should be excluded from school for wearing headscarves and emphasised that the real problem was that of the integration of Muslim women, not the headscarf itself. Expressions Maghrebines au Feminins planned to tear up a veil in public to symbolically reaffirm their belief in individual liberties (*Libération*, 1 November 1989).[13]

Hayette Boudjema, one of the leading lights of SOS Racisme, organized a petition supporting this same view, which was signed by a number of prominent women some of whom were involved in the women's movement.[14] This acknowledged that the headscarf symbolized the oppression and constraint of Muslim women, but opposed their exclusion from school. Hayette Boudjema feared that antiracists had been misled by the debate between religious and secular fundamentalists and that women, who had the most to gain from education and subsequent integration, would be the ones to lose. Exclusion from school would leave them further marginalized. A similar position was sustained by women from *France Plus* (Zahia Ramani and Nadia Amioni) who emphasized that nothing should prevent women from being integrated within republican values, 'School is a space of liberty for children brought up in the North African community' (*Libération*, 1 November 1989). That is why they argued, allowing the headscarf in school would be a mistake, a backward step for young women who surreptitiously changed into fashionable jeans on their way to school, away from the supervision of their families. They feared that the affair was a gift for the extreme-right *Front National* leader Le Pen because the publicity given to the headscarf would fuel a racist backlash.

Etienne Balibar was one of the few to comment on the hidden gender dimension of the headscarf affair, 'it is simultaneously omnipresent, but obstinately denied, while giving rise to gross stereotypes'(*Libération,* 3 November 1989). The head-scarf signified the institutionalized inferiority of women, was one of the ways in which male-dominated Western societies were able to convince themselves of their collective superiority. He wrote, 'Fatima, Leila and Samira were taken as hostages and became pawns between two antagonistic phallocracies' (*Libération*, 3 November 1989).

The really important issue for antiracists lay in the widespread refusal to accept the children of immigrants in school. This interpretation led away from the specific problem of young women wearing headscarves. Regardless of their motives, which could be religious conviction, a way of managing tensions at home, or even youthful rebellion against family or school authorities, it was assumed that the girls were being manipulated by fundamentalist male authority figures. Later, some studies did try to understand these motivations and produced a more nuanced analysis (Gaspard and Khosrokhavar 1995).

The debate about the place of headscarves in schools continues, fuelled by international developments, changes of government or local protests (*Le Monde,* 28 March 1997; *Le Monde,* 10–11 January 1999; *L'Express,* 20 January 2000). But there are indications of changes in attitudes to women who have been affected both by fundamentalism and by racism in France. A mediator, Hanifa Cherifi (an official of the Education Department who is herself of Algerian origin) has intervened in all such cases since her appointment in 1995 to help with the implementation of the Bayrou circular (1994) which allows headteachers to make decisions about how to deal with the headscarf but these provisions still do not take into account the situation of young women who are attempting to express themselves by wearing the *hijab* or who are attempting to manage their relations with their families. Their voices are increasingly heard through a multiplicity of associations at local, regional and national level.

The Growing Importance of the *Mouvement Associatif*

In the early 1980s two developments freed some space for women's mobilization in general. The first was a great impetus given to local associational life when the 1901 law regulating associations was reformed to allow foreigners to lead formally recognized associations (Conseil d'Etat 2000).[15] The second development, the decentralization of many government structures and policies after 1981 provided a new institutional terrain within which local associations could develop (Negrouche 1992). These new structures provided a sympathetic environment in which women could operate, gaining or using their experience in these expanding and wide-ranging associations. There were fewer barriers to their advancement than in more established structures.

The new associations built on earlier more political youth antiracist groupings, which had developed as the children of primary migrants began to come of age. Their activities were oriented to their lives in France, whereas their parents' political activity had often been focused on their countries of origin. This was a significant development. At the end of the 1970s a youth movement developed against racist violence, mobilizing around grass-roots initiatives such as *Rock against Police*. This was largely dominated by young men, and was linked into a masculine popular culture of rock music. In 1983 many activists mobilized around the March for Equality (Bouamama 1994). The participants in the March were relatively politically inexperienced and women found that the media was just as interested to hear their stories as their male counterparts. One or two forceful personalities (such as the film maker Farida Belghoul) became well known media performers. They emphasized cultural production, drama, writing and visual representations.

During the late 1980s the associations began to situate themselves within the French political structure, around the debates about the nationality code, the crisis of violence, discrimination and exclusion in the *banlieues*,[16] questions of identity as raised in the Islamic headscarf affairs. In the most recent phase (late 1990s and early 2000s) commentators suggest that associations are on the one hand increasingly focused on local, neighbourhood problems and on the other more effectively linked to national associations (Wihtol de Wenden and Leveau 2001).

Through their different manifestations, young women found it easier to enter these relatively unformed structures than the more rigid male hierarchies of established political organizations. Employment open to migrant women remains extremely limited: the main areas of work being the domestic and related service sector (cleaning, and other forms of domestic labour) and largely unskilled posts in manufacture (Migrations Etudes 2002; Leonetti and Levi 1979; Morokvasic 1975). To make things worse, there are a large number of posts in the French public services (which is still a major employer), which are reserved for French citizens.[17] Others, especially asylum seekers may have experienced a dramatic fall in status as a result of migration, forced to leave professional jobs for uncertainty, unemployment or voluntary work. The most important source of such voluntary employment for many is to be found in associations.

One of the best known of these organizations set up specifically by young women from immigrant families from the Maghreb is the *Nanas Beurs* established in 1985. They describe themselves as:

> Bringing together young women of Maghrebien immigrant origin . . . having in common the will to combat their oppression. This is a specific oppression common to all women throughout the world (as a sex) and also an oppression which is experienced by women with an Arab-Muslim background. We believe that to have a consciousness of this oppression was insufficient. It was necessary to take some action.

A more recent summary of their activity (July 2000) shows the association providing services for some 1,500 people every year, specializing in help to migrant women who have family difficulties (they cite forced marriages, forced return to the country of origin, denial of their chances for education or sequestration). From their base in Boulogne-Billancourt, on the outskirts of Paris they provide psychological counselling with individual and group work, social work support, and language classes in Arabic and English. They also undertake out-reach activities in schools, colleges and universities.

A small group of Turkish women set up ELELE[18] at about the same time as Nanas Beurs. The association is avowedly feminist and nearly all of those working there are women, and the organization sets out to serve the Turkish and the wider community (especially in the 11th and 10th *arrondissements* of Paris where they are based). The objectives of the organization are to support the integration of Turkish migrants into French society and much of their expertise is used to providing advice for women and men alike about dealings with French bureaucracy, housing, employment and immigration problems. What is special about ELELE is the very welcoming environment they provide for women for whom they provide language training (literacy in Turkish and basic French conversation) but also run seminars on matters of interest to their female clients (they say that the most popular sessions are about health and dieting) and also arrange outings and visits. They also provide advice for agencies which intervene in domestic disputes My observations and interviews at ELELE showed how a resourceful, voluntary organization like this can give support to newly arrived migrants who may take voluntary responsibilities there which can prepare them for paid employment. ELELE does not challenge the basis of French society except where it discriminates or makes unjustified assumptions about migrants from Turkey, and it is recognized by the authorities as an important base for integration.

Both Nanas Beurs and ELELE in their different ways addressed the general problem of the contradiction between the respect for family tradition and European culture, which is increasingly centred on relational exchanges, leaving most of the emotional, affective part of lives and social organization of immigrants to the community (Rude-Antoine 2000). Women from Morocco, Algeria, Tunisia, Senegal, Mali, Mauritania and Turkey face quite intractable problems. Women are faced with the choice of either submitting to 'traditional' practices or a radical break with their family (ELELE 1992; ELELE 1998). They may be ambivalent, torn between their violent opposition to a marriage and the fear of betraying their family and these associations can help them to find accommodation, and social support. The situation, paradoxically, becomes more difficult as young women succeed: in schools, colleges, universities they are doing better than boys in terms of qualification, and are more likely to take responsibilities in class, in municipal youth councils or in their neighbourhoods, despite often having to shoulder additional family responsibilities.

The women leading in these associations are attempting to project a positive image of Muslim women in France. They tended to be from middle-class or well-educated families but often because of political activities, were conscious of their responsibilities to those less powerfully positioned than themselves. A similar approach has been adopted by women elected to local authorities or who worked as 'cultural mediators', playing a central role in the cohesion of migrant communities (Andizian and Streiff 1982; Oriol 1982). They have been portrayed as operating at the interface of contemporary French and Maghrebi societies: 'Cultural mediation work based on the situations of daily life which could turn into a crisis through misunderstandings due to inadequate communication . . . they try to restore the links between culture and identity' (Delcroix 1994). This work, which provides an interface between French and migrant communities, can be illustrated by the response of women's associations to the campaign of the *sanspapiers*.

West Africans, Housing and the *Sanspapiers*

Some of the advances (and the inherent limitations) of this associative movement can be seen in the *sanspapiers* movement of the late 1990s, and continue today. The movement developed in the context of restrictive legislative measures (described above) which increased the regulation of migrants, deprived new categories of people of residence permits, or denied legal status to others who had lived and worked legally in France for many years. The media linked *clandestins* (who were often migrants who had entered legally but who had lost their residence status) to crime, drug dealing and terrorism. In particular, West African migrants were targeted in discussions about the limits of integration, which focused on the presence of polygamous families in France. West African women occupied a very low status, they had lost their autonomy on migration to France, and only gradually redeveloped their social networks, so important in finding work, and sustaining sociability (Nicollet 1991; Quiminal 1991; Quiminal 1995a; Quiminal 1995b).

In the early 1990s West African women had led demonstrations for better housing conditions, setting up a tent city at Vincennes (Lloyd 1997). Most of those involved in initiating and sustaining this protest were women and they made a major symbolic impact by bringing their daily lives into the public arena. The sight of women and men attempting to provide for their families in what looked like a refugee camp on the esplanade of the Chateau de Vincennes in Paris, was a visible indictment of the inhumanity of current immigration policy. Their visibility began to challenge media stereotypes of the African male migrant worker. However it was not easy to sustain the unity of this protest as the media focused on the 'colourfulness' of the women and emphasized their family role at the expense of the single people involved in the protest. As the summer protest dragged on into autumn and winter, the French housing authorities began to pick off 'worthy' families for housing offers. An imaginative squat at the rue du Dragon, in the Saint Germaine area of Paris continued the protests during 1995. This captured media headlines with theatrical campaigning, and broadened the reach of the campaign by linking the struggle for migrants' rights with those of all homeless people notably through the housing rights group Droit au Logement (DAL) campaign (Droits Devant! 1995). There had also been a series of hunger strikes organized by rejected asylum seekers.

On 18 March 1996 a group of 300 West African families occupied the church of Saint Amboise, Paris XI, to highlight their claims for residence papers. They were rapidly evicted from the church but found a temporary home in the church of Saint Bernard, Paris XIII. In mid-August, a time when political France normally closes down, the church was unexpectedly raided at dawn by CRS riot police, and hunger strikers, children and all the other *sanspapiers* were evicted, some in chains. The government badly miscalculated with this move. There was a furore: film stars such as Emmanuelle Béart were photographed being dragged out of the church while still chained to the other protestors. Public opinion responded to the breach of the sanctity of the church, but mainly to the sight of women and children being terrorized by the riot police.

The raid on Saint Bernard helped to galvanize a wider coalition of support for the *sanspapiers*. They led a nomadic existence, living in a succession of local buildings owned by the church, trade unions, and later the radical theatre at the Cartoucherie in Vincennes. They turned this to advantage by broadening their base of support among radical media workers and trade unionists, and within a month had been joined by a college of mediators who helped to negotiate with the authorities, while they kept up media attention by the use of protest actions and hunger strikes.

Women from West Africa played a prominent role: giving interviews to the press about how they came to France and revealing the impoverished conditions in which they were obliged to live. Most of the women interviewed had been left alone in France following the deportation of their husbands, and now faced destitution, especially if they were not fluent in French. But there were also highly educated women among them, such as Madjiguène Cissé who revealed herself to be a talented orator. In defending herself and others against deportation she reminded the tribunal of the role of women in the railway workers strike of 1947 during the Senegalese struggle for independence from France.

In dealing with the press the *sanspapiers* had a difficult path to tread. West African women were portrayed suckling babies, wearing colourful clothes and dancing at the front of demonstrations. These images challenged the criminalized stereotype of *clandestin*. They disrupted the public/domestic division that underscores gender relations in political life to the detriment of women (Rosaldo and Lamphere 1974). It was important to remind the French public that many of the children involved in the *sanspapiers* protest would be legally entitled to French citizenship at the age of maturity. So protective attitudes towards children and respect for family life could come into play, a tactic often used in immigration hearings to assert the right to family life under article 16 of the UN Universal Declaration of Human Rights (Prencipe 1994).

This use of discourse about the family also gave rise to disquiet among the *sanspapiers* and their supporters. The media equated the family with the Western-style nuclear family. The privileging of the family meant that people not living in a married relationship would be seen as less worthy of support. It was much more difficult to influence the media agenda to favour the rights of single people, and it was difficult to prevent the issue being defined in terms of 'traditional' French values. And yet these values did not prevent them from using physical violence against female and male protestors alike. In her account of the protest, Madjiguène Cissé (1999: 142–3) wrote:

> For some it was far too much to have a woman who was foreign, Black, and a *sanspapier*, especially when she could prove that she was as able to think, analyse, and organise. Men often prefer submissive and docile women. In the collective, the only way they could prove their superiority was to show their muscles. When they can't control the way the argument is going, men tend to use violence . . . The employees of the *PJ*[19] or the *RG*[20] used a different violence to inflict damage, this time it was verbal. Insults when there are no witnesses, there you are alone, with two, three, or six police sometimes, who are there to remind you that you are just a poor little woman!

These problems from 'outside' the protest were not the only ones faced by the women involved. The way the protest was organized involved people living in close proximity to one another, in highly stressful circumstances. In order to press their point of view women had to impose themselves. Cissé describes this as a learning process – members of the collective learned that women were capable of analysing a situation, expressing their point of view and making interesting suggestions. She points to a number of significant changes, including those involved in domestic roles – notably a man took charge of the cooking in Saint Bernard. As in many moments of intensified activity, there was conflict, but there were also heightened understandings between the *sanspapiers*.

Important solidarity came out of the experience of the associative movement I have discussed above. During the 1980s and 1990s, activists had gained experience, structures and developed networks and the earlier form of the *sanspapiers* struggle had alerted them to some of the key issues involved (Simeant 1998). Some of the long-established antiracist organizations set up their own committees to focus on the position of migrant women.[21] Most migrant organizations have developed sections or committees to focus on women: this is certainly the case with Turkish and Kurdish associations I met in the spring of 2000, who were actively seeking to develop these sections. In 1998, the RAJFIRE (Reseau pour l'autonomie des femmes immigrées et refugiées) was set up. It was composed of representatives of many different associations,[22] having links with the Collectif pour les droits des femmes and the Comité de Suivi des lois sur l'Immigration, based in the National Assembly. They participated in the World March for Women in 2000 and work closely with the different *sanspapiers* collectives and other migrants defence groups.

Cissé writes especially about the impact of this solidarity between women. She evokes all sorts of contact, at the level of everyday concern and presence and the high-profile media presence of celebrity supporters. The contact between French women's organizations and the *sanspapiers*

> was a mutual enrichment. Some French women had never had such a close relationship with foreign women before. It was a great discovery for us all that women could establish such a contact so easily. There was no doubt that women were the stabilising factor in this struggle, they gave it renewed life. They showed an attachment and unsurpassed faithfulness which depended on women's mutual complicity, I think that their effectiveness came out of their profound respect for the equality for which we were struggling. (Cissé 1999: 146)

Conclusions

It would appear that the basis for women's solidarity started to be built around the *sanspapiers* struggles for rights, particularly for the equal rights of women migrants. There has been a struggle for the recognition of their situation, over many years, which in the French context has taken place in a situation where the discourse of human rights is too frequently articulated as the rights of *man,* and the bonds of solidarity too often rendered as *fraternity.* With significant changes in the way in which women are represented generally in French politics a space has begun to open up for women migrants to challenge the way in which they too are ignored, or constructed as appendages of their families. This has involved a double burden, a dual oppression whereby women are oppressed both within their immediate family or ethnic group and discriminated against by French society because they are migrants or asylum seekers through repressive and insensitive laws. Struggle within these circumstances has been full of pitfalls as the media tends to portray such a group as vulnerable victims, and thus to diminish their own capacities for action. This was illustrated by the headscarf affair, where French society debated the place of Islam and the future of secular education, with scant regard for the young women who were at the centre of the storm. But through struggles like that of the *sanspapiers*, women migrants have been able to build on the organizational capacity and networks of associations set up in the 1980s. It is important not to overstate their achievements: the *sanspapiers* have not been able to achieve all they had hoped, their main aim to gain regular papers has been thwarted by a cynical government and obstructive officials (CIMADE 2000). But a significant step forward has taken place especially for women migrants who are less isolated than before. More organizations are aware of the multiple oppressions engendered by their position in France, but they are less likely to underestimate the capacity of women migrants to take effective action on behalf of themselves and their communities.

Acknowledgement

Much of the material for this chapter was collected under the auspices of a research project funded by the ESRC (award no L213 252016): 'Civic Stratification, Exclusion and Migratory Trajectories in Three European States'. My co-researchers were Eleonore Kofman and Rosemary Sales.

Notes

1. The *sanspapiers* or undocumented migrants movement made an important impression on French public opinion in the late 1990s. Through a very public demonstration of their plight (occupation of churches and theatres, hunger strikes and a high media profile) they helped to change the terms of discourse from one of 'illegal' migrants to one of being 'undocumented', which took into account the circumstances in which migrants could lose their legal status. (See Fassin et al. (1997; Lloyd 1997).

2. There are long-standing antiracist organizations in France, dating back to the immediate post-war period, such as the MRAP (Mouvement Contre le Racisme et Pour l'Amitié entre les Peuples) and more recent groups formed in the 1980s, such as SOS Racisme – see Lloyd (1998a). The women's movement, such as the official MLF (*Mouvement de liberation des femmes*) had few activities

relevant to migrant women – see Lloyd (1998b), but more recently important partnerships have developed between feminists mobilizing at the grass roots and migrant women, notably the RAJFIRE, a feminist network. See RAJFIRE (1999).

3. It was said that women had 'earned' their right to vote because of their heroic role in the Resistance, thus denying their inherent right.

4. Law of 6 June 2000

5. *New Ways* 4/98 (European Network: Family and Work EC Employment and Social Affairs).

6. In the case of Morocco, the *Mudawwana*, formulated in 1957, revised in 1993, with a more liberal version currently under debate, the controversial Algerian *Code de la Famille* (1984, amended in 1988) and the Tunisian *Magâlla* first set out in 1956 and revised in 1993.

7. Law of 17 July 1984.

8. Law of 9 September 1986, 'loi Pasqua'.

9. Law of 2 August 1989, 'loi Joxe'.

10. Law of 22 July 1993 on nationality, 10 August on identity, 24 August and 30 December 1993 on entry and settlement.

11. Although not all these new entries are women: Turkish associations in Paris pointed to the position of male fiancés who enter France to marry women who have been brought up in France. This can alter power dynamics within the family to the advantage of the partner familiar with French society, ELELE

12. GISTI, http://www.gisti.org.

13. We should note that for many women of Algerian origin the struggle around the headscarf was an unwelcome reminder of the conflict in Algeria in which Islamic fundamentalists targeted women living independent lives. The headscarf was an important marker in this conflict, which was taking place at roughly the same time.

14. They included Nora Zaidi (MEP); Marguerite Duras, Edmonde Charles Roux; Nora Allami (author of *Voilées dévoilées)* and Simon Iff (Member of Economic and Social Council and head of the French Family Planning Movement (MFPF)); the Member of Parliament Ségolène Royal and Marie-France Casalis (Family Planning).

15. The restrictions were introduced in 1936 against the activities of extreme right-wing militias. The new law was passed on 9 October 1981. Until then, migrant associations operated with the help of French citizens who allowed their names to be used. Recognition in law gives mainly financial benefits as well as an official status to associations.

16. Banlieux, or suburbs, where many ethnic minority people live in dense housing estates.

17. This does include migrants from the DOM-TOM.

18. ELELE is Turkish for 'hand-in-hand'.
19. Judicial police.
20. *Renseignements géneraux*: police who specialize in the collection of inform-
    ation, like the British Special Branch.
21. For instance, in April 1997 the MRAP (Movement Against Racism and for
    Friendship between Peoples) set up a collective, Femmes Immigrées en Lutte,
    as a result of concern about the large numbers of migrant women seeking legal
    advice. They also hoped to position themselves to influence the policies of
    the new government (*Différences* no. 223, November 2000).
22. FASTI, Maison des femmes de Paris, ASFAD, Puri-elles Algérie, reseau femmes
    Ruptures; groups Femmes Libres, Radio Libertaire and individual women.

Bibliography

Andizian, S and Streiff, J (1982), 'Transformations and Reintegrations of the
    Traditional Female Role in an Immigrant Situation', in Unesco (ed.) *Living in
    Two Cultures. The Socio-cultural situation of Migrant Workers and their
    Families*, London: Gower/ Unesco.
Bouamama, S. (1994), *Dix ans de marche des Beurs. Chronique d'un mouvement
    avorté*, Paris: Desclee de Brouwer.
CIMADE (2000) 'Le pouvoir du guichet', *Causes Communes (les hors series)*:
    60: 189.
Cissé, M. (1999), *Parole de sans-papiers*, Paris: La Dispute.
Comitè de Suivi des Lois sur l'Immigration (2000), 'Femmes Etrangères et
    Immigrées en France', Paris: Assemblée Nationale.
Condon, S. (2000), 'Female Migration from Portugal and Activity on Arrival in
    France: a Variety of Personal and Family Strategies', *Population,* 2: 301–5.
Condon, S. and Ogden, P. (1991), 'Afro-Caribbean Migrants in France: Employ-
    ment, State Policy and the Migration Process', *Transactions of the Institute of
    British Geographers* 16: 440–57.
Condorcet (1983 [1790–1]) *Memoires sur l'instruction publique*, Napoli: Biblio-
    polis.
Conseil d'Etat (2000), 'Rapport public 2000. Jurisprudence et avis de 1999. Les
    associations et la loi de 1901, cent ans apres', Paris: Conseil d'Etat.
de Gouges, O. (1989 [1791]), 'The Rights of Women', London: Pythia.
Delcroix, C. (1994), 'Emergence de sujets (Feminins) originaires du Maghreb a
    la jonction de l 'immigration et de la Societe Francaise, rapport du CDIS/
    ADRI', Toulouse: Université de Toulouse le Mirail.
Droits Devant! (1995), 'Effets Pasqua: Les Faits', *Droits Devant* 5 (9 June, 2–3).
Editorial (1990), 'Edito', *Carnets des Nanas Beurs,* 1: Summer, p. 5.

ELELE (1992), 'Les femmes originaires de Turquie. Vie quotidienne, projets, avenir', Report, Paris: FAS/Secretariat d'etat aux droits de femmes et a la vie quotidienne.

ELELE (1998), 'Honneur et Violence. Fatalite ou conjuncture pour les femmes turques?' in ELELE (ed.) *Actes du Colloque organise a l'Unesco*, UNESCO: Elele.

ELELE (2000), *Rapport d'activite 1999*, Paris: ELELE.

Fassin, D., Morice, A. and Quiminal, C (1997), *Les lois de l'inhospitalite. Les politiques de l'immigration à l'épreuve des sanspapiers*, Paris: La Decouverte.

Fraisse, G. (1994), 'Quand gouverner n'est pas représenter', *Esprit*, March–April: 103–14.

Gaspard, F. and Khosrokhavar, F. (1995), *Le foulard et la République*, Paris: La Découverte.

Guillaumin, C. (1992), *Sexe, Race et Pratique du pouvoir*, Paris: Côté-femmes.

Guillaumin, C. (1995), *Racism, Sexism, Power and Ideology*, London: Routledge.

Institut Panos (1993), *Quand les immigrés du Sahel construisent leur pays*, Paris: L'Harmattan.

Kofman, E., Phizacklea, A., Raghuram, P. and Sales, R. (2000), *Gender and International Migration in Europe*, London: Routledge.

Leonetti, I. and Levi, F. (1979), *Femmes et immigrées: insertion des femmes immigrées en France*, Paris: La Documentation Francaise.

Lloyd, C. (1997) 'Struggling for Rights: African Women and the 'Sanspapiers' Movement in France', *Refuge*, 14, (2): 31–4.

Lloyd, C. (1998a), *Discourses of Antiracism in France*, Aldershot: Ashgate.

Lloyd, C. (1998b), 'Rendez-vous manqués: feminisms and antiracisms in France: a critique', *Modern and Contemporary France*, 6, (1 February): 61–74.

Lloyd, C. (2001), 'The Transformation of Family Life and Sexual Politics', in M. Guibernau (ed.), *Governing Europe*, Milton Keynes: Open University Press.

Long, M. (1988), *Etre Français aujourd'hui et demain*, Paris: 10/180.

Migrations Etudes (2002), 'Les Femmes Migrantes et la Creation d'activité, un apport à l'économie française', *Migrations Etudes*, 104, (January).

Morokvasic, M. (1975), 'L'émigration des femmes et quelques unes des transformations sociales qu'elles entrainent, envisagées du point de vue des femmes yougoslaves', *Migration*, 125–38.

Negrouche, N. (1992), 'L'échec des associations franco-maghrébines issues de l'immigration 1980-1990', *Esprit*, (January): 41–52.

Nicollet, A. (1991), *Femmes d'Afrique noire en France*, Paris: CIEMI/ L'Harmattan.

Nicollet, A. (1994), 'Les enjeux féminins d'une migration Africaine', *Migrations Société* VI, 35, (September–October): 27–42.

Observatoire de la parité entre les femmes et les hommes (2000), *La parité en politique*, Paris: Observatoire de la parité entre les femmes et les hommes.

Oriol, M. (1982), 'Introduction: the research on a 'lost generation', educating women migrants in industrialised countries', in Unesco (ed) *Living in Two Cultures. The Socio-cultural situation of Migrant Workers and their Families*, London: Gower/ Unesco.

Pateman, C. (1988), *The Sexual Contract*, Oxford: Polity.

Prencipe, L. (1994) 'Famille-Migrations-Europe. Quelles relations possibles?', *Migrations Société*, 6 (September–October): 27–42.

Quiminal, C. (1991), *Gens d'ici, gens d'ailleurs*, Paris: Christian Bourgeois.

Quiminal, C. (1995a), 'Les associations de femmes africaines', *Regards – Femmes d'ici et d'ailleurs*, 75 (October): 1–30.

Quiminal, C (1995b), 'Mobilisations associatives et dynamiques d'intégration des femmes d'Afrique subsaharienne en France', *Migrations Etudes*, 9 (October–December).

RAJFIRE (1999), 'Brochure du RAJFIRE', Paris: *RAJFIRE*:

RAJFIRE (2000), 'Brochure No 2', Paris: *RAJFIRE*.

Reynolds, S. (1987), 'Rights of Man, Rights of Women, Rites of Identity', in J. Bridgford (ed.) *France, Image and Identity*, Newcastle upon Tyne: Newcastle upon Tyne Polytechnic.

Rosaldo, M. and Lamphere, L. (1974), *Women, Culture and Society*, Stanford: Stanford University Press.

Rude-Antoine, E. (2000), 'Le mariage des Marocains et des Vietnamiens en France: contrainte, persuasion ou liberté', *Hommes et Migrations*, (September–October): 303–8.

Sayad, A. (1999), *La double absence: Des illusions de l'émigré aux souffrances de l'immigré*, Paris: Seuil.

Silverman, M. (1992), *Deconstructing the Nation. Immigration, Racism and Citizenship in Modern France*, London: Routledge.

Siméant, J. (1998), *La cause des sanspapiers*, Paris: Presses de Science Po.

Spensky, M. (1990), 'Identités multiples: l'affaire du foulard', *Modern and Contemporary France*, 42: 126–34.

Stora, B. (1991), *La Gangrène et l'oubli. La mémoire de la guerre d'Algérie*, Paris: La Découverte.

Tapinos, G. (1992), 'Immigration féminine et statut des femmes étrangères en France', *Revue Française des Affaires Sociales*, 46: 29–60.

Vovelle, M. (1985), *La mentalité révolutionnaire*, Paris: Editions Sociales.

Walby, S. (1994), 'Is Citizenship Gendered?', *Sociology*, 28, (2): 379–95.

Wihtol de Wenden, C. (1988), *Les Immigrés et la Politique*, Paris: Presses de la Fondation Nationale des Sciences Politiques.

Wihtol de Wenden, C. and Leveau, R. (2001), *La beurgeoisie. Les trois âges de la vie associative issu de l'immigration*, Paris: CNRS Editions.

Part III
Gender, Ethnicity and Islam

6

Shifting Meanings of Islam and Multiple Representations of Modernity: The Case of Muslim Women in Italy
Ruba Salih

Introduction

Muslim migrants in Europe are often represented as people who move from one bounded cultural and physical location to the global and modern world where they are seen as either resisting or absorbing global (Western) cultural traits. This holds particularly true when it comes to representations of migrant women from Islamic countries. Indeed, in popular and, often, in academic understandings there is a growing tendency to perceive Muslim women who adopt Islamic symbols as embodying an 'authentic' and traditional culture, as opposed to secularized Muslim women who, on the contrary, often come to be seen as hybrid or Westernized and, therefore, as modern. This kind of understanding is reinforced by a frame of reference, especially visible in multicultural perspectives, that sees Muslims as by and large embodying an essence, claiming respect for a set of static and immutable traditions that they would automatically and uniformly reproduce in continuity with supposedly past practices and beliefs. Although disguised by the narrative of respect for cultural difference, these representations as Al-Azmeh aptly puts it, 'reduce the *history* of the present to the *nature* of an invariant essence'(Al-Azmeh 1996 [1993]: 62).

These reductive discourses, however, find an echo in a trend that is forcefully taking place in the Middle East. In the last few years, there have been a plethora of arguments holding that, by combining Islamic behaviour with the quest for self-determination, Muslim women are attaining a more 'culturally authentic' identity, which rejects Westernization and the homogenizing processes inherent in globalization (see Duval 1998).

While it is undeniable that behaviour, symbols and ways of life labelled as 'Islamic' are increasingly embraced as a cultural alternative frame to Westernization by many young educated women both in Europe and in the Muslim world, these new Islamic identities emerge out of a complex intertwining of global, local and historical factors and more often constitute a modern phenomenon than the retrieval of old and traditional practices. Moreover, the contentions (sometimes sadly violent) occurring in the Muslim world among Islamic reformers, secular constituencies, feminists and other subjects show that Islam is not simply an ensemble of static and uniformly practised religious duties pertaining to the private sphere of individuals, but emerges as a political terrain, which opposes different constituencies and their concerns about how state, society and gender relations should be orchestrated. In this context, the roles and facades Islam assumes in the lives of migrant women in Italy mirror global processes in the Arab-Muslim world and elsewhere.

This chapter is an attempt to go beyond formal and normative sociological descriptions of Islam and Muslim women, to unveil and bring to surface the very distinct political, cultural and social projects that being a Muslim woman in Europe (specifically in Italy) implies. Most writing on Muslims in Italy, indeed, tend to reproduce a normative understanding of Islam, seen as an ensemble of religious and cultural norms transplanted in a new context, through which Muslim women's social realities are filtered and explained (see, for example, Saint-Blancat 1999). The paper is based on ethnographic work carried out in several mosques, but which focused predominantly on a mosque where a group of 15 to 20 women used to meet every Sunday.[1]

One of the aims of the chapter is to show how, far from being a shared identity, to be Muslim implies a battlefield for contesting and opposing discourses around authenticity, tradition and modernity.[2] Very often, at stake in these representations is the definitions of the boundaries that mark the belonging to a 'community' or national group. In the Middle East, secular oriented women's movements have been historically accused of threatening the cultural homogeneity of the national community by introducing Western models and behaviour, and therefore, they were and still are labelled as culturally inauthentic by the establishment (Al-Ali 2000). For Muslim migrants in Europe, the processes of contestations around 'authenticity' and 'traditions' may be amplified, because the boundaries of the 'community' are more in danger of being jeopardized and therefore certain Islamic symbols may be actively chosen or imposed as crucial markers of cultural difference.

This chapter suggests that an understanding of Muslim women's multiple attitudes towards Islam cannot dismiss the role played by migration and travel (Eickelman and Piscatori 1990) and by the new place women inhabit (Metcalf 1996). Growing transnational migratory movements together with the rapidity of flows of ideas, commodities and cultural forms, force social scientists to rethink processes of cultural, religious and social formations and the nature of their relations to 'place' and 'space' (Appadurai 1991; Fog Olwig and Hastrup 1997; Gupta and Ferguson 1997).

Muslim Migrants in Italy

Traditionally an emigration country, Italy became only quite recently an important country of immigration and the presence of Muslims started to be visible at the beginning of the 1980s. At a general level, contemporary international migration flows to Italy occurred within a frame of changing socio-economic conditions with respect to the industrial expansion of the 1950s and the 1960s in France and other European countries (see Harvey 1989). Changes have occurred both at the demographic and economic levels. In particular, the increasing need for migrant labour should be located in the globalization processes affecting local economic processes and in the demographic decline of the local population. However, while European industrial societies in the postwar period were characterized by a high level of recruitment within an expanding Fordist industrial sector, in the 1990s, in Italy and elsewhere, migrant labour is employed in highly segmented, flexible and precarious jobs that are unfilled by the local labour supply (De Filippo and Pugliese 1996). In particular, to be competitive within an internationalized and globalized market, small industries in Emilia Romagna (an economically flourishing region in Italy) have been encouraged to reduce labour costs and to introduce flexibility to their recruitment policies. Many such industries, nowadays, employ only seasonal workers.

Migrant women, on the other hand, are increasingly filling the gaps left by the crisis of the welfare state in post-industrial societies through their (often illegal) jobs in the domestic sector and in care-related occupations (Andall 2000). Moreover, the need for migrant women's labour is a reflection of demographic trends in Italy where death rates outnumber birth rates. The rapidly increasing percentage of elderly people in Italy has been accompanied by a major restructuring of the Italian welfare system, due to cuts in public expenditure. By way of confirmation, most migrant women I talked to are employed within the domestic and cleaning sectors and, in very few cases, in small industries. Most of them are employed 'cash in hand'. Migrant women are thus substituting Italian women in their reproductive roles (Andall 2000).

Italy has been generally described as a weak nation due to deep internal historical, cultural, economic and social differences.[3] As we know from Benedict Anderson, all nations are first of all constructions by members who conceive themselves as part of an imagined community of similar individuals. In Italy, the lack of a solid nationhood has its extreme reflection in the emergence of populist movements such as the Northern League. This party seeks secession of part of the North from the rest of Italy (the South and immigrants) on the basis of the retrieval of the ethnic and historical specificity of the northern regions of 'Padania'. Its adherents are at the forefront of an anti-Islamic battle for a re-Christianization of society. On the one hand, the challenge posed by this secessionist movement and its political expressions forged attempts to create political federalism while, on the other hand, it reinforced counter nationalist claims aimed at affirming the unity of the Italian nation on the basis not so much of ethnic and cultural homogeneity, but of a 'common past' (see Rusconi 1997).

Italian political and popular constructions of Muslims reinforce an imagined historical and cultural homogeneity of the Italian-Christian nation, which is represented at once as reinforced and threatened by the penetration of Islamic symbols. Differences within Italy are dismissed or forgotten in the language and images promoted by politicians, newspapers and media that display narratives whereby a culturally homogeneous Italian nation is opposed to a culturally homogeneous community of Muslim immigrants.

In this context, women's representations and behaviour become central to processes of ethnic and national differentiation (Anthias and Yuval-Davis 1989) and this comes forth quite clearly within political and popular discussions around Muslim women's claims to express their religious identity by covering their heads in the public spaces of the European societies where they reside or where they are indeed citizens (Bloul 1996). In such circumstances, the profoundly gendered logic at the base of the various rubrics of modernity and tradition comes to surface. The latter often assumes women's bodies as icons or threats to the integrity of the nation.[4]

For example in 1998 an image of Flavia Prodi (the wife of the former Prime Minister Romano Prodi) wearing a *hijab* during an official visit to Iran, set the stage for debates in the media. The magazine *Liberal* addressed the topic with a special issue on the *hijab,* which discussed whether Muslim women are to be left free to wear veils in a society such as Italy, where, it was suggested, 'women are emancipated'. The implicit question revolved around how much multiculturalism is tolerable within Italian society. Opponents and supporters were called upon to express their opinion on the matter. Similarly to what happened in France, considerations crosscut political affiliations (see Bloul 1996). With few exceptions, all the people interviewed shared the opinion that the veil, in whatever form, is a symbol of oppression and is intrinsically anti-modern. The well-known liberal intellectual Ernesto Galli della Loggia was sympathetic with the right to wear the *hijab*, although he would not accept the teaching of the Arabic language in Italian schools, because 'If we are to allow all groups or minorities to study their own cultural-religious language . . . it is equivalent to a first step towards the end of any attempt to call for Italian society's historical unity'. Cultural and religious differences, evidently, serve the aim of restoring an imagined historical and cultural unity of the Italian nation, which is represented as threatened by the introduction of gendered Islamic symbols.

Muslims and Islamists

According to scholars such as Nielsen (1992: 65), the ethnic and cultural variety of Muslims in Europe has compelled them to universalise Islam, since 'it became necessary to identify those aspects of the way of life which were culturally relative and to categorise them apart from the central Islamic core which must remain absolute.' This process is not so obvious in Italy where, due to the plurality of national and cultural origins of Muslims, the tension between universalization and ethnicization of Islam is quite tangible.

Muslims in Italy are estimated to number around 600,000 (Muslim organizations estimate 1,000,000) and they come from a wide range of countries, where Islamic traditions are very different. The more numerically relevant countries of origin are Morocco, 135,650; Albania, 67,000; Tunisia, 48,664; Senegal, 33,089; Egypt, 25,553; Algeria, 13,324; Somalia, 10,818; Pakistan, 11,320 and Bangladesh, 11,021.[5] These figures however, are deduced from the number of migrants from countries where Islam is professed by the majority of the population, and do not tell us, therefore, how people identify themselves.

Although, as we shall see, a process of universalization and transnationalization of Islam is taking place amongst Muslims in Italy, on the other hand contentions might arise due to differing political and social views on the socio-political role of Islam in a non Islamic society. Through diverse ideologies of Islam, larger arenas of conflict are expressed, which could be generational, political, gendered and ethnic. Or, more simply, they could bear witness to divergent ways of conceiving oneself as Muslim in a non-Muslim place, and thus express conflicting ideologies of place and space. Indeed, the articulation between Islam and discourses around authenticity and tradition is also a significant arena through which the diverse identity renegotiation processes through which Muslim women respond to a new life in a new place could be grasped.

Aziz Al-Azmeh draws a distinction between Muslims and Islamists. The former are concerned with ordinary and day-to-day practices and beliefs, while the latter endorse Islam as a political and militant project and are involved in what he calls an 'overislamization of Islam' (1996 [1993]: 56; see also Abu-Lughod 1998a). Although boundaries are often more blurred, it is useful for analytical reasons to draw a similar distinction to describe the attitudes towards Islam of the Muslim women I worked with. Whereas for some Moroccan women, and indeed also for some Italian women converts or other Arab Muslim women, Islam is the crucial aspect of their identity, for other women Islam is but one among their other identifications. Therefore, I will mainly use the word 'Islamist' to indicate a group of young, well-educated women who regularly meet in the mosque and who endorse what could be defined as an Islamist discourse. I will generally refer to those women who are not involved with activities in the mosque, who usually do not wear a *hijab*, and only sporadically practise some or all of the pillars of Islam, as simply 'Muslim'.[6] The latter are indeed Muslim, because they consider themselves spiritually, culturally and socially as such. This is important since it is a first way to stress that, although they negotiate religion in various ways *vis à vis* Italian society, these women are neither hybrid, as they are sometimes defined in other contexts (see Khan 1998), nor Westernized. The term 'hybridity', used to describe these secular attitudes, is misleading, because it assumes Islamism as historically more 'authentic', denying its political and profoundly modern nature, whereas women who adopt secular stances are described as deviating from the 'norm' (see Salih 2000).

As we shall see, Islamic practices are shaped by the new local space they inhabit, but Islamist women claim that their life in a new country where Muslims represent a minority did not play a role in their rediscovery or reinforcement of an Islamic identity. They perceive themselves as part of the *Umma*, an imagined transnational community, scattered all over the world and often insist on defining Islam as a universal religion, with no local variations. On the other hand, for other women, being Muslim in Italy either remains or becomes a generic sign of belonging. They might define themselves first as Moroccans or Arabs, and then Muslims, although their reflections and thoughts about themselves and others often revolve around Islam because, in their day to day life in Italy, Islam is the primary frame through which their identities are filtered.

As mentioned above, I suggest that by attributing different meanings to Islam, women display and articulate different narratives of modernity. For Islamist women, modernity is possible only through knowledge and the devout practice of Islam, which is nonetheless presented as a break with past traditions. This new Islam represents their way to progression and to social, cultural and spiritual self-fulfilment. Other women, however, are engaged with modernity as a fracture, a process of ongoing crisis between past certainties (or habitus) and current challenges, between the refusal to assimilate and the impetus for secularization, and they express this through a constant negotiation and reflection around diverse cultural models.

Islamizing the Local and Localizing Islam

Mosques symbolize the appropriation of space by some Muslims who increasingly perceive Italy as the country where they and their children are likely to live in the future (see Werbner 1996; Nielsen 1992). Since the end of the 1980s and the beginning of the 1990s, with the flow of migrants mainly from the Maghreb, the number of mosques multiplied. The number of official and unofficial mosques[7] is around

130 (Caritas 1998). In comparison with the institutional Centro Islamico d'Italia, recently built in Rome principally thanks to Saudi funding, the Islamic centres I visited claimed to be entirely financed with donations collected among the 'community'.

Since the 1970s, mosques in Italy have changed their roles from rooms fulfilling religious aims and mainly attended by Middle Eastern students to places that, by promoting different activities and offering several services, are now trying to become a point of reference for Muslims from different parts of the world. The shift in the organization of mosques, thus, also marks the passage from a phase characterized by the temporary project of settlements of students, to one of permanent dwelling of entire migrant families.

Most of the recent mosques have a small library, an office and, in a few cases, rooms equipped for Arabic lessons and small conferences. The bigger mosques also organize pilgrimages and provide services such as Islamic weddings, funerals and rites of conversion to Islam. The need to explain Islam to locals in order to counteract the denigration of Islam in the media, moreover, has urged activists to place special importance on the image of the mosque and its activities. Especially during Ramadan, debates, meetings and conferences are addressed to the local population. As a consequence of control and limitations in their countries of origin, activists often argue that they can proselytize and disseminate their *da'wa* (invitation to embrace the Islamic religion) more freely in Italy (see Nielsen 1992). Many Muslims lament the tendency in many Arab countries to repress completely forms of Islamic institutionalization. In Tunisia, one informant argued, mosques are controlled by the secret services, women can not publicly wear *hijabs* and men with beards are considered as persons potentially subverting the system. In Morocco, too, mosques are subject to increasing controls and special permission from the government has to be issued to carry out activities other than praying (Rouadja 1997).

Islamic centres are also shaped by the presence of Italian converts, amongst them many women, who place specific expectations on the mosque and are often engaged in organizing activities addressed at locals. Italian Muslim women converts in particular, but also other Muslim women, often lamented the lack of space for children and youths within Islamic centres. They see this as necessary for creating and promoting among them the sense of being part of a group, the only way to overcome the isolation in which Italian and non-Italian Muslim youths live and where, thus, they would be able to experience confidently their differences from mainstream youth ideologies and social habits.

In some ways, the participation of educated Italian Muslims in the organization and representation of the mosque is valued by non-Italian activists because it emphasizes the universality of Islam and guarantees useful mediation with the local councils and, more generally, with the state. Converts, however, often propose a textual version of Islam, reinvented as a universal and transnational religion, disassociated from the various local traditions in which Islam developed. More often than those of Muslims by birth, converts' discourses are imbued with references to 'authenticity' and adoption of the texts as the only reliable sources. However, converts themselves are not a monolithic entity. Their organizations reflect a wide range of ideologies and schools that could be at odds with each other.

Among those I used to visit during my fieldwork, the mosque in Reggio Emilia was the only one where a group of women, including both converts and Muslims by birth, met regularly every week to attend classes on Islamic doctrine.[8] Most of them did not go to the mosque in their country of origin. It is in Italy that the mosque increasingly starts to represent a public space inhabited also by women, although for a minority of women, an absolute identification with an Islamist project is in continuity with the lifestyles they held in their country of origin.

In a plurally ethnic environment such as the mosque, Egyptian, Tunisian and Moroccan women (who represent the main national groups within the mosque) used a fusion of written or classic Arabic and the Egyptian dialect in order to communicate, the latter being very popular due to the availability of Egyptian soap operas on satellite TV.

In this context, it is clear how the kind of Islam being shaped and produced in mosques in Italy is not the simple recreation of a familiar environment where individuals privately carry on their prayers or rituals in continuity with habits held in the country of origin. In a context of migration, Muslim identities and organizations are increasingly forged by, and are part of, a collective identification with a global *Umma*, an imagined transnational community, whose existence is actualized in several ways, from satellite television's programmes on Islam, to books published in England, the United States or Egypt and by the actual interaction of Muslims with other Muslims from different parts of the world (see Metcalf 1996). So, too, is the role played by Italian Muslims in the construction of an Italian Islam and in the attribution of new roles to the mosque – a concrete instance of how Islam in Italy does not pertain exclusively to the realm of immigrants' religion or culture of origin.

Veiling and Studying: Islam as Performance of Modernity

'I don't wear it [the *hijab*] as my mother does: as a custom handed down from one generation to another. I wear it because I feel a sort of responsibility as I studied and I know how important it is.' This quotation from a young Moroccan woman reflects the sentiments of several other women I met in the mosque who explained how, since they had studied, they were able to realize and develop a consciousness of what being an authentic Muslim woman implies. That the veil no longer signifies oppression and seclusion for a large number of women who don it has been amply documented by several studies in different countries. To signify the rupture with its past meanings the *hijab* is now described as the 'new veil'. For the Jordanian women studied by Jansen (1998: 90), the new veil 'expresses transnational anti-Western sentiments in its international uniformity' (see also Afshar 1996; Azzam 1996; Watson 1994). Concerning women wearing the veil in contemporary Morocco, Leila Hessini (1994) suggested that the *hijab* is increasingly deployed as a 'liberating force' for some Moroccan women, especially as through it, women acquire a higher degree and freedom of mobility and respect from mainstream society.[9]

Being a Muslim transcends national affiliations and becomes a transnational identity inscribed in the *Umma*, a global imagined community whose members are supposed to share universal practices and values. Explaining the reasons why Muslim women have to be covered, an Italian woman convert energetically stated:

> Muslim women who live in a foreign country should wear the *hijab* because it is a duty where the majority of people are non-Muslims. The *kafirun* [those who do not believe] have no problems if they do not, so it is the [Muslim] woman's responsibility to protect her dignity because men who are *kafirun* do not care about this. They are not like our Muslim men who protect women's dignity.

She is sharing with her migrant Muslim sisters the sense of being a foreigner, despite the fact that Italy is the country where she was born and grew up. This feeling of displacement, however, is also rooted in the attitude of perceiving the world and the society in which she lives as divided between believers and *kafirun* (sinners).

The idea of the *Umma* is often materialized in metaphors that emphasize synchronicity and accordance of Muslims in the world. During a *Khutba* (Friday sermon) where the topic was the practice of fasting during Ramadan (*As-Saum*), for example, it was emphasized how, through the mechanism of time based on the lunar month (on which the Islamic time is based), Muslims from the north to the south of the hemisphere will fast the same number of hours.

For Islamist women, only the practice of an authentic and pure Islam could give birth to a real *Umma* that is often referred to in functionalist terms, recalling Jamal el Din Al Afghani's conceptualization. The well-known Muslim thinker, who lived in the second half of the nineteenth century, defined the nation as a body whose vitality depends on the activity of its single parts. A young Moroccan woman, for instance, represented the *Umma* in the following terms: 'We, Muslims, should be a unique body, a single organ. Even if a single part is sick the whole body should be affected. We are not like this, because we are not practising an authentic Islam, we are not a real community!'

Islam as Knowledge, Islam as Modernity

Young educated women interpret their involvement in learning and knowing the texts as the modern way of being a Muslim woman. At the same time it seems that only by being truly Muslim, can a woman be modern. Study is synonymous with knowledge and modernity. But knowledge can only be Islamic. As one Moroccan woman stated:

> The atmosphere in our families is not really and completely Islamic. Instead of taking a break in our days from our duties to read and study the Quran, we are always watching television, handling the remote control. If we continue behaving in such a way, we will remain ignorant, at a low level, we won't learn anything.

Aicha, the Muslim name of a Greek woman married to a Syrian whom she met at university in Italy 20 years ago, blamed the 'so-called Muslim countries' for women's illiteracy problems: 'Arab régimes who define their countries in principle as Muslims are not at all Muslim when it comes to practice. In a country like Morocco, women are kept illiterate; the doors of knowledge have not been opened to them. This keeps women ignorant and far from Islam.'

As I have already noted, although the Sunday meeting is also a way to meet and let their children play, the younger and more committed women are keen to explain that the reason for these meetings is to learn and exchange erudition on Islam and they are keen to counteract the popular image of women's gatherings as places of gossips and subversion. A young Moroccan woman graduate, Kalthoum, explained that she only attends the mosque to participate in the classes. Shelves in her home are full of books on Islam. When Kalthoum does not agree with the Shaikh on a particular interpretation, she studies books addressing that topic to assess whether her thesis is correct. If this is the case, she discusses it with him on the following Sunday.

By engaging in a sort of *ijtihad* (interpretation) women defy an unquestioned male authority on religious issues, which for centuries kept them outside the domain of the Islamic doctrine. Women are extending their role within the public sphere of Islam by also claiming the respect of those same rules of separation that were historically imposed on them. For example, after they had attended a conference on the 'Muslim family' organized for women, they criticized the presence, both as observers and speakers, of men in the conference. A Moroccan woman argued that, if men carried on attending the conferences organized for women, their husbands would prevent them from participating in future events such these. Another Egyptian woman then asked the Shaikh why women themselves could not be the speakers in conferences, given that Islamic history provided examples of prominent female who played such roles.

Islamist women's conceptualization of modernity also invests the family sphere (see Abu-Lughod 1998b). Women in the mosque often describe the relationship with their husbands in idealized terms. This is described as a relationship of devotion, complicity and respect, as opposed to the traditional patterns of wives' and husbands' roles identified with the extended family. Leila, for example, argued that the marriage between *Ibn 'Amm* (paternal cousins) is decreasing in Morocco and it is practised only among rural populations. Her husband, Kasem, belongs to a large traditional extended family from Settat. Kasem's father is polygamous, because he married another woman when his first wife, Kasem's mother, became very seriously ill. Leila explained that Kasem decided to marry 'outside the family' and wanted to live far away to avoid family control and interference, adding that some families interfere too much in the life of newly married couples: 'They do not leave you alone, they comment on everything that happens between wife and husband.' Leila and her sister however, were given as spouses soon after they finished school in Casablanca to Kasem and his brother, at that time already residing in Italy. The union was arranged through the mediation of a family acquainted with both her and her husband's families.

Women's methods of learning about and appropriating Islam suggest that a crucial issue for them is to interpret, to participate in, and to know matters from which they have been traditionally excluded. A deep knowledge of Islamic religion (*'Ilm*), and the capacity to decide what is correct as Muslims (*fiqh*)[10] is central in the case of young educated Muslim women in Italy who regularly attend the mosque. By engaging in such a project, women engage in a project of modernity that rejects the Western version expressed by a secularized and disordered society where, it was often stated, the family is fragmented and women's bodies are exhibited as objects. Indeed, as Zygmunt Bauman (1990) has argued, 'modernity' is ambivalent, searching for order, but simultaneously needing chaos. Islamist women in Italy construct their order, embodied by an Islamic morality, by opposing it to the disorder, fragmentation and immorality of the Other. At the same time, the model of woman they propose represents a shift from traditional practices associated with rural and illiterate women in their respective countries.

Counternarratives: Secular Modernities

Whereas Islamist women in the mosque feel that there cannot exist different ways of being Muslim because the Quran says clearly what being a good Muslim implies, many Moroccan women consider themselves Muslims and adhere to the general principles of the Islamic religion but show flexibility in practising them and admit to different behaviour. However, Muslim women who display more secular behaviour are not necessarily less embedded within traditional practices.

More importantly, women who renegotiate Islam construct their own versions of authenticity by reformulating and accommodating diverse cultural and religious practices. While in Morocco they celebrated religious rituals, once in Italy, where daily life is transformed, the significance of religious practices may shift. Some women and their families may, at the beginning of their experience of migration in Italy, fast and pray in continuity with their habits, but they may later renegotiate the importance of these performances. When it comes to children's education, these women also show a shifting attitude. They may want their children to be aware that they are Moroccans or Muslims but without imposing on them normative behaviour. In other cases, although keen on reminding them of Arab origins, families may not want to emphasize Islam as central in their education, stressing other cultural traits.

In these cases, women do not feel part of a particular 'community'. They tend often to underline differences and heterogeneity with respect to other Moroccans instead of insisting on a shared culture or roots. In many cases, these women try to develop relationships with Italians, and are more affected by the local dimension of the place they now inhabit. For example, some women may allow their children to eat pork, and working mothers may send their children to Catholic schools, which often keep children for the whole day instead of half a day. These women might well observe Ramadan, yet also prepare a Christmas tree at Christmas.

The secular demeanour displayed by these women does not represent a capitulation to a Western hegemony, to which they become assimilated. Migration is certainly part and parcel of women's compulsion for change, as it constitutes a major turning point in their lives, where the confrontation with a different model of living and interpreting religion amplifies their reflections about themselves, their culture and their roots. However, women's renegotiation of Islam also reflects the historical processes of adaptation, negotiation and reformulation of cultural and religious identities that have occurred in postcolonial societies (see Bennani-Chraïbi, 1994). Indeed, processes of renegotiation of cultural and religious practices are more rooted than the more recent Islamist call for a return to the texts as sources of authenticity. Hence, whereas some women turn to Islam as the only possible path to either maintain or indeed achieve both personal and social or collective advancement, other Moroccan women endorse a diverse renegotiation process and contest Islamist women's authenticity.[11]

Rather than seeing authenticity reflected in the respect for strict and fixed cultural and religious rules and roles, several women described as inauthentic certain uses of Islamic symbols. For example, different women provided me with diverse examples of how the veil both in Italy and Morocco is often used as a way to gain the trust of the family and the society and to take part more freely in anti-Islamic conduct. A common narrative alludes to women who 'leave the house with the veil and enter the bar without'.

Mariam, for example, stated that wearing a veil in order to gain freedom of movement is a widespread phenomenon among young girls in Morocco. Indeed, Mariam argued, 'many of these girls were lying to their parents and in fact were going out at night, conducting a sort of double life . . . There are many . . . some time ago, some of them have been discovered! Samia called for an economic explanation arguing that the veil and more generally, Islamic dress, is adopted by women who cannot afford other styles and thus justify their outfits in terms of religious choice. To Samia, especially in Italy, the adoption of the Islamic outlook is a way of hiding inadequate economic conditions. She was adamant in accusing the practice of wearing veils and Islamic dresses as being hypocritical: 'I have yet to see a rich woman wearing a *hijab* or an Islamic dress, they wear them just because they can not afford a different life . . . If they become rich, I am sure they will change!'

Women displaying secular attitudes are not automatically able to free them-selves from dominant constructions of gender roles, which they have internalized. These are sometimes more deeply rooted in women who adopt secular attitudes than in those who are engaged in the process of learning and studying Islam in the mosque. This could also be attributed to the major appeal that Islamist discourses have exerted on middle-class and lower-class university students in Morocco since the 1970s.

Ziba, who is now 30 years old, belongs to a 'traditional' family. Her four older sisters have not received any education because their father at that time thought school was not important for his daughters. However, Ziba and her youngest sister studied as far as the baccalaureate thanks to her mother who eventually convinced the father of the importance of education. Ziba grew up with traditional values concerning sexual intercourse and husband/wife relationships. In accounting for the arrangements preceding her wedding, she revealed her deep respect for her husband, when, despite having met her only once, he declared his serious intention to marry her and approached her father for permission. On another occasion, she told me how she regretted her husband not having been present when she gave birth. She thought that witnessing women's suffering in the process of giving birth increases men's respect for their wives. Her conceptualization of her role as mother and wife is not articulated with explicit reference to Islam. Although she perceives her culture as entangled with religion, discursively, Islam does not emerge as a rigid set of beliefs and practices that should govern her life.

Women's efforts to affirm their own subjective positions suggests a power struggle to interpret and define cultural aspects and performances and highlights their contestation of dominant perceptions of cultural authenticity. In one of our last conversations, Ziba shared with me her anxieties and reflections about two models and dominant discourses, articulated as the 'Western' and the 'Islamist', both of which she felt ultimately alien to her identity. For Ziba, for example, authenticity is not a mere hypocritical respect for some religious norms, but is rather about positioning herself through genuinely recognizing cultural negoti-ations as inescapable outcomes of living in a different society.

Conclusion

Many Muslim women in Italy appropriate Islam as the alternative to assimilation and cultural homogenization. This reflects a global phenomenon whereby Islam is increasingly constructed as an arena untouched by Western globalization and colonialism and is propounded as the 'culturally authentic' alternative to Western modernity. However, the observation of microdynamics and discourses among Moroccan women brings to light a multiplicity of paths and unfolds contestations and opposing practices embedded within notions of authenticity and cultural identity. Indeed, my aim in this chapter was to portray the voices and agencies of those Moroccan women who seek to affirm a more subjective and secular way of living Islam (whether in continuity or not with the outlooks they hold previous to migrating), refusing nonetheless the label of 'assimilated' or 'inauthentic'.

These ethnographic accounts defy the conventional perception of the opposition between Islamist and secular constituencies in terms of a clash between traditional and modern views. These kinds of dichotomic representations, as the Comaroffs (1993: xii) have suggested 'reduce complex continuities and contradictions to the aesthetics of nice oppositions'. In this chapter I have suggested that Muslim women's cultural and social identities in Italy are neither simply in continuity with a past tradition or in opposition to homogenizing processes, nor are they symbols of adaptation to the West. Muslim women's manifold, and often opposing dis-courses around Islam, authenticity and tradition convey contestation over opposing projects of 'modernity'.

According to Leila Ahmed (1992) both the narrative of the veil as oppression and the counternarrative of the veil as resistance are misperceptions grounded on, and reinforcing, the premises of Western, colonial discourse. Indeed, the veil is identified also by orientalist feminists, either as the emblem of women's repression or as a marker of women's resistance to Westernization or even to sexism within Muslim societies. I totally agree that the veil, like other symbols and practices, has been and indeed still is the core of a misplaced attention in Europe and in many Muslim countries. Nevertheless, partly because of this, it is often a central topic among Muslim women in Europe. This is partly due to the fact that migrant women's representations of themselves and their choices are also deeply informed by the ways they feel they are perceived and represented within the European societies where they live. Those women who criticize its use and those who con-sider wearing a *hijab* a fundamental duty of Muslim women both often engage in discussions around its meanings that are grounded in a complex web and dialectic of Western images and representations and counterimages and counterrepresent-ations. However the *hijab*, as one among other symbols and practices, is becoming a transnational emblem used to display a specific representation of modernity that differs from the Western one and denotes a global identification with an Islamic identity. As Abu Lughod (1997: 126) has argued, 'For rural Egyptian, as for urban lower- and middle-class women since the 1980's, to become "modern" and urbane has meant taking on a more identifiable Islamic look and sound.'

In my account I have shown that 'tradition' and 'Islam' are often erroneously seen as overlapping and, like Abu Lughod, I have suggested that many Moroccan and other Muslim women endorsing Islamist discourses in Italy are well-educated women who aspire to and embody a modern project. Women embrace Islam in Italy as an attempt to distinguish themselves from Western society, asserting a project of self-fulfilment through an alternative (Islamic) morality. However, Islam also represents for these women a way of overcoming what they label as backward and traditional features of their cultures. To a certain extent it could be said that the endorsement of a Muslim agenda and the process of studying and learning becomes a terrain whereby women negotiate their aspirations for autonomy and self-realization in a sort of public sphere without challenging their husbands' trad-itional supremacy in the private sphere. Women who actively engage with Islam in Italy constantly confront other Muslim women who, according to them, remain in the realm of ignorance or tradition, or whom they see as loosing their identity by compromising with Western values and behaviour.

These narratives, however, are highly contested by other women who invoke a notion of modernity which endorses secular ideas and behaviour and affirm a diverse notion of authenticity. They define themselves as Muslims but refuse Islamism as the only political and cultural frame leading to self-determination without assimilation.

Notes

1. The analyses expressed in this paper are the result of extended field research, carried out between September 1996 and October 1998, predominantly in Italy and partially in Morocco, the country from where the majority of Muslim migrant women in Italy come. Data for this paper are based mainly on part-icipant observation of the meetings of a group of Muslim women taking place in a mosque located in the Emilia-Romagna region of Italy. More formal

interviews were carried out with local Muslim leaders of several other mosques. The general research, however, was conducted among some 20 Moroccan families whose views on religion and identity also constitute the background against which these analyses are built.

2. I am not engaging here with the debate on the emergence, nature and meaning of the term 'modernity'. An extended version of this chapter which deals with the complex question of the relation between modernity, gender and Islam can be found in Salih (2002).

3. For an analysis of the question of the 'failed nationhood' in Italy see Pandolfi (1998).

4. In June 2000, after a declaration from the Italian Ministry of Education that the headscarf in school should be allowed by virtue of the freedom of religious expression affirmed by the national Constitution, an online discussion on the website of the national newspaper *La Repubblica* was initiated. Amongst the hundreds of people who wrote to express their opinion on the Muslim head-scarf, the majority were Italian males.

5. The list of 18 numerically important countries of origin of Muslims in Italy includes: Iran (6,814); Turkey (6,630); Nigeria (6,447); Yugoslavia (6,500); Bosnia (5,339); Iraq (4,519); Macedonia (4,126); Croazia (2,264) and India (2,154) (Pacini 2000).

6. Other scholars would refer to a further distinction between High Islam and popular forms of Islam, expressed by Sufi cults such as magical practices and rites of possession (Gellner 1992). Yet, in people's practices, popular and High forms of Islam have coexisted historically, especially in Morocco where the former have been tolerated more than in other North African countries.

7. These are flats, houses and rooms that are rented or purchased and are formally called Islamic Cultural Centres, since the *Intesa* (covenant), which, according to Italian law, should regulate the relationship between Muslims and the Italian state, has not yet been signed. The *Intesa* would regulate many aspects related to deaths, weddings and the official recognition of mosques.

8. The Shaikh running the mosque and teaching is a young Egyptian. He decided to provide specific classes for women on Sundays when he realized that a few women were auditing the Saturday classes of their husbands from their separate room. Although at the beginning very few women regularly attended these classes, Shaikh Tareq never gave up until a regular group of 10 to 20 women was formed. Thanks to this attitude, Shaikh Tareq gained a great deal of respect among women.

9. However, Hessini (1994: 54–5) rightly calls attention to a paradox whereby the wearing of *hijab* 'perpetuates the old dual vision of women as both temptresses and blameless pillars of sustenance for men. The *hijab* serves a paradoxical purpose: it simultaneously challenges and underscores the notion of the unchanging, eternal female and her associated traditional roles.'

10. Islamic jurisprudence.
11. See Bennani-Chraïbi (1994) for an analysis of the changing attitudes of young Moroccans in Morocco around Islam and cultural values.

Bibliography

Abu Lughod, L. (1997), 'The Interpretation of Culture(s) After Television' *Representations,* 59: 109–34.

Abu-Lughod, L. (1998a), 'Introduction. Feminist Longings and Postcolonial Conditions' in L. Abu-Lughod (ed.) *Remaking Women. Feminism and Modernity in the Middle East*, New Jersey: Princeton University Press.

Abu-Lughod, L. (1998b), 'The Marriage of Feminism and Islamism in Egypt: Selective Repudiation as a Dynamic of Postcolonial Cultural Politics', in L. Abu-Lughod (ed.) *Remaking Women. Feminism and Modernity in the Middle East*, New Jersey: Princeton University Press.

Afshar, H. (1996), 'Islam and Feminism: An Analysis of Political Strategies', in M. Yamani (ed.) *Feminism and Islam. Legal and Literary Perspectives*, Reading: Ithaca Press.

Ahmed, L. (1992), *Women and Gender in Islam*, New Haven and London: Yale University Press.

Al-Ali, N. (2000), *Secularism, Gender and the State in the Middle East: The Women's Movement in Egypt*, Cambridge: Cambridge University Press.

Al-Azmeh, A. (1996 [1993]), *Islams and Modernities*, London: Verso.

Andall, J. (2000), *Gender, Migration and Domestic Service. The Politics of Black Women in Italy*, Aldershot: Ashgate.

Anthias, F and Yuval-Davis, N.(eds) (1989), *Women, Nation, State*, London: Macmillan.

Appadurai, A. (1991), 'Global Ethnoscapes: Notes and Queries for a Transnational Anthropology' in R.G. Fox (ed.) *Recapturing Anthropology*, Santa Fe: School of American Research Press.

Azzam, M. (1996), 'Gender and the Politics of Religion in the Middle East', in M. Yamani (ed.), *Feminism and Islam. Legal and Literary Perspectives*, Reading: Ithaca Press.

Bauman, Z. (1990), 'Modernity and Ambivalence', in M. Featherstone (ed.), *Global Culture. Nationalism, Globalization and Modernity*, London: Sage.

Bennani-Chraïbi, M. (1994), *Soumis et Rebelles: les jeunes au Maroc*, Paris: Editions du CNRS.

Bloul, R. (1996), 'Engendering Muslim Identities. Deterritorialization and Ethnicization Process in France' in B. D. Metcalf (ed.), *Making Muslim Space in North America and Europe*, Berkley, Los Angeles and London: University of California Press.

Caritas (1998). *Immigrazione, Dossier Statistico '98*, Roma: Edizioni Anterem.

Comaroff J. and Comaroff J. (1993), 'Introduction', in J. Comaroff and J. Comaroff (eds), *Modernity and Its Malcontents. Rituals and Power in Postcolonial Africa*, Chicago and London: University of Chicago Press.

De Filippo, E. and Pugliese, E. (1996), 'Le nuove migrazioni internazionali e i modelli migratori nei paesi del Sud Europa', *Inchiesta*, Luglio-Settembre: 49–57.

Duval, S. (1998), 'New Veils and New Voices: Islamist Women's Groups in Egypt', in K. Ask and M. Tjomsland (eds), *Women and Islamization. Contemporary Dimensions of Discourse on Gender Relations*, Oxford and New York: Berg.

Eickelman, D.F. and Piscatori, J. (eds) (1990), *Muslim Travellers: Pilgrimage, Migration and the Religious Imagination*, London: Routledge.

Fog Olwig, K. and Hastrup, K. (eds) (1997), *Siting Culture. The Shifting Anthropological Object*, London and New York: Routledge.

Gellner, E. (1992), *Postmodernism, Reason and Religion*, London: Routledge.

Gupta, A. and Ferguson, J. (1997a), 'Beyond "Culture": Space, Identity, and the Politics of Difference', in A. Gupta and J. Ferguson (eds), *Culture, Power, Place: Explorations in Critical Anthropology*, Durham and London: Duke University Press.

Harvey, D. (1989), *The Condition of Postmodernity*, Oxford: Basil Blackwell.

Hessini, L. (1994), 'Wearing the hijab in contemporary Morocco: choice and identity' in F. M. Göçek and S. Balaghi (eds), *Reconstructing Gender in the Middle East. Tradition, Identity, Power*, New York: Columbia University Press.

Jansen, W. (1998), 'Contested Identities: Women and Religion in Algeria and Jordan' in K. Ask and M. Tjomsland (eds), *Women and Islamization. Contemporary Dimensions of Discourse on Gender Relations*, Oxford and New York: Berg.

Khan, S. (1998), 'Muslim Women: Negotiations in the Third Space,' *Signs*, 23, 2: 463–94.

Metcalf, B. D. (ed.) (1996), *Making Muslim Space in North America and Europe*, Berkley, Los Angeles and London: University of California Press.

Nielsen, J. (1992), *Muslims in Western Europe*, Edinburgh: Edinburgh University Press.

Pacini, A. (2000), 'I Musulmani in Italia. Dinamiche organizzative e processi di interazione con la società e le istituzioni italiane' in S. Ferrari (ed.), *Musulmani in Italia. La condizione giuridica delle comunità islamiche*, Bologna: Il Mulino.

Pandolfi, M. (1998), 'Two Italies: Rhetorical Figures of Failed Nationhood', in J. Schneider (ed.) *Italy's 'Southern Question' Orientalism in One Country*, Oxford: Berg.

Rouadja, A. (1997), 'La moschea nel paesaggio urbano del Maghreb' in AA.VV. *Città e società nel mondo arabo contemporaneo. Dinamiche urbane e cambiamento sociale*, Torino: Fondazione Giovanni Agnelli.

Rusconi, G.E. (1997), *Patria e Repubblica*, Bologna: Il Mulino.

Saint-Blancat, C. (1999), 'Le donne fra transizione e alterità', in C. Saint-Blancat (ed.) *L'Islam in Italia. Una presenza plurale*, Roma: Edizioni Lavoro.

Salih, R. (2000), 'Shifting Boundaries of Self and Other. Moroccan Migrant women in Italy', *European Journal of Women's Studies*, 7, (3): 309–23.

Salih, R. (2002), 'The Gender of Modernity. Narratives of Muslim and Islamist Migrant Women', *Journal of Mediterranean Studies*, vol. 12 (1): 14–169.

Watson, E. (1994), 'Women and the Veil: Personal responses to global processes' in A.S. Ahmed and J. Donnan (eds) *Islam, Globalization and Postmodernity*, London: Routledge.

Werbner, P. (1996), 'Stamping the Earth with the Name of Allah: Zikr and the Sacralizing of Space among British Muslims' in B. D. Metcalf (ed.), *Making Muslim Space in North America and Europe*, Berkley, Los Angeles and London: University of California Press.

7

'Nowadays your Husband is your Partner': Ethnicity and Emancipation as Self-Presentation in the Netherlands

Joke van der Zwaard

Interviewing is asking the interviewee to present herself. In the self-presentations of the Turkish and Moroccan immigrant women I interviewed, several interrelated meanings of gender and ethnicity were communicated. The themes I will discuss in my contribution to this book are: the distribution of domestic tasks between husband and wife, the sexual freedom of young women and the broken-off school career. I will analyse the arguments and expressions used as reflections and reactions regarding the dominant discourse on 'Muslim' women in the Netherlands, in which these women are portrayed as extremely dependent on men, particularly their fathers, brothers and husbands. Before doing this I will give some information about the political and practical research context and explain the main theoretical sources of inspiration.

Related Worlds and Power Differences

Turks (312,000) and Moroccans (265,000) are two of the five largest groups of migrants from non-European countries in the Netherlands (16,000,000 inhabitants). The other three groups are migrants from Indonesia, Surinam and the Antilles, three former Dutch colonies. Turkish and Moroccan migrants are often discussed in one breath by the so-called autochthons. This one-group construction is linked to their common migration background, their economic position in the Netherlands and to Dutch preoccupation with their 'Eastern' religion, Islam. The migration of both Turks and Moroccans began in the period 1964–1974. During this time there were annual recruitment contracts between the Dutch government and Turkish and Moroccan governments for male unskilled workers. Older or educated people were not sought; rather, candidates were selected on the basis of physical health and strength. The Moroccan 'guestworkers' were recruited from the very poor Rif region in the north of Morocco. A third of those selected did not have any formal education. Only 25 per cent of the first generation of Moroccan male migrants was educated beyond primary school level. These were principally men who had migrated without a contract after having worked in Italy or France. The Turkish workers came from the central area of Turkey and the Black Sea Coast. While the majority had some formal education, 75 per cent were educated only to primary school level and the majority came from a farming background. In 1974, a period of economic recession followed the oil crisis and the Dutch government forbade further recruitment. By this time, there were 50,000 Turks and 25,000 Moroccans living in the Netherlands. Although they were recruited on a temporary basis and despite the fact that they had no intention of settling in the Netherlands, the majority stayed given the lack of opportunities in the sending country.

Secondary migration occurred a few years later as the majority of these men had a family in their country of origin. The family reunification process was primarily initiated by the wives. They wanted both independence from their in-laws and fathers for their growing children. Generally these women were less educated than their husbands. For example, more than 50 per cent of first-generation Moroccan mothers were unable to read or write. Following arrival in the Netherlands, Turkish women began to participate in the labour market as unskilled factory workers or cleaners. Moroccan women were more usually full-time housewives/mothers. They had arrived some years later than the Turkish women, as the women of the Moroccan Rif region were more accustomed to their husbands working and living away for long periods.

The more recent migration of Turks and Moroccans consists of the spouses of the first generation's children. Approximately 75 per cent of these young men and women marry someone from the original sending region/country. The educational level within this group of partners from abroad varies from virtually illiterate to academics and includes both men and women. The problem and injustice is that – unlike for instance American and Japanese qualifications – these foreign degrees are not recognized by Dutch institutions. For example, a qualified and experienced Turkish or Moroccan nurse has to start her professional training all over again to obtain a job in her profession in the Netherlands.

At the same time, the vast majority of first-generation male immigrants are unemployed and the average level of income of these households is low. Their (grand)children are labelled as 'risk-groups' by policymakers and professionals because of their average low level of education and the high rate of school dropouts and unemployment. One could point to the educational progress these children – particularly the youngest children of first generation migrants – have made in comparison to the starting position of their parents. However, this type of observation is nowadays labelled as 'politically correct' optimism or relativism. The current acceptable standpoint is to speak of a 'multicultural tragedy' and to define and attribute educational and social inequality to a lack of 'integration'. In political, professional, academic and public discussions the disadvantaged position of inhabitants with a Turkish and Moroccan background is totally or partly explained by 'cultural deviance'. Turks and Morrocans are supposed to have the same culture to a great extent because of their common religion, Islam. Notwithstanding (or thanks to) advanced secularization in the Netherlands, the Dutch discourse on 'multicultural problems' focuses on classical Islam/Christianity dichotomies, such as rationality versus irrationality, developed versus backward, individual responsibility versus subordination to the group, modern equal versus traditional unequal gender relations (Said 1978; van der Zwaard 1992, 1999b). Consequently signs of modernity, emancipation and educational achievement are labelled as 'Westernization'. Adopting the same line of reasoning, the migration of spouses from Turkey and Morocco is problematized as a backlash in the integration/modernization process of the second-generation and their offspring. The new centre-right government currently under formation is formulating proposals to raise the minimum age and minimum income necessary for marriage to a partner from abroad. These measures are of course intended to prevent or reduce migration (from certain countries) in general, but in the context of my account it is interesting to see what strategies of legitimization are used.

Working as an independent researcher in the field of social policy, I travel between the institutional world of policymakers and professionals (district nurses and welfare workers) and the world of daily life experiences of the main objects of social programmes, women of low-income groups. In some research projects I study political documents and institutional practices to investigate the 'interpretative repertoire' (Potter and Wetherell 1987) of professionals and policymakers, the systems of terms that are used for explaining social inequality and characterizing cultural differences, and the effects of these constructions on professional and bureaucratic attitudes and procedures. In other projects I interview women/mothers, mainly immigrant women living in Rotterdam, to find out their perceptions of their social economical position, their ways of surviving and efforts to improve their situation, and their assessment of existing professional provisions.

The image of travelling between two worlds is mainly an expression of my irritation about the apparently self-evident problematizing and pathologizing of these women's ways of life by professionals and policymakers. I frequently use this metaphor to intervene in this massive and dominant political discourse, to influence the professional ethnocentric gaze and to enable the experience of these groups of women to be taken seriously and seen as legitimate and valuable.

From a strictly analytical perspective, however, the postulation of two divided worlds or two different vocabularies does not clarify the situation. The ways women of low-income groups organize their lives are also a reaction to legal rules and restrictions, institutional programs and professional approaches. An example is the use of post restantes for partners to prevent the reduction of social security given stricter controls on household composition. Another example is the participation of immigrant mothers in parental education programmes, not primarily to improve their motherhood, but to gain contact with people who might help them to find a job. On the one hand my interviewees criticize the expressions professionals use to label them or to explain their behaviour; on the other hand their way of speaking about themselves is clearly mediated through the dominant discourses. Children of migrants may call themselves, for instance, foreigners or *allochtone*, the Dutch policy term for immigrants and their children and grandchildren. When a Turkish woman does not much want to participate in a mother's course, a very popular professional strategy to 'integrate' migrant women in the Netherlands at the moment, she may use the excuse of having a 'traditional Turkish husband' to prevent further questions and insistence.

To take into account the dominant discursive context in the analysis of interview texts of immigrant women the concepts of De Certeau (1988) and Harré (1979) proved to be useful. De Certeau introduced the term 'tactics' to interpret acts that are determined by the absence of power, in addition to 'strategies' (Foucault 1986) that are organized by the postulation of power. Tactics constantly manipulate events to turn them into opportunities; they have more to do with constraints than with possibilities. It is 'backstage' behaviour that offers informal forms of influence and perhaps has the potential to confront the existing discourse, but does not yet challenge the overarching power structure and beliefs. Macleod (1991) used this concept to interpret the revival of veiling among lower middle-class women in Cairo as a reaction to the hardships of their overburdened life as working mothers with little opportunities to improve their situation, either at home or in the office. She describes this new fashion as 'accommodating protest' against existing gender relations and class relations. Skeggs (1997) used the concept to understand the humour and the flirting behaviour of white working-class women in 'caring courses', as a reaction to and an escape from the sexist approach and the 'classing gaze' of their teachers. Both authors found that respectability and respect are central issues in the accounts of their interviewees. Respectability is analysed as part of the excluding self-definition of higher middle-class women. In the accounts of the excluded and pathologized women of lower classes, this meaning of femininity is connected with feelings of frustration and humiliation as well as with ideals of social mobility. Respect has to do with the wish for self-determination and the need for recognition of their contributions and worth, both in the household and in society.

Theoretically these meanings of respect and respectability can be linked to Harré's concept of the expressive order of social life. Harré makes a distinction between those aspects of social activity that are directed to material and biological ends, which he calls 'practical', and those directed to ends such as the presentation of the self as rational and worthy of respect, and belonging to a certain category of beings, which he calls 'expressive'. According to Harré, in many social interactions the expressive order is more dominant than the practical order. In his words: 'The pursuit of reputation in the eyes of others is the overriding preoccupation of human life' (Harré 1979: 3). Therefore he considers self-presentation first of all as part of the 'impression management' people use to accommodate their social reputation to their self image. So by investigating interview texts as self-presentation, one may firstly find out the interviewees' social knowledge, their ideas about the social stratification in the society they live in and the dominant norms and values. Secondly it may be possible to reconstruct their estimation of their public social reputation and their 'moral career',[1] and their tactics to improve their social reputation. An inspiring research example of such an 'account analysis' is the discussion of life stories of German and Italian immigrant women in Canada by Freund and Quilici (1997). Confronted with some puzzling standard themes in these accounts, such as the description of rather isolated maid-servant work as a suitable way to integrate in the new country, they analyse them as constructions that help the interviewed women to reconcile discrepancies between life experiences and ideals and to maintain feelings of autonomy and self-respect.

The Research Context: Group Discussions and Individual Interviews

The accounts I discuss here are taken from two research projects. In the one project I organized group discussions between women/mothers of different ethnic groups living in the same 'working-class' neighbourhood. There were 48 participants: Dutch, Surinamese, Turkish and Moroccan women, one Capeverdian and one Croatian woman. The groups were composed on the basis of common involvement on an upbringing issue. The themes were: the role of the grandmother, daily practice in large families, upbringing in a new country and childcare services. By bringing together mothers from different ethnic backgrounds we hoped to clarify similarities and differences between mothers, without attributing these *a priori* to 'culture' or 'ethnic background' or 'immigration'. We deliberately did not introduce these categories into the discussion, as we wanted to know which categories these women use themselves and how they position and identify themselves. The discussions were structured as focus-group discussions, a research method in which participants are asked to react to statements or presentations and in which interactions between participants are stimulated (Kitzinger 1994). The theoretical argument was that in daily life people form their ideas and opinions in reaction to the statements or the behaviour of other people. The intention was to analyse rational and emotional responses. The central theme in my research report is the complex coherence between the life stories of the women, their assessment of their current social and material circumstances and different meanings of motherhood

(Van der Zwaard 1995). I will focus here on the unplanned hilarious intermezzi about 'men' in the group discussions.

The other project consisted of group discussions and individual interviews with (150) Surinamese, Antillian, Dutch, Turkish, Moroccan women, one Croatian, one Pakistani and one Iraqi woman. The group discussions were used to detect the main themes in their life stories. In the individual interviews these themes were used to reflect on changes in the recent past and to fantasise about the future. The main purpose of this research project was to gather more information about the ways women/mothers of low income groups in Rotterdam try to survive and to improve their situation, and whether they are (sufficiently?) supported by their informal social network and professional provisions. The overall findings and conclusions are published in Van der Zwaard (1999a). Here I will focus on accounts about the broken-off school career. This is a frequently recurring theme in the interviews with Turkish women who migrated to the Netherlands as children under the 'family reunion' opportunities of male labour migrants.

As interview texts are analysed here as self-presentations towards another person, I should state that I am a Dutch white middle-aged woman. I am the eldest daughter of parents of low education and I attained university by a roundabout way involving secretarial jobs. Class differences are an essential part of my own life story. But I do realize that for my interviewees I am in the first place white/ Dutch and well-educated and vaguely related to official institutions. I do not have a standard personal introduction for my interviews. Normally I start by explaining why I am going to ask all these questions and what I will do with the information. Depending on verbal and nonverbal reactions during the conversations I might reveal something of my background or my current situation. For example sometimes interviewees wanted to know whether I have children (no) and where I live (in a comparable neighbourhood in Rotterdam). For some migrant women it was the first time they had 'such a personal conversation' with a Dutch woman at their home. Some took the opportunity to ask me all kind of practical information, about housing, education, medical services and so forth. If possible I gave answers or I provided contacts later on.

Finally it is important to note that 45 per cent of the population of Rotterdam (600,000) has an immigrant background, in the sense that they were either born abroad or have at least one parent who was born abroad. There are currently 40,000 Turks and 30,000 Moroccans living in Rotterdam.

Intermezzi about 'Men': Explicit Quarrels and Implicit Messages

The participants of the focus group discussions about child-rearing issues enjoyed talking about their daily experiences and did not seem to be afraid to bring to the fore questions, difficulties, different experiences or disagreements. An answer from one often provoked a 'yes, but . . .' reaction from another. Consequently different sides of an issue, different circumstances and different considerations came into discussion quite naturally. Besides, there were moments of recognition, sometimes leading to emotion and expressions of understanding, sometimes leading to hilarity.

The introduction of the word 'men' was always cause for hilarity. It struck me that as soon as somebody used that word the atmosphere in the group changed from a rather serious discussion to a somewhat giggling women-among-women conversation. There was always someone who reacted with a remark like 'an extra child' or 'an extra problem', which was irrevocably followed by a series of anecdotes of (often failed) efforts to attain a more equal distribution of domestic tasks and responsibilities. Turkish and Moroccan women participated notably with more enthusiasm in these lively conversations than Dutch women. The accounts of the Turkish and Moroccan women often consisted of a mixture of indignation about the current state of affairs. They were triumphant about small successes and expressed (self-)ridicule over failed efforts to change the situation. Dutch women remained more serious. They did not react or they intervened with questions expressing dilemmas and contradictory feelings.

My first thought was that 'the power of self-evidence' might be more effective in Dutch households than in immigrant households. This power-concept of the Dutch social psychologist Komter (1985), based on research on decision making in (white) Dutch families, refers to the implicit consensus about how things go, which maintains the existing unequal distribution of tasks and decision power in 'modern' families. Komter showed that this consensus is based on women's habit of adjusting their wishes and needs to those of her husband to avoid difficulties and quarrels and to maintain the idea of a modern, equivalent and harmonious marriage. Young immigrant women, busy designing their household structure in a new situation, might lack some self-evidence. They explained that their own mothers could only partly serve as role models, because of different circumstances and different ideas about staying in the Netherlands. Therefore problems regarding a more honest distribution of domestic tasks might be fought out more openly.

My second thought was that the effusions of the Turkish and Moroccan participants should not only be understood as actual descriptions of domestic power conflicts but as a way of self-presentation towards the Dutch audience: the Dutch participants and the Dutch researcher. So what was the impression management aim of this self-presentation? In view of the many times the words 'Turkish', 'Moroccan' and 'Dutch' were used one thing was clear. The individual self-presentations were also connected with the social reputation and cultural identity of different ethnic groups.

Identifying as a New Generation of Young Modern Turkish Women/Mothers

I will illustrate this combination of individual and group presentation with text fragments from a group discussion about childcare services. There were seven Turkish, one Moroccan, one Croatian and two Dutch women in the group. All the Turkish women came to the Netherlands during their childhood. They were all full-time housewives. Most of them stopped working after the birth of their second child. In the first hour of the meeting there was extensive discussion about the problems encountered trying to find suitable employment that could be combined with the responsibilities of motherhood.

The conversation about men and the distribution of domestic tasks followed after a discussion of youth experiences with childcare. Some Turkish women talked indignantly and, at the same time, understandingly about the way their own mothers solved childcare problems. Most of their mothers did cleaning work or factory work during the first 10, 20 years in the Netherlands. Sometimes the problem of childcare was (partly) solved by giving the eldest daughter responsibilities at a young age or by sending one or more children back to Turkey for a few years. One woman explained in detail the different positions and ideas of Turkish parents then and those of young parents nowadays. Important arguments in her account were: there was no one who could help because we were the only Turks in our street then; our parents came here for a temporary stay to earn money, while for us young Turkish women living in the Netherlands is the normal situation.

Esma, another Turkish woman, completes her argument by saying: 'Nowadays you do everything together with your husband. I may safely say: I don't like cooking and I actually do not cook at home. My mother would not be allowed to say this.' Sibel, also Turkish, reacts: 'No, a women ought to cook, that was how it was, but this has all changed now.' Dubravka, the Croatian woman says: 'Yes, at present women and men are equal. They both work, they both do their things at home. In former days it was quite different.' Karin, a Dutch woman, disagrees: 'That's not altogether true. When my child is ill, I take a day off, my husband will not do it.' She has five children and she had explained earlier how she and her husband organize childcare in shifts. He works during the day from Monday to Friday and she works in the evenings and on the weekends. Suna, Turkish, admits immediately: 'That's the only thing we could not change yet.' Carla, a Dutch woman asks: 'But do we want to change that? If I answer honestly, it is no. After all I want to be the central person and the central manager. In this respect I resemble my mother.' Selma, Turkish, reacts: 'It's the same with me. I think all mothers have those feelings.'

By positioning themselves as a new generation of Turkish (migrant)women/ mothers they include themselves in the group of modern young mothers in the

Netherlands. By doing this they also appropriate the well-known contradictions between the ideology and the daily practice of modern mothers. Family research in the Netherlands has demonstrated that the essential difference between mothers/ housewives with 'modern' opinions and women with 'traditional' ideas about motherhood is situated in what they say, and not in what they do (Knijn and Verheijen 1988). In Harré's terms you might say: a modern mother puts up with the undesirable unequal distribution of tasks in order to maintain practical family-organization, but at the same time she tries to keep the reputation of a modern emancipated woman. The women interviewed suggest that more has changed in the domain of house keeping than in the domain of childcare. Where children are concerned contradictory feelings seem to handicap the realization of the ideal of modernity. Some of these feelings had been discussed earlier in relation to the issue of combining labour and childcare, such as guilty feelings, the feeling of not being a 'real' mother, jealousy towards the grandmother/baby sitter, the wish to be a better mother than their own mother. All mothers presented themselves as mothers with a great sense of responsibility. This 'responsible mother account' undermines their accounts about the modern distribution of tasks at home.

Refusing the Compliment of being a Model Moroccan Woman

Souad, the Moroccan participant, had not reacted yet. Asked for her comments, she happened to have a different opinion and practice. Souad migrated to the Netherlands as a young adult to marry a Moroccan man. First she recounts the strict arrangements about domestic tasks she made with her husband and children the moment she started working outside the home. A Dutch woman asks her how she solves complicated situations, for example when her children are ill. She answers that she will not stay at home automatically and illustrates this with a recent event: 'Last week my son was ill, but my husband was also ill, so there was no reason for me to stay home.' As if she wants to illustrate how strong a woman must be to achieve equality she continues by narrating a quarrel with her brother-in-law. He became angry with her, because one evening she stuck to her plan of going to a party instead of welcoming him and his wife. During the postponed visit, one week later, he was still angry with her. She stated:

> I said to him: 'Mohammed, I was invited to that women's party[2] two weeks before. So I went. But the kitchen is always open. You can make a meal together. You come for your brother, don't you!' He said: 'Yes, but my wife . . .' I answered: 'Your wife may easily talk with you. I am not going to stay home for that.'

The mentioning of women's parties provoked a series of hilarious remarks from the Turkish women about going out with women, I will return to these later.

Souad took up the thread of her own serious argument again: 'In Turkey or Morocco you can easily go out with your husband. There is always a mother, aunt or sister who can take care of the children. Here we do not have family. So one has to stay home when the other wants to go out in the evening.' Carla, Dutch, and living in the same street as Souad said: 'But you are an exceptional ideal woman.' Souad did not accept the compliment. She immediately started telling a story about a conflict with her husband about the distribution of tasks at home.

> My husband said recently: 'The doors are dirty.' I had a day off, but cleaning the doors belongs to his task. If I clean them, he will never do it again. I may have time to do it, but I go out, to friends. Some time ago we quarrelled about it again. Then I said: 'OK, I will resign from my job, I will stay at home and take care that dinner will be ready on time each day and that everything is always clean.' The following week I was free; it was the school holidays but he did not know that. So Monday I stayed at home and said to my children: 'What are we going to do?' My husband asked: 'Did you really resign!?' He asked my children, but they didn't know either. They asked me: 'What will we do for money?' I answered: 'Your father will take care of that.' I succeeded making up idle stories for another two days, but of course I couldn't keep up. Then I told him that it was not true. He said: 'You are really a mean pig-headed woman.' I said: 'You are pig-headed too, you always try to throw the work on me, but I want enjoy my free time too. Not always running, running . . .'

The other participants are impressed by her story. Esma, Turkish, concludes: 'Men always try to throw work on women.' Carla, Dutch: 'It does not matter, Turkish, Moroccan, Dutch men, it's all the same.' All ladies in chorus: 'All men!' They start giggling about so much harmony, but Souad continues seriously: 'But in former days Moroccan men really did nothing at home. Just eating and playing the boss. Nowadays it's different.' Carla states:

> You educated your husband. But if you only look in our street, how little Moroccan women come on the street. That causes conflicts. The children want do otherwise, the mother too, but she does not do it because of her husband. But those fathers have problems too. They came here thinking that all would be going on the familiar way. But you and your husband are different, you mix with other people.

A Turkish women interrupts with a remark about the first generation of migrants who hold onto the idea of Turkey and Turkish norms of 30 years ago. Other Turkish women join in and once more they emphasise the big difference between their parents and themselves concerning life story and norms. Souad does not join this conversation. She mentions changes among Moroccans, but does not speak in separate generations and categories. Neither does she react to Carla's suggestion that her being a 'model woman' is the result of her mixing with other ethnic

(Dutch, I suppose) groups. Her reaction to the initial compliment by narrating the heroic quarrel story is ambiguous. On the one hand, it might be interpreted as a way to explain that her situation at home is no more ideal than that of the others; that she is not a model woman at all. On the other hand, she deliberately tells a heroic and impressive story about the tenacious and successful struggle with her husband. Taking the two interpretations together, the conclusion may be that she does not only say something about herself, but that she also want to improve the social reputation of 'Moroccans' as a group. She clarifies to the others that the Moroccans nowadays are not the same as the Moroccans in former days. Something is changing, but definitely not automatically. It requires tactics as well as perseverance and tenacity from the women; and that is the same for all women.

Fun, Freedom and Morality

Both interventions from the Turkish women in the serious argument of Souad have to do with fun, freedom and morality. The words 'women's parties' causes the following conversation:

Esma:	Women's parties, in my mother's time that was not possible. But we young women, we really go out on Saturday evening, women together. And the men stay home to take care of the children.
Hürya (enthusiastic):	That's a big fashion lately. We take the very sexiest clothes from our wardrobe. The party starts at seven and we keep on to one or two at night. Some even go to discotheques afterwards, but we behave a bit properly.
Esma:	Maybe the next time . . .
	(*Sniggering.*)
Sibel:	I know Dutch women who say: 'My husband would not do that, give up his Saturday.' Women you wouldn't expect to say that at all.

Immediately the Dutch women present let us know that their husband would take care of the children. However Dubravka, the Croatian woman, says that she would not at all like going out 'on my own, without my husband'.

Esma:	But among women, that's really big fun. All the things we do!!! (screaming) And it remains proper!
	(*Laughter, much talking over each other*).

Later, they broach a related topic to illustrate the conservatism of the 'first generation labour immigrants' – their sticking to the idea of Turkey and Turkish of 30 years ago. They talk about confrontations with Turkish youth in Turkey:

They thought we were free, because we were from Europe. Europe, that is saying sexual freedom. They thought we did all kinds of things. But actually we girls from Europe were behind the times compared with the girls in Turkey. Our parents were quite rigid about going out and having boy friends. They always said: 'Turkish girls don't do that' and we fell for it. But during our holidays we found out that the girls in Turkey had a lot more freedom than we had. Turkey changed altogether, even the villages changed. But our parents do not want to see that and they do not take it from us.

The self-presentation of these Turkish women as 'second generation migrants' consists of different identifications or self-categorizing. In the first place they present themselves as 'established', women who know no other life than living in or belonging to the Netherlands. This is in contrast to their parents who retained the idea of a temporary stay in the Netherlands for a long time and hence were or still are 'outsiders' in the Netherlands.

In the second place they present themselves as European Turks who are behind the times compared with Turkish Turks. For a long time their Turkish identity was filled in with accounts from their parents about norms and customs in Turkey, which could only be verified during holidays. All the examples talk about morality and sexual freedom. In most of the Dutch literature about Turkish and Moroccan immigrants rigidity in this domain is explained by the concept of 'honour' in combination with 'Islamic culture'.[3] However, these women emphasize that their parents' restrictions are consequences of social isolation effected by emigration and immigration. Moreover, they clarify their parents' sticking to old norms as a reaction against negative images of European moral standards. In Turkey, European Turks are admired, but also suspected of moral deterioration. The accounts of the young Turkish women do not make clear how they dealt with their bad reputation in Turkey. What they emphasize is that their holiday experiences resulted in disputing their parents' definition of 'being a Turkish girl'. Remarks like 'they do not take it from us' suggest that their parents are stubborn, particularly concerning moral issues. For in other domains, the women mention changes in their parents' attitudes. For instance regarding the equivalence of sons and daughters, Hürya says:

Young people do not mind any more, a boy or a girl. But in former days . . . my father in law had two sons. When his third child happened to be a daughter he did not come home for three days. Now he thinks it's mad. Now and then his daughter says: 'Go away, you may not sit next to me, because you did not see my mother for three days.' He really loves his daughter. He feels ashamed.

This emphasis on current consensus between parents and (older) children may be an expression of efforts to find a new collective orientation and identity in circumstances that have been changed by migration. It may also be interpreted as softening the negative picture they gave of their parents and older Turkish immigrants in general. These two interpretations do not necessarily exclude each other.

The third identity theme in the second generation account is linked with 'being behind the times' and may be called 'recovering'. They definitely make clear that they are no longer backward girls and that they have worked off arrears concerning their freedom of movement at a rapid tempo. Women's parties on Saturday evening are not only presented as a warlike deed in the struggle with their husbands, but also as proof that they are no longer behind the times, in relation to both Turkish women in Turkey and Dutch women in the Netherlands. In Harré's (1979) terms: the women describe their moral career as an upward tendency. Based on the theoretical framework of De Certeau (1984) one might add that humour is used as a tactic to criticize dominant images of Muslim women in a non-confrontational way.

The Broken-off School Career

There is another domain in which these eldest daughters of labour immigrants have to work off arrears: education. Arriving in the Netherlands in the middle of primary school they were confronted with Dutch schools that were poorly equipped to take care of pupils with another mother tongue. Consequently most of them ended up in so called 'international linking classes'[4] in secondary girls' schools leading to very restricted qualifications. Many of them did not finish school. They left school the moment compulsory education ended and some gave up before that age. In those days (1980s) there were two explanations for the broken-off school career of Turkish and Moroccan girls. On the one hand, the parents were blamed for having traditional ideas about girls and education. Turkish and Moroccan parents would not attach great importance to educated daughters because, after all, their future would be restricted to being a (house)wife and mother, probably not living in the Netherlands. Besides they would be afraid that their daughters might come into contact with boys. This 'cultural' account was the most dominant explanation among professionals and policy makers. On the other hand, some education researchers pointed out the restricted perspectives of the schools these girls were assigned to and identified comparable attitudes among Dutch pupils in these schools. Their conclusion was that at least a part of the immigrant girls stayed away from school or left school, through a 'lack of motivation'. The girls did not see what good it was to take a diploma of so little value. Besides, some were disappointed because in Turkey or Morocco they were successful pupils with high ambitions.

In my interviews with the Turkish 'second generation' women both explanations were brought to the fore. Some women emphasized that their parents (mother and/ or father) did not allow them to attend school, because of the boys and because they thought it was not of great use for a (Turkish) girl to obtain a (Dutch) diploma. Some revealed that they were very angry with their parents at that time. Some said that they easily tolerated their parent's opinion because they did not feel at home at school or in the Netherlands. Some said that their parents had not explicitly forbidden them from finishing school, but 'you hear your family talking about girls going to marry and you draw your own conclusions.' Most of them added that their parents changed their mind in later years. They mentioned younger sisters who did get the chance to finish school and who have diplomas of greater value: 'My mother regrets what she did then, she feels sorry for me now.' 'My mother started learning Dutch recently, she always says to me and my sisters: you have to learn ladies, it's never too late'.

At least as many women tell quite another story. They emphasize that it was their own choice to leave school and that they did this against their parents' (particularly fathers') will. The reasons they give were variations on 'I did not feel at home at school' and 'I did not see what good it was to finish (that) school'. They explain their lack of motivation by pointing to the limited value of the diploma and to the lack of career opportunities for migrants in the Dutch labour market. 'I thought, we as foreigners will never get a chance to get a higher position than our parents.'

On the one hand, the complexity of most accounts brought me to the overall conclusion that, for the most part, the broken-off school career was the result of a mixture of circumstances, assessments and conflicting feelings, of both the parents and the girls themselves. On the other hand, it struck me that either dependence or autonomy was the central theme in the accounts. Re-analysing the accounts as self-expressions towards a Dutch researcher, the emphasis on dependence and Turkish traditional ideas about femininity might be interpreted as giving an explanation that fits within the dominant discourse and the supposed interpretation repertoire of the interviewer. This is completed by a deliberate effort to improve the social reputation of Turkish immigrants by adding that their parents' opinions have changed. The emphasis on 'my own choice', autonomy and the progressive ideas of their parents about girls and education might be interpreted as a critical reaction against dominant discourse about 'Islamic' gender relations, in which the unequal chances of (female) migrants in the Netherlands are neglected.

Epilogue

This analysis of interview texts of Turkish and Moroccan immigrant women as self-presentation towards a Dutch audience reveals in the first place their social knowledge, their assessments of their social reputation as 'Islamic' woman in the Netherlands. Implicitly and explicitly the women react against dominant ideas about their 'culture': their traditional family relations, lack of freedom and restricted autonomy. Differentiating the category of Turkish and/or Moroccan women into subgroups, such as first- and second-generation migrants, and emphasizing change are both tactics to improve their social reputation. However, by positioning and identifying themselves as 'modern' women, wife and mother they clearly appropriate the complexities and contradictions of this position and identity too. For example, the presentation of marriage as partnership, the combination of the glamorous idea of freedom with female decency and the complicated idealization of autonomy. Moreover, their reactions reveal that for migrant women, individual social reputation is always connected with the reputation of the ethnic group. Therefore, being judged as an exceptional modern model women is not considered a compliment.

Notes

1. Harré's definition of a moral career is: 'the social history of a person with respect to the attitudes of respect and contempt that others have to him and of his understandings of these attitudes' and 'a life trajectory defined in terms of public esteem' (1979: 312). Harré borrowed this concept from Goffman (1959).
2. The social equivalent of a 'girls' night out'.
3. For a critical review of this literature see Lutz (1991).
4. In 'international linking classes' newcomer children mainly receive language teaching.

Bibliography

De Certeau, M. (1984), *The Practice of Everyday Life*, Berkeley: University of California Press.

Foucault, M. (1977), *Discipline and Punish. The Birth of the Prison*, London: Allan Lane/Penguin.

Freund, A. and Quilici, L. (1997), 'Die erforschung von Mythen in den Erzählungen von Frauen: Italienische and deutsche Einwanderinnen in Vancouver 1947–1961', *Bios, Zeitschrift für biographieforschung und oral history* 10, (2): 209–28.

Goffman, E. (1959), *The Presentation of Self in Everyday Life*, New York: Doubleday.

Harré, R. (1979), *Social Being. A Theory for Social Psychology*, Oxford: Basil Blackwell.

Kitzinger, J. (1994), 'The Methodology of Focus groups. The Importance of Interaction between Research Participants', *Sociology of Health and Illness*, 16, (1): 103–21.

Knijn, G.C.M and Verheijen, C.M.L.H (1988), *Tussen plicht en ontplooiing*, Nijmegen: ITS.

Komter, A. (1985), *De macht van de vanzelfsprekendheid in relaties tussen vrouwen en mannen*, Den Haag: Vuga.

Lutz, H. (1991), *Welten verbinden. Türkische Sozialarbeiterinnen in den Niederlanden und der Bundesrepublik Deutschland*, Frankfurt am Main: IKO.

MacLeod, A. (1991), *Accommodating Protest. Working Women, the New Veiling and Change in Cairo*, New York: Columbia University Press.

Potter, J. and Wetherell, M. (1987), *Discourse and Social Psychology. Beyond Attitude and Behaviour*, Newbury Park: Sage.

Said, E. (1978), *Orientalism*, London: Routledge & Kegan Paul.

Skeggs, B. (1997), *Formations of Class and Gender. Becoming Respectable*, London: Sage.

Zwaard, J. van der (1992), 'Accounting for Differences. Dutch Training Nurses and their View on Migrant Women', *Social Science and Medicine* 35, (9): 1137–44.

Zwaard, J. van der (1995), *Hoe vrouwen moederen. Buurtgesprekken over opvoeding*, Utrecht: SWP.

Zwaard, J. van der (1999a), *Met hulp van vriendinnen. Vrouwen uit lage inkomensgroepen over rondkomen en vooruitkomen*, Utrecht: SWP.

Zwaard, J. van der (1999b), 'The Obstinacy Stage. Reconstruction of a Culturally Defined Child-rearing Problem', *The Netherlands' Journal of Social Sciences* 35, (1): 23–36.

8

Gendered and Racialized Experiences of Citizenship in the Life Stories of Women of Turkish Background in Germany

Umut Erel

Women of Turkish background in Germany[1] are a group that holds a particular place in public discourse and the imagination of 'foreigners'. The role of migrant women is a key topic in discursively creating the difference between a German collectivity and justifying the exclusion of its 'Others'. This is reflected in the focus of social research on women of Turkish background, which far exceeds the number of studies on other immigrant nationalities (Lutz and Huth-Hildebrand 1998). Both in quantitative and qualitative terms, images of women of Turkish background have come to represent migrant women: 'From the 1970s onwards, a clear tendency towards the orientalization of migrant women can be identified: the debate on "foreign women" (*Ausländerinnen*) became a debate on Turkish women' (Inowlocki and Lutz 2000: 307). The key themes that have structured such research for the last three decades have been that of 'the (uncivilized) stranger, the victim of patriarchal honour and being "twice rootless"' (Inowlocki and Lutz 2000: 307). This seems particularly significant because social research, social policy and public discourse converged to construct a homogenized image of women of Turkish background as essentially oppressed by their fathers, husbands or brothers (see below). This image posits women of Turkish background firmly in a subordinate position, both vis-à-vis men of Turkish background and the wider society. While mainstream social research is beginning to recognize a 'pluralization' of the 'Turkish community', the tendency to cast the object of research as constituting a social problem (Räthzel 1994) still remains alive in this recognition of diversity (Heitmeyer, Müller and Schröder 1997; Sen and Goldberg 1994). Moreover, in these approaches gender continues to be neglected as constitutive of ethnic identity, and the essentialized image of the downtrodden woman of Turkish background who is outside of German society still forms a tacit but powerful point of reference. The effects of gendered racism, on the other hand are often overlooked. While these representations can still be seen to dominate public and private representations of Turkishness and Turkish femininities (Schneider 2001; Laviziano, Mein and Sökefeld 2001), here I would like to give a brief and necessarily selective overview of recent research contesting such representations.

Feminist research on migrant women during the last decade has contributed hugely to deconstruct these representations. A path-breaking work has been Lutz's (1991) study on Turkish women social workers in Germany and the Netherlands. It challenged the assumption that Muslim women's identity and behaviour can mainly be explained on the basis of their culture of origin, narrowly defined as religious and 'traditionally' patriarchal. This view is reductionist in several ways. First, it prioritizes the supposed ethnic or cultural identity of women of Turkish background over all other possible identificatory elements such as gender, class, political orientation, or educational status. Second, it reduces Turkishness to a unified totality, within which traditionality and religion are seen as the determining structures. This is part of a construction of the Muslim 'Orient' as the Other of Europe, which imagines itself as modern, dynamic, secular and rational (Said 1978; Lutz 1991).[2] Elsewhere, Lutz (n.d.) coined the term of 'Other Other' to describe the complex interplay of gender and ethnicity in the representation of Muslim women: women are constructed as the Other of a male norm, while the Orient is constructed as the Other of Europe. At the same time, the study highlighted the significance of institutional and interpersonal racism for the educational and professional development of Turkish women. The study emphasized Turkish women's strategies and their agency to negotiate and overcome these restrictions. Thus it challenged the notion of Turkish migrant women as passive victims. Moreover, it showed the diversity of Turkish migrant women as well as the complex web of gendered, ethnocized and class-specific social relations.

Other research has deconstructed specifically anti-Muslim racism and the centrality of images of women, as dehumanized victims of patriarchal oppression on the one hand and sexually luring objects of desire on the other (Pinn and Wehner 1995). The focus on the family as a site of oppression of previous research has given way to a wider range of research questions. Thus, the internal differentiation of women of Turkish background has been raised. Otyakmaz (1995) has argued that the generalizing notion of the second generation as caught up 'between two cultures' is untenable. Although the young women she interviewed experienced conflicts with their parents, they did not see them in terms of cultural conflicts but as generational difference. Moreover, these conflicts were held in balance by shared values and parental support, for example for their educational progress. Researching inter-generational change from the perspective of first-generation migrant mothers, Krüger and Potts (1995) find that an expectation for the daughters to marry goes hand in hand with strong support for the daughters' education. Yurtdas (1995) has explicitly sought to correct the image of first generation migrant women as passive and unable to adapt to the changing situation of migration. Her biographical study of Kurdish rural women migrants argued that they have paved the way for subsequent migrants and participated in the creation of a migrant subculture. This is in contrast to previous research, which presented poorly educated rural migrants as passive victims of patriarchal oppression within the family and helpless victims of modernization in Germany. Toksöz (1991) has examined the working lives of women of Turkish background and their participation in trade unionism. She found that despite the women's high rates of trade-union membership and their militant activism, the structures of the trade union failed to accommodate and represent their interests. Many researchers explain the low levels of labour market participation[3] of migrant women from Turkey through culturalist arguments and thus as a reflection of Muslim gender segregation and women's restriction to the home. As recent research reveals, this view is not tenable and women's life plans and aspirations include paid work, not as an alternative but together with motherhood (Erdem 2000; Gümen and Westphal 1996).

While Islam has often served as a culturalist explanation of the difference of women of Turkish background, little in-depth qualitative research has been done into the subjective meanings and practices of religion for them. Public discourse centres on religion as an obstacle to integration, as a source of patriarchal oppression and as a threat to democracy through political Islam, so-called fundamentalism. Such reductionist views of Muslim women and their practice of wearing a headscarf contrast sharply with what in-depth research can reveal. Thus, in her study on Muslim women of Turkish background studying for educational professions, Karakasoglu-Aydin (1999) found a wide range of different orientations regarding religion. She differentiates between atheists, spiritualists, laicists, pragmatic or idealist ritualists. In her study, the wearing of the headscarf expresses a variety of attitudes. Her findings alert us that the practice and orientation of religion are far more differentiated than the public representations suggest.

In the imaginary space, Muslim women in general and Turkish migrant women in particular are juxtaposed to German women, whose lifestyle is seen to embody Western democracy and liberal values. In this view, German women constitute the symbols of the free and democratic constitution.[4] The argument most often used to explain the assumed 'backward' character of gender roles of people of Turkish background is based on evolutionary assumptions that picture gender equality as a civilizatory achievement, granted by German democratic institutions. The social participation of migrant women therefore is another issue that has been difficult to conceptualize within the dominant Orientalist paradigms. In their examination of the social participation of migrant women Rodriguez (1999) and Akashe-Böhme (2000) draw attention to the continuing structural subordination and exclusion of migrant women in both the labour market and the political domain. Democracy, they argue, needs to be progressive in the sense of increasing the participatory element and increasing the group of participants. Research has however not yet taken up these concerns to discuss the concept of citizenship from the standpoint of migrant women's subjectivity and social participation.

In this chapter, I would like to suggest that the lifestories of women of Turkish background can inform new notions of community, belonging and social participation that are constitutive of citizenship. This includes two moves: first, epistemologically I place the subjectivities of migrant women of Turkish background centre stage. Secondly, I include them in debates on citizenship, a concept that, in the German context, is not yet inclusive of these women. I begin by discussing the construction of gendered ethnic and national identities. Then I move on to discuss the literature on citizenship identifying the gap regarding migrant women's social participation. In the final part, I present two life stories of women of Turkish background and their conceptualizations of issues of 'membership in a community'.

I shall be focusing on the relationship between citizenship, nation and the subjectivities of ethnocized women. This draws on research, carried out in 1996, in which I conducted nine life story interviews with single, educated women of Turkish background in Germany.[5] The sample includes first- and second-generation migrant women,[6] situated within varying professions. Here, I will focus on the life stories of Nilgün, a second generation migrant and Ayten, a first generation migrant. Central themes in Nilgün's lifestory relate to her education, where she had to resist racist classifications as a low achiever by her teachers in order to achieve qualifications enabling her to study. The decision to leave the parental home was another key event in her life story. This entailed conflicts around divergent views on gendered lifestyles. At the time, experiences of racism and her dis-identification with parental gendered norms led Nilgün to reject Turkishness. As a young adult, Nilgün encountered politically active Left-wing people of Turkish background, with whose gender concepts she could identify more readily and she began to relate to 'Turkishness' more positively. However her process of politicization also entailed conflicts: thus, she contested the homeland orientation of many Left-wing groups from Turkey and the Eurocentrism of the German feminist movement. Finding a place for herself through her social and political activism therefore constituted another key theme in her life story that I will discuss below. A key theme in Ayten's lifestory is individualism. She grew up in a European-oriented, urban middle-class family in Turkey. While Ayten's family supported female education, she was the first woman in the family to go abroad for study. She presented this as an instance of her curiosity and wish for self-development. In her professional life, she develops the theme of resisting authorities through her choice to become self-employed. When she married a German man, she decided to stay in Germany. There, she became active in cultural events and also in a Turkish community organization. Ayten's lifestory elaborates on the key theme of developing herself through individualism and care for others. While gender and ethnicity are constitutive of this process, she challenges essentialist concepts of community, as I elaborate below.

Nilgün's and Ayten's lifestories articulate specific notions of social participation and community. Below, I suggest how these can be useful in challenging essentialist notions of Turkish femininity, Germanness and also nationalised citizenship.

Gendered Constructions of German and *Ausländer* Identities

I now turn to examine the relational construction of Germanness and Turkishness in relation to gendered narratives of identity. Here, my concern is how Germanness is constructed via the racialized Others and the gendered implications of this.[7] I will examine the concept of *Ausländer* (foreigner, but linguistically expressing the outsider status) as central for the construction of German national identity. For a long time, the term *Ausländer* has been regarded as synonymous with 'Turk', and indeed, research reveals that Turkish people are imagined as a socially and culturally distant group (Forsythe 1989).

With reference to Germany, Kalpaka and Räthzel (1990) conceptualize racism and nationalism (Räthzel 1995) as forms of hegemonic societalization. By this, they mean that racism functions as a practice of constructing boundaries of belonging to the German collectivity. At the same time, however, it is the basis of normalizing practices to establish the content of Germanness. If *Ausländer* are seen as exhibiting undesired behaviour, this also serves to control Germans' behaviour. The difference between Germanness and *Ausländer* is crucial for the construction of the boundaries of Germanness, although both categories are not unitary or homogenous in themselves. There is not a single German national identity but rather, different and contradictory versions of national identity are put forward by different groups. Different political and social groups may try to hegemonize competing versions of national identity (Johnson 1993). These may include varying degrees of plurality and diversity of who may be recognized as 'German'. However, for all constructions of national identity, an exterior Other is crucial to determine its boundaries. In the German context, this external Other takes the form of *Ausländer*.[8] Although legally anyone without German citizenship is an *Ausländer*, socially the term coincides with racialization so that white West-Europeans are only occasionally regarded as *Ausländer* (Forsythe 1989). On the other hand, for example black Germans may often experience being labelled as *Ausländer*, despite their formal German citizenship and cultural competence (Oguntoye et al. 1997). Among migrants, so-called 'guest workers' and their children, asylum seekers, refugees, undocumented immigrants, students, business people, and so forth, are regarded as *Ausländer*. While class, educational status and generation are factors that may qualify the racialization of an individual *Ausländer* situationally, this does not render the categorization ineffective for the ethnic collectivities. Different groups of *Ausländer* are differentially and hierarchically positioned in different discourses and practices. For example, labour migrants may be seen as more legitimately belonging to a locality than asylum seekers, refugees or undocumented immigrants by Germans, and may indeed participate in local racist practices of exclusion.[9] Despite this 'differential racialization' (Brah 1996) the dichotomy between Germanness and *Ausländer* is effective. In my view, the recent emergence in the German media of a new discourse on second and third generations as hyphenated 'Turkish-Germans' constitutes a refinement of the category of *Ausländer*, not its dissolution, because the constitutive assumption of difference remains intact (Erel 1999).

Until recently, the concept of racism had hardly been recognized in dominant German discourses. Instead, the concept of *Ausländerfeindlichkeit* – 'enmity to foreigners' – was used. This concept mainly refers to a personal, emotional attitude and is not seen as linked to structural racism and racist state practices. The principal reason for 'enmity to foreigners' is seen in the difference of *Ausländer*. The dominant approach of political parties, social workers and social scientists therefore is centred around promoting 'integration'; however 'integration' most often amounts to assimilation. Thus, immigrants are expected to physically and metaphorically close a huge gap in order to catch up with Germans (see Blaschke 1994). However all integrationist approaches ignore the fact that there is already a basic structural inequality,[10] thus making the *Ausländer* and their 'cultures' responsible for *Ausländerfeindlichkeit*. The construction of the cultural difference of the *Ausländer*, a pretext for their exclusion from full social, political and economic participation, is however crucial for maintaining the boundaries of Germanness.

Gender, Ethnicity and Nation

I am arguing from a point of view that regards gender, 'race', ethnicity and class as intermeshing social divisions (Anthias and Yuval-Davis 1992; Hill-Collins 1990). My focus here is on the interrelated constructions of 'Turkish' femininity and ethnicity. Women's roles in ethnic or national communities are often constructed only in relation to and depending on men. They are viewed in family metaphors such as mothers, sisters or daughters. As mothers and wives, women's role as biological and ideological reproducers of the nation or ethnic group is pre-eminent. At another level, women and their appropriate (sexual) behaviour serve as signifiers of ethnic and national difference (Anthias and Yuval-Davis 1989). The construction and guarding of the boundaries of ethnic groups is a constitutive element of ethnicity, thus I see the construction of gender roles as central to the construction of ethnicity (both, materially and symbolically). This is valid for the dominant German group as well as for subordinated groups, such as Kurdish and Turkish people in Germany.

Sexuality is a key theme in women's role as signifier of the ethnic group. For example, in the life stories of second-generation migrant women from Turkey, the decision of a young woman to leave the family home, not for marriage, but to live independently, is often viewed by the parents and also by the young women, as 'leaving' Turkishness and turning to Germanness. Parental fears of pre-marital sexuality in this context have come to be a signifier of Germanness and the transgression of the boundaries of Turkishness. For example, Nilgün's mother threatened her and her sister: 'if you go away I'll tell everybody that you are prost-itutes, you know. And we said, "yes, do so." We were hurt, you know, but that wouldn't have prevented us anymore, it was simply too late, you know' (pp. 9–10).

Sexuality here was used to demonize the daughters and to ostracize them from the Turkish community, although the conflict at hand was one of parent-child relationships and conflicting life plans. Sirin recounts that, at the time, her first sexual relationship with a German man meant to her that she could not go back to being 'Turkish'. To her, sexual experience symbolized the trespassing of the boundary to Germanness. To her it meant that she had to accept a German lifestyle, even though she did not like many aspects of what she perceived to be a German lifestyle and even though her sexual relationship was not known to anybody and she did not receive sanctions for her sexual behaviour from Turkish people. In her own consciousness, pre-marital sexuality and being a Turkish young woman were incommensurable.

Sometimes, this dichotomization of gender roles as ethnically bound can be internalized by women of Turkish background. Suzan, a 29-year-old student of literature, recounts that, as a young girl who wanted to be independent from her parents without marrying, the only option seemed to be to become German. She felt that her German friends ignored her experiences of racism and saw her as one of them because they saw her as 'not really Turkish'. On the other hand, her wish to live an independent lifestyle, which she perceived to be exclusively possible for a 'German', in conjunction with the strong and debilitating experiences of vulnerability and helplessness in the face of violent racism, made her feel she had to make a choice:

> Before, for me, it was either you're a Turkish [woman], so you've got to get married, you've got to do what your parents say, you've got to stay respectable, blah blah blah. Or, you are thus like virgin – whore, but in this case like Turkish-German. You're German, you've got a boyfriend, you can [have a] profession, blah blah blah. It was all extremes, it was divided, either-or, there was no being in-between . . . in order to be with Germans, you had to reject everything that was Turkish absolutely, there was no way of keeping anything . . . And I could not imagine having Turkish friends, I did not know any others who were like me . . . I ran away from home when I was eighteen, didn't have any contact with my parents, didn't speak any Turkish – I nearly forgot all my Turkish and didn't want anything to do with it. And I moved out – [I] ran away with the idea . . . that my parents would reject me. I never thought that instead they would mourn me. [My idea was] that my leaving home would mean giving up my Turkish identity, giving it up completely. (p. 34)

In these examples, a clear-cut dichotomy between Germanness and Turkishness and a homogenization of 'Turkish' and 'German' lifestyles is prevalent. Later on in their lives, these women came to challenge such concepts, but at the time they exerted a very strong power over them and their view of themselves. However, the image of the 'Other Other' is also a crucial element of Germans' behaviour towards women of Turkish background. Often, they ignore the actual personal history and circumstances of women of Turkish background and relate to the pity-provoking, victimized image they have of them rather than to the person's actual behaviour. On the other hand, there is a tendency to incorporate women of Turkish background who do not fit into the image of the 'Other Other' into Germanness, thus denying them the possibility of also partly representing Turkishness. The stereotypical expectations that Germans have of women of Turkish background are most obvious regarding education, professional status and gendered lifestyles. Ayten, a first-generation migrant, who is a doctor, experienced disbelief from colleagues regarding her wide-ranging and specialized qualifications, as a woman from Turkey. But also in everyday life, she is often not identified as Turkish, but as a foreigner from a 'higher status country'. Being an unmarried woman does not correspond to gendered ethnocized images of women of Turkish background either. Here, Nilgün refers to German people's reactions to her being unmarried and living on her own:

> With the Germans I've got the feeling [that they think] 'What? Her too?!' well, that they don't expect something like that at all. That really they've ascribed another role to you and it surprises them that you've got a different role. I find this – I distance myself from them, I have the feeling this is not equal. I – well, my status is being put in the foreground. Just as if I had a disability or so, and that one is being disabled through this. (Nilgün p. 44)

German people's normative assumptions about women of Turkish background's lives, are powerful factors that may constrain their negotiations of gender roles by ethnocizing them. This is often felt as 'disabling' by women of Turkish background, rather than confirming the purported role of German culture as an emancipatory force. However, the women have found different ways of dealing with and overcoming these constraints.

Citizenship and Subjectivity

The issue of citizenship in Germany has become particularly topical through the debates on dual citizenship and the new citizenship law. In 1999, the new Social Democrat/Green government amended the citizenship law against vehement opposition by the conservative Christian Democrat parties. The most significant changes in my view have been on a symbolic level. Thus, the previous citizenship law (1913), had based the *right* to German citizenship exclusively on *ius sanguinis*, granting non-residents of German origin the right to citizenship while all other residents of Germany did not have any entitlements to naturalization. Their naturalization was made contingent on 'German interests' and was seen as an exception. This has been changed in favour of a mixture of *ius sanguinis* and *ius soli*. From January 2000, children born in Germany have the right to German citizenship if one of the parents has been living in Germany legally for eight years and has secure residence status. The practical effects of this amendment are limited.[11] For the purposes of this chapter, however my concern will not be with these recent changes to the formal citizenship law. This is because the interviews took place before the current developments. Moreover, I think that a focus on formal citizenship is insufficient for making sense of the women's experiences. Instead, I shall discuss citizenship in its wider meaning, as 'membership in the community' (Marshall 1953). My main concern is with the ways in which communities are defined and negotiated within ethnocized and gendered parameters. Most debates about both formal and substantial aspects of citizenship in Germany are dominated by a dichotomizing logic; on the one hand there are the migrants and their interests; on the other hand there is German society and German interests. While those who support the inclusion of migrants into German society may argue that German and migrants' interests converge in certain respects, the epistemological basis for distinguishing these interest groups on the basis of ethnicity is taken for granted. Thus, such accounts often enumerate the benefits migrants have brought or are likely to bring to German society.

Academic debates on citizenship tend to exclude migrant women by focusing one-dimensionally on migrants, generically defined as male (Mackert 1999), or by examining the articulation of gender and nationality only in terms of their effects on women nationals (Appelt 2000). I take a contrasting epistemological starting point by putting the subjective accounts of women of Turkish background centre stage. Most theorists agree that citizenship is a status that bestows rights and obligations. At the same time, each system of citizenship also constructs its ideal-typical subject as those who are best able to fulfil their obligations and are presumably thus best equipped to exercise their rights. As Léca points out, 'those individuals who consider their interests as properly served through citizenship are recognized as the best citizens, and those who possess the most "capital" (material, cultural or technological) are recognized as the most competent' (Léca 1992: 20). I would add however, that for women of Turkish background in Germany, much of their social and cultural capital is not recognised by the ethnically dominant society (Lutz 1991).

Citizenship is a multidimensional concept and different theorists have pointed out that there are different levels of citizenship (legal, social, political (Marshall 1953)), different aspects of citizenship (active/passive and public/private (Turner

1990)) as well as different tiers of citizenship: local, regional, national, transnational (Yuval-Davis 1997). Despite the universalist claims of contemporary democracy, different members of the community are positioned very differentially with relation to all of these dimensions of citizenship, according to gender, ethnicity, ability and legal residence status.

For different categories of citizens or denizens,[12] different capacities and statuses *vis-à-vis* the state and society are prioritized. Soysal (1994) argues with respect to migrants in Germany, that although they may not be formally citizens, they share the same social rights as full citizens. She views this as an example for the emergence of 'post-national citizenship' in Europe, which privileges human rights over nationally, bounded citizenship rights. While I agree with her normative view that human rights should usefully supersede nationally bounded citizenship rights, I do not see the basis for such a development put into practice yet. On the one hand, I would agree with Kofman (1995) that political rights are indispensable to ensure and sustain migrants' status. Political rights are also important for any attempt to transform and redefine the substance and form of rights and obligations. On the other hand, I cannot agree that migrants enjoy social rights to the same degree as full citizens (see Mackert 1999). Migrants' residence status is still contingent: thus, migrants who are long-term unemployed, who commit a crime or whose political activities endanger 'the interests of the Federal Republic of Germany' may lose their residence permit and be deported.[13] Migrants' lack of political rights also has an impact on their social rights. Without political rights, denizens have few possibilities of co-determining the content of social rights. Moreover, the reduction of migrants to bearers of social rights structurally fixes them as recipients of services.

First, such a view does not take into account the economic contributions to German society, both through their labour and through their taxes to the state system (Cohn-Bendit and Schmid 1992). The unpaid labour of migrant women in the home is not taken into account, neither is their caring labour of bringing up children. Often women working full time, especially in the past, had to rely on relatives in Turkey to bring up their children, thus 'outsourcing' this labour for lack of adequate childcare facilities, housing and income in Germany. Secondly, it structurally reifies what Avtar Brah (1996) calls 'minoritization': the construction of ethnocized or racialized groups as 'minors in tutelage' (1996: 187). Radtke (1993) has argued that the state and in particular associated social work agencies have been central in homogenizing culturally, linguistically and socially diverse populations into distinct ethnocized groups. These social work agencies have constructed migrants primarily as recipients of state services on the basis of their ethnicity. Thirdly, a reductionist view of migrants' citizenship as primarily social does not take account of migrants' cultural, political and social contributions to civil society. Finally, all of these contributions can only be fully taken into account if we do not collapse national identity and citizenship and conceptualize migrants as part of civil society (see Yuval-Davis 1997).

In the following section I will focus on two issues, first the construction of communities and second, its implications for conceptualizing women's social participation. For this purpose, I suggest a broad notion of 'quotidian politics' (McClure 1992: 112) that does not reduce citizenship to rights-claiming activities *vis-à-vis* the state, but includes other social arenas and social relations in the analysis. Such a view accepts that power relations, and processes of inclusion and exclusion take place across a range of social relations and are not limited to the arena of formal or state-oriented politics. A broadened notion of citizenship, not entirely contingent on the nation state in its conception, could also usefully question the exclusivity of the privileges conferred by formal citizenship.

Social Participation and Belonging

So far I have outlined some key factors regarding the positioning of women of Turkish background in dominant German discourse and practices. As *Ausländer*, they are seen as exterior to German society and only perceived of in terms of problems. Germanness and Turkishness are seen as mutually exclusive, incommensurable and essentially distinct. Turkishness in this dichotomy holds an inferior position. Gender plays a crucial part in this construction. Women of Turkish background are only conceivable as victims of a violently patriarchal 'Turkish culture'. If they do not fit into these images, they are either seen as 'atypical', and thus irrelevant, or they are constructed as Germanized and not competent to represent another version of Turkishness. The construction of these women, both as exterior and as victimized, makes it impossible to see them as active subjects who participate in and shape German society. This view is based on a collapsing of German society with the nation. It ignores racism as a constitutive element of national definitions and does not acknowledge any participation in this society that challenges the unity of society and nation through claiming a place in the society without subjecting oneself to national assimilation. All of the interviewees participated actively in social relations, in different ways, and with different aims. Their activities ranged from being active on committees, organizing professional exchange programmes, voluntary work in community organizations, activity in women's centres and single issue campaigns. The ways in which the interviewees conceptualize their social participation and in particular the notion of community may shed some light on the constitution of citizenship and throw up some questions regarding a national basis for social participation and belonging. With brief extracts from two lifestories, I will discuss some of the ways in which the interviewees negotiated and contested their positioning as exterior and subordinated in German society.

Nilgün

Nilgün is a 29-year-old social worker. A main theme in her life story is finding a place for herself. During her adolescence, like many other second-generation women of Turkish background, she reworked meanings of Turkishness. She struggled with denigrating racist definitions of Turkishness by her German environment as well as with her own and her family's conflicting perspectives on gendered lifestyles. In different left-wing and women's community centres for people of Turkish background, she found ways of living out a Turkish femininity that were closer to her own ideas and ideals than either dominant German or her parents' notions of appropriate Turkish femininity. When, as a reaction to increased nationalism and violent racist attacks in the course of German unification, an anti-racist migrants' movement began to form, Nilgün became involved in it. She describes herself as a 'migrant', a term that was developed in the migrants' movement as a political term, similar to the notion of political blackness in 1980s Britain, to encompass racialized people in Germany (Café Morgenland 1993). This term challenges the dichotomizing logic of either assimilating to Germanness or belonging to the nation of origin, and instead tries to create a community whose political stance is based on challenging German nationalism and claiming a place in German society, as 'the place where one lives' without being German. Nilgün sees her social marginality as an analytically central vantage point for understanding and challenging the place in which she lives:

> I am also quite happy not to belong somehow . . . politically, too. I'd like it if there weren't any nations and if people would define themselves differently. I'd find that better, I feel that [national belonging] is a barrier . . . Rather, it is important to . . . substantiate a commonality with different values. I find it much closer to life . . . instead of some abstract rulers' definitions, [such as] nation or religion or capitalism (laughs). (p. 42)

In her biography of migration, Nilgün sees a chance to question structures of national belonging and perceives the position of non-belonging as a potentially privileged vantage point providing one with:

> possibilities so that you can deal critically with your environment, also with yourself. So that you can question certain things about yourself, is this really mine or have I just adapted it . . . What are these values, really? When you are excluded you start thinking. Do I want to be like them, or what are they really doing? . . . I actually find it very positive if one can use it consciously. (p. 42)

In this sense, marginalization can provide a more critical view of the naturalized notions of community, such as national or ethnic boundaries. It can enable her to define belonging in a politically conscious way as well as make it easier to decide against dominant values and create different values since 'you don't belong anyway' (p. 42). Moreover, her view of national belonging as a 'rulers' definition' interprets the decision not to belong as an act of resistance against dominant structures of subjection.

Nilgün's conceptualization of national belonging as a form of power relation becomes quite clear in her commitment against the war against Kurdish people in Turkey. When some women of Turkish background came together to form a group to protest against the war, they wanted to define themselves:

> what are we, Turks or how are we defining ourselves (laughs). I have never defined myself as a Turk, but if somebody says 'Fucking Turk' I would defend them. That's different, but I wouldn't voluntary call myself that . . . I don't know what it's like to be Turkish. And then . . . we analysed nationalism and what it means . . . there were big discussions, and some even left. And that's the first time I said, I agree that we call ourselves 'Turkish women' (laughs). Because I became convinced about using it as a political tool, because in Kurdistan the Kurds are oppressed and we are the privileged society. It makes no bloody difference if I live here or not . . . I would use it again if it were to mirror these relations of oppression . . . However in very specific situations, when it is only about this issue. Not because I advocate it, but because it's a fact. (p. 41)

Nilgün views Turkishness as a relational entity. In this case, Turkishness in the context of the Kurdish-Turkish conflict is a subject position that requires a specific expression of solidarity with Kurdish people. Highlighting her Turkishness amounts to admitting a relative position of privilege in Germany as well as in Turkey, it also serves to subvert the naturalization of Turkishness as the only ethnicity of people in or from Turkey, as well as subverting a national, Turkish consensus on the legitimacy of the war against Kurdish people. In this quotation, not only the politically purposive use of a national definition is highlighted, but I also want to underline the fact that Nilgün actually chooses a national name or chooses not to use it in other situations. This is because in other situations she does not want to 'advocate' the concept of national belonging itself.

Nilgün uses the term migrant throughout the interview. This concept expresses social relations of ethnocization but does not evoke national identity. She values this subject position of migrant since it allows for a critical evaluation of dominant values of assimilation into the ethnic majority at the same time as questioning a national identity basis with ethnic minority communities.

Ayten

Ayten is a 49-year-old doctor who runs her own practice. She has a teenage daughter. She migrated to Germany in order to complete her education. After a period of two years during which she worked in Turkey, she decided to return to Germany, in order to join her German partner there. She has been living in Germany for more than 20 years. A main theme in her life story is her search for self-realization and self-development. This means developing her professional and artistic skills, but also an involvement in social issues.

Over the years, she has been active in a large number of voluntary organizations and groups, many of whom provided services for migrants from Turkey. When asked how she became involved in these different groups, and in particular in the Turkish community organization where she held two terms of office as vice president, she responds:

> I think it's got to do with personality. It happened and I did not say I do not want to do it; but I was there and looked forward to doing something . . . Yes, I also wanted to meet people here, the people who live normal lives here, what their wishes are and what pains they have. And I've met a lot of people and exchanged ideas with them. That was a very interesting experience. Yes . . . and we have tried from a particular political direction to bring in our political opinion. I think, this [is] sort of being a dissenter, or that one does not live in conformity with the authorities. (pp. 25–6)

Ayten describes her commitment to social projects as a feature of her personality, as a result of her curiosity and her non-conformism to authorities. This way of conceptualizing participation in society draws on a notion of self that is directly connected to the social. It does not resound with liberal notions of citizenship and the state or society, in which individuals are conceived of as strangers to each other and only connected through their shared responsibilities or rights claims towards the state. Rather, commonality is sought outside the authorized modes of self. This refers mainly to ethnocized modes of citizenship, as her political work in that community organization involved contesting hegemonic discourses on (formal) citizenship, national belonging and ethnocization.

> *Ayten*: I am still a Turk, I have not taken on German citizenship. Well, I must say maybe I stayed loyal to myself due to my early beginning here and through luck, but it is really luck.[14] Because inside myself, I have always rejected getting a German passport, because I've said with a passport I am also giving up my identity. I do not claim Turkish identity, either, but I am myself. Maybe I am a hybrid or I am a human being of this universe . . . I have smiled [when people have said] 'Oh! We wouldn't have thought so, we thought that you were Israeli or French or I don't know what, Greek.' And I've said 'I am staying Turkish! I do have this passport!' Even if Turks are not categorized as cultured people, I am a cultured person, but with my passport. I am staying this way. And I am still Turkish, and despite this I have a German doctors' certificate, so I can work here . . . in my own surgery . . . maybe it's utopian, still I don't want to take up a passport; no man with a black beard and Anatolian looks is going to become German with a German passport . . . I could disguise myself easier and disappear or slip through as a non-Turk.

But not at all! . . . First of all, the people don't need that or shouldn't need that. I think it's really great that they maintain their first generation, their Anatolian or Turkish identity . . . I didn't want to go with the mainstream.

In this quote, Ayten makes clear her views on formal citizenship. Although her Turkish passport does not signify belonging for her, she sees it as a part of herself that signifies a part of her identity, and this is something she does not want to give up. By maintaining her Turkish passport, she also wants to maintain that she is a person from Turkey. This is contextualized as rejecting being Germanized or to be ascribed a nationality that in the German context signifies greater value than Turkishness.[15] It is an attempt to challenge economic and social mechanisms of ethnocization that do not allow for a successful, highly educated, well-off doctor to be from Turkey. She may – according to the system of ethnocization – become German, thus elevating her ethnic status to match that of her socio-economic and educational positioning.

Her defiance also extends to other people, with her argument operating on two levels. First, she opposes the fact, that rights and legitimacy to live in German society should be conditional on becoming German, be it through acquiring formal citizenship or in the implied assimilation to Germanness. Second, she contests the equation of formal citizenship with the assumption that a 'man with a black beard and Anatolian looks' will not be discriminated against. Thus, the assumption of equality due to shared citizenship is challenged on the grounds that racist ascriptions of lower status and legitimacy will continue to be effective. Her wish to keep a Turkish passport and her support for people who want to keep up a Turkish, Anatolian or first-generation identity, is, however, not an expression of 'ethnic absolutism' (Gilroy 1993). Ayten argues for enabling individual choices and allows for the possibility of assimilation, however without pressure. Ayten sees her own identity as a very individual mix of influences. This leads her to say that she has a 'hybrid' (p. 24) or a 'twin identity' (p. 27):

I am a twin . . . I speak both languages well. I sometimes feel at home in Germany as well as in Turkey, but I would rather decide on Germany for my future. But half of my life has been formed by my Turkish . . . life and I don't know whether I have lived a typical Turkish life, but I would say that my identity is a twin identity . . . I like being in A-town, I have a social task in this society which I have been practising for twenty years and I feel fine here. (p. 27)

She favours a dimension of personal lived experience, with its 'changes', 'transitions' (p. 28) and 'migrations' (p. 24) over nation or ethnicity as formative for her identity. However, she does not view this individual identity as outside of social factors, but emphasizes her participation in German society through her professional contribution.

Ayten additionally argues that she is: 'a European person and I don't want to be here as a Turk, a German, Frenchwoman, I want to be accepted as an integrated Central European and I don't need to change my passport. As an integrated person I want to have all political rights in this society and free movement in Europe' (p. 11). Thus, her argument challenges absolutist and exclusionary notions of national identity and its link to citizenship from various vantage points: she argues for a supra-national, European identity, which is determined by place.[16] She also argues for a local identity, when she describes herself as a 'A-town Turk' or an 'A-towner of Turkish descent' (p. 27). This is also a place-bound argument, which is based on what Massey (1994) calls the multiple identity of places. In this sense, she lays claim to decide what 'A-town' means, and tries to determine that 'A-town' is not coterminous with 'Germany' or 'Germanness'. On the other hand, she argues for a hybrid identity and thus displaces notions of pure national or ethnic identities.

These different ways of challenging ethnic absolutism and exclusion may be contradictory if argued through stringently. For example, one might question her notion of Europeanness as entitling her to political rights and free movement within Europe from a perspective that favours local identities and ask 'what about A-towners of Ghanaian descent, are they not also entitled to political rights?' Or one may, from a perspective which favours hybridity, disentangle the notion of Europeanness (see Nederven Pieterse 1994). However, this is not to say that her argument is not valid or cannot be taken seriously. It is a common feature of life stories, and also of identity, that they are not without contradictions, and that they take on meaning in context. Therefore, the different arguments can be seen as different strategies that Ayten employs in different contexts.

All these arguments, however, lead to Ayten's demands for political rights and her stance against racist discrimination. I think it is important to note, that she demands full political rights for immigrants. Thus, her argument points beyond the 'human rights discourse' (Soysal 1994), in which social and civil rights are in the foreground. Soysal argues that, at the civil and social level, migrants in Europe already enjoy citizenship rights. I would argue however, that she overlooks the fact that these rights are conditional for migrants. Moreover, Ayten's emphasis on political rights entails an argument for a non-nationally, non-ethnically defined, place-bound notion of participatory citizenship that sees the local as a favoured setting of citizens' activity.

(Dis-)articulating Subject Positions

Throughout the analysis of the interviews it has become clear that women of Turkish background are constituted through different discourses in varying and at times contradictory subject positions. The women negotiated these subject positions and gave new meanings to Turkishness, Germanness, and their gendered constructions.

The legitimate subject of citizen is implicitly and at times explicitly based on nationalist and patriarchal premises. These have to be challenged in order to construct a notion of citizenship which is not exclusive and hierarchical on the lines of gender and ethnicity. As Chantal Mouffe (1992: 236) puts it: 'The critique of the liberal notion of pluralism entails a critique of the conception of rights, too. Since all rights have been constituted on the exclusion of rights of others, it is not possible to include new groups into citizenship without deconstructing the identities of those who benefited from their former exclusion.'

This is, I think, a crucial point, which is expressed by most of my interviewees through challenging either pure, national-ethnic-citizen identities and communities or any form of national or ethnic identification. For many of the interviewees, challenging everyday racist and sexist discrimination was important. They were – albeit mostly not in formal political parties – involved in political groups and campaigns, voluntary work, in professional organizations and so forth. The level of their activities ranged from the neighbourhood level to the transnational level. The broad range of social participation that was apparent in the interviews makes a clear point. Although these women are not considered to be part of Germanness (though some held formal citizenship), they actively take part in the construction of this society on various levels, in the process constructing different communities both within and across ethnic boundaries. This argument seems important to me in redressing the dominant *Ausländer*-research paradigm, which constructs *Ausländer* as a particular and external element of German society, and therefore irrelevant to it. What becomes quite clear is that all of my interviewees, through their own lives, contest a concept of citizenship that is built on systematic exclusion through ethnic criteria.

Acknowledgements

I would like to thank the Gender, Ethnicity and Social Research Reading Group, Helma Lutz, Nira Yuval-Davis and the editor for very helpful comments on earlier drafts of this chapter.

Notes

1. I use the expression 'women of Turkish background' to allow for the multiplicity of ethnic allegiances and identities of migrants from Turkey. Moreover, I would like to emphasize that not all migrants from Turkey are ethnically Turkish, the most politicized ethnic difference being that of Kurdish people

who constitute a fifth of Turkey's population. Turkey's population is multi-ethnic, although the official state doctrine does not acknowledge this. The residence status of interviewees was varied. Some had German citizenship at the time of the interview, but not Ayla and Nilgün, whose stories I present later in the chapter. The legal situation of those holding citizenship and those without differs, social discrimination is a constitutive experience regardless of the passport they hold.

2. Although, Turkey has occupied an ambiguous role in the construction of the Europe-Orient dichotomy as a place in between (Kevin 1996).

3. Erdem states that in 1996, only '27.1% of women aged 15–64 were employed.' (Erdem 2000: 7). She argues that the effect of foreigners' policies have not been sufficiently taken into account in previous explanations of these figures.

4. The German is: *Freiheitlich demokratische Grundordnung*. Kalpaka and Räthzel (1990) point out that the *Freiheitlich demokratische Grundordnung* and other elements of the German, but in fact every democratic state, are frequently asserted by media and in every day discourse as expressions of German national character or ethnicity.

5. In my sample, except for two interviewees, all identified as Turkish, one identified as coming from a Kurdish-Turkish family, and another one identified as coming from a family with Macedonian origins. The interviews were conducted in summer 1996. All quotations from the interviews are my translations, either from German or from Turkish. The page numbers refer to the transcripts of the interviews.

6. The terminology of 'second or even third generation migrant' is contentious because some of the people termed thus have not migrated themselves but are born in their country of residence. However, their belonging to the country of residence is not accepted unequivocally by the state or the ethnically dominant society.

7. By racism I mean discourses and practices that exclude and subordinate people who are constructed as a 'race' or ethnic group. Racialization means the social process by which this group is constructed through a biologistic or culturalist language (Anthias and Yuval-Davis 1992).

8. There are also internal Others, in opposition to which West-Germanness has been constructed, notably the Nazi past, and the former German Democratic Republic (GDR).

9. Thus, in research carried out in a borough of Hamburg in 1995, I found that local police, business people, residents, housing officials as well as national and local media colluded in constructing Romani refugees as the most problematic criminal group that ought to be controlled. Labour migrants, including Romani families, were regarded as also being victimized by the Romani refugees' anti-social behaviour.

10. Third-country nationals have only limited rights of residence in Germany, they lack the right to vote and be elected. In the labour market, a law prescribes that each vacancy has to be filled firstly with Germans, and if these are not available then with EU citizens and only if these are not available can non-EU citizens be employed. These are but a few examples of legally inscribed inequalities.

11. Naturalization for residents, in particular for people under 23, has been made easier since the 1990s. The new citizenship law does not constitute a significant improvement in practical terms. First, only a small percentage of migrant residents will be able to benefit. Second, those who decide to take up German citizenship are not entitled to keep their second citizenship. Therefore, many may not be able or willing to take up German citizenship.

12. A 'denizen' has been defined as one who enjoys full civil and social rights, but not political rights. This arguably applies to those who entered Germany as guestworkers.

13. The immigration officials have some discretion and only those who serve prison terms longer than six months may be deported. Nonetheless, residence is conditional on 'good behaviour' rather than seen as a right.

14. When Ayten refers to herself as having been lucky to be able to keep her Turkish passport, she implicitly refers to the fact that she has obtained a licence to practice medicine. In the 1980s this was very difficult for non-German citizens to obtain, when there were many unemployed German doctors. This is another example of the way in which professional protectionism operates along racialized and ethnocized lines.

15. As the earlier quote on her being perceived by Germans as Greek, or French shows.

16. She includes Turkey in Europe, a notion that is contested because placing Turkey within or outside Europe bears a strong relationship to different, often contradicting political projects.

Bibliography

Akashe-Böhme, F. (2000), *In geteilten Welten: Fremdheitserfahrungen zwischen Migration und Partizipation*, Frankfurt a.M: Brandes und Apsel.

Anthias F. and Yuval-Davis N. (1989), 'Introduction', in F. Anthias and N. Yuval-Davis (eds), *Woman-Nation-State*, London: Macmillan.

Anthias F. and Yuval-Davis, N. (1992), *Racialized Boundaries,* London: Routledge.

Appelt, E. (1999), *Geschlecht – Staatsbürgerschaft – Nation: politische Konstruktionen des Geschlechterverhältnisses in Europa*, Frankfurt/Main: Campus Verlag.

Blaschke, J. (1994), 'Internationale Migration. Ein Problemaufriss', in Knapp, M. (ed.) *Migration im neuen Europa* (Internationale Beziehungen Bd 5), Stuttgart: Franz Steiner Verlag.

Brah, A. (1996), *Cartographies of Diaspora. Contesting Identities*, London: Routledge.

Café Morgenland (1991), *Deutschland im Herbst 1991: Rassismus als Norm. Redebeitrag zur Veranstaltung über Rassismus*, Universität Frankfurt. Manuscript.

Cohn-Bendit, D. and Schmid, T. (1992), *Heimat Babylon. Das Wagnis der multikulturellen Demokratie*, Hamburg: Hoffmann und Campe.

Erdem, E. (2000), 'Mapping women's migration: A case study of the economic dimensions of female migration from Turkey to Germany', paper presented at the conference 'Assimilation – Diasporization – Representation: Historical Perspectives on Immigrants and Host Societies in Post-war Europe', Second Workshop on Contemporary Migration History, Humboldt-Universitaet, Berlin, October 27–29.

Erel, U. (1999), 'Grenzüberschreitung und kulturelle Mischformen als antirassistischer Widerstand?', in C. Gelbin, K. Konuk and P. Piesche (eds), *Aufbrüche. Kulturelle Produktionen von Migrantinnen, Schwarzen und jüdischen Frauen in Deutschland*, Königstein/ TS: Ulrike Helmer Verlag.

Forsythe, D (1989), 'German Identity and the Problem of History', in E. Tonkin and M. Chapman (eds), *History and Ethnicity*, London: Routledge.

Gilroy, P. (1993), *The Black Atlantic: Double Consciousness and Modernity*, Cambridge MA: Harvard University Press.

Gümen, S. and Westphal, M. (1996), 'Konzepte von Beruf und Familie in den Lebensentwürfen eingewanderter und westdeutscher Frauen', *Frauen in der Einen Welt*, 1: 44–69.

Heitmeyer, W., Müller, J. and Schröder, H. (1997), *Verlockender Fundamentalismus*, Frankfurt M: Suhrkamp.

Hill-Collins, P. (1990), *Black Feminist Thought. Knowledge, Consciousness, and the Politics of Empowerment*, Boston: Unwin Hyman.

Inowlocki, L. and Lutz, H. (2000) 'The "Biographical Work" of a Turkish Migrant Woman in Germany', *European Journal of Women's Studies*, 7, (3): 301–20.

Johnson, R. (1993), 'Towards a Cultural Theory of the Nation: A British Dutch Dialogue', in A. Galema, B. Henkes, H. te Velde (eds), *Images of the Nation. Different Meanings of Dutchness 1870–1940*, Amsterdam: Rodopi.

Kalpaka, A. and Räthzel, N. (1990), *Die Schwierigkeit nicht rassistisch zu sein*, Leer: Mundo Verlag.

Karakasoglu-Aydin, Y. (2000), *Muslimische Religiösität und Erziehungsvorstellungen. Eine empirische Untersuchung zu Orientierungen bei türkischen Lehramts- und Pädagogik-Studentinnen in Deutschland*, Frankfurt: IKO Verlag für Interkulturelle Kommunikation.

Kevin, R. (1996), 'Interrupting Identities: Turkey/Europe' in S. Hall and P. du Gay (eds), *Cultural Identity,* London: Sage.

Kofman, E. (1995), 'Citizenship for Some but not for Others: Spaces of Citizenship in Contemporary Europe', *Political Geography,*14, (2): 121–37.

Krüger, D. And Potts, L. (1995), 'Aspekte generativen Wandels in der Migration: Bildung, Beruf und Familie aus der Sicht türkischer Migrantinnen der ersten Generation', *Zeitschrift für Frauenforschung,* 13, 1 and 2.

Laviziano, A., Mein, C., Sökefeld, M. (2001), '"To be German or not to be . . ." Zur Berliner Rede des Bundespräsidenten Johannes Rau', *Ethnoscripts* 3, (1): 39–53.

Léca, J. (1992) 'Questions on Citizenship', in C. Mouffe (ed.) *Dimensions of Radical Democracy: Pluralism, Citizenship, Community,* London: Verso.

Lutz, H. (1991), *Welten verbinden. Türkische Sozialarbeiterinnen in den Niederlanden und in der Bundesrepublik Deutschland,* Frankfurt: Verlag für interkulturelle Kommunikation.

Lutz, H. (n.d.), *Migrant Women from so called Muslim Countries,* University of Amsterdam: Occasional Papers, Institute of Social Science

Lutz, H. and Huth-Hildebrand, C. (1998), 'Geschlecht im Migrationsdiskurs. Neue Gedanken über ein altes Thema', *Das Argument,* 40, (1/2): 159–73.

Mackert, J. (1999), *Kampf um Zugehörigkeit. Nationale Staatsbürgerschaft als Modus sozialer Schließung,* Opladen: Westdeutscher Verlag.

McClure, K. (1992), 'On the Subject of Rights: Pluralism, Plurality and Political Identity', in C. Mouffe (ed.), *Dimensions of Radical Democracy, Pluralism, Citizenship, Community,* London: Verso.

Marshall, T.H. (1953), *Citizenship and Social Class,* Cambridge: Cambridge University Press.

Massey, D. (1994), *Space, Place and Gender,* Cambridge: Polity Press.

Mouffe, C. (1992), 'Democratic Citizenship and the Political Community', in Mouffe, C. (ed.), *Dimensions of Radical Democracy. Pluralism, Citizenship, Community,* London: Verso.

Nederven Pieterse, J. (1994), 'Unpacking the West: How European is Europe?' in A. Rattansi and S. Westwood (eds), *Racism, Modernity, Identity,* Cambridge: Polity Press.

Oguntoye, K., Opitz, M. and Schultz, D. (1997), *Farbe bekennen. Afro-Deutsche Frauen auf den Spuren ihrer Geschichte,* Frankfurt/ M.: Fischer Taschenbuch Verlag.

Otyakmaz, Berrin (1995), *Auf allen Stuhlen. Das Selbstverstandnis junger turkischer Migrantinnen in Deutschland,* Koln: ISP Verlag.

Pinn, I. and Wehner, M. (1995), *Europhantasien. Die islamische Frau aus westlicher Sicht,* Duisburg: DISS Verlag.

Radtke, F. (1994), 'The Formation of Ethnic Minorities and the Transformation of Social into Ethnic conflicts in a so-called multi-cultural Society: The Case of Germany', in J. Rex and B. Drury (eds), *Ethnic Mobilisation in a Multi-Cultural Europe*, Aldershot: Avebury.

Räthzel, N. (1994), 'Harmonious "Heimat" and disturbing "Ausländer"', *Feminism and Psychology* 4, (1): 81–98.

Räthzel, N. (1995) 'Nationalism and Gender in Western Europe: the German Case', in H. Lutz, A. Phoenix, N. Yuval-Davis (eds), *Crossfire*, London: Pluto Press.

Rodriguez, E.G. (1999), *Intellektuelle Migrantinnen – Subjektivitäten im Zeitalter von Globalisierung. Eine postkoloniale dekonstruktive Analyse von Biographien im Spannungsverhältnis von Ethnisierung und Vergeschlechtlichung*, Opladen: Leske und Budrich.

Said, E. (1978), *Orientalism*, London: Routledge & Kegan Paul.

Schneider, J. (2001), Deutsche in der Berliner Republik, *Ethnoscripts* 3, (1).

Schwartz, T. (1992), *Zuwanderer im Netz des Wohlfahrtsstates.Türkische Jugendliche und die Berliner Kommunalpolitik*, Berlin: Edition Parabolis.

Sen, F. and A. Goldberg (1994), *Türken in Deutschland: Leben zwischen zwei Kulturen*, München: Beck.

Sharp, I. (1994), 'Male Privileges and Female Virtue: Gendered Representations of the two Germanies', *New German Studies*, 18, (1/2): 87–106.

Soysal, Y. N. (1994), *Limits of Citizenship: Migrants and Postnational Membership in Europe*, University of Chicago Press.

Toksöz, G. (1991), '*Ja, sie kämpfen – und sogar mehr als die Männer.' Immigrantinnen – Fabrikarbeit und gewerkschaftliche Interessenvertretung*, Berlin: Verlag für Wissenschaft und Bildung.

Turner, B. (1990), 'Outline of a Theory of Citizenship', *Sociology,* 24, (2):189–217.

Yurtdas, H. (1995), *Pionierinnen der Arbeitsmigration in Deutschland. Lebensgeschichtliche Analysen von Frauen aus Ost-Anatolien*, Hamburg: LIT-Verlag.

Yuval-Davis, N. (1997), 'Women, Citizenship and Difference', *Feminist Review,* 57: 4–27.

Zentrum für Türkeistudien (1995), *Migration und Emanzipation*, Opladen: Leske und Budrich.

Part IV
Gender, Ethnicity and Identity

towns are at different geographical distances from the capital (200–1,450 kilometres), but all are remote from Moscow in terms of attitudes and lifestyles. They
are also small – with populations of 5,500 to 8,300 – and three to four hours bus
journey from the nearest city, so they are all quite deep into the 'depths'.

The research is based mostly on interviews with 107 women and 34 men in
1999–2000.[2] Respondents were all members of the intelligentsia – chiefly teachers,
but also journalists, arts centre employees and librarians, plus a few doctors. These
professions are highly feminized. Of the 141 interviews, 124 were with the 'core'
intelligentsia of each town – people still working in education, the media, culture
or health. This was 10 per cent to 15 per cent of the total number of such people in
each town. I also interviewed 27 members of the 'fringe' intelligentsia, typically
ex-teachers.[3]

It was suggested above that women have a special role in transmitting the
national cultural heritage to the younger generation and to their communities at
large. This is partly because they are mothers. However, in the case of this
particular group of Russian women, it was their professional status that conveyed
a special responsibility for the cultural health of the local community. Naturally
teachers of history, geography and Russian have the most direct input into the
process of teaching about the nation. However, built into the Russian concept of
the 'intelligentsia' is the assumption that its members should serve the wider
community, by virtue of their superior education and greater awareness of issues
of national importance. All three communities continue the Soviet practice of
involving a much wider range of women than just teachers in 'patriotic education'
of children and adults. For example, Pushkin's bicentennial celebrations in 1999
included exhibitions at libraries, concerts in houses of culture and various activities
in children's arts centres; they received wide coverage in the local press.

The three towns are in different regions of Russia. Achit is in the Ural Moun-
tains on the fringes of Europe. The name, which may derive from 'hungry dog' in
Tatar, is said to refer to the greed of the eighteenth-century Russian fortress from
which the settlement originates. The fortress was built on the Siberian Road, the
link between European Russia and the prison camps of Siberia. The modern
trunkroad across the Urals brings many travellers into the district. For example,
traders from Azerbaidjan buy up spare potatoes from the local people's allotments,
or barter them for water melons. The influx of traders from outside the region
creates a certain tension, for example because of worries about drug trafficking
and the destruction of local forests for timber export. Prejudice against Roma and
people from the Caucasus no doubt also plays a role. On the other hand, my
interviews suggested little evidence of tension between the various local peoples
resident in the district. At the time of the last census, in 1989, Russians formed
79.8 per cent of the district's population. The other 20 per cent belonged to Muslim
Turkic or Finno-Uralic nations. The largest groups were Tatars (10.8 per cent) and

Mari (6.7 per cent).[4] Both groups tend to live in separate villages and have their own schools and libraries. The regional leadership, headed by ethnic German governor Eduard Rossel, has been encouraging the revival of ethnic minority cultures. Russian culture has also experienced a revival insofar as, in 1997, a Russian Orthodox chapel opened in Achit in a cramped wing of the former church building, now used as a children's arts and sports centre.

Bednodemyanovsk, in Penza region, is only a few kilometres from the Republic of Mordovia, another Finno-Uralic language area. The Mordvin influence in Bednodemyanovsk is to be seen in some of the architecture, and Mordvins form the most substantial ethnic minority in the town. According to the 1989 census, 89 per cent of the town were ethnic Russians, 9.2 per cent were Mordvin, and Tatars, Ukrainians, Chuvash and 'others' each constituted less than one per cent.[5] Mordvins are the most Russified minority in the Middle Volga area (Frank and Wixman 1997: 175) and Bednodemyanovsk itself is predominantly Russian. It possesses an imposing Russian Orthodox Church. The seventeenth-century name of the town, Spassk, meaning 'Saviour', is preferred by many local people. Spassk was renamed in 1925 in honour of the Stalinist hack poet Demyan Bednyi, and this link with the worst of *Soviet* as compared to *Russian* culture is resented. The name of the town is commonly abbreviated to Bednyi, meaning 'poor'.

Finally, Zubtsov, 200 kilometres west of Moscow, is located in an almost completely ethnically Russian region. It used to have a tiny Jewish minority but they have emigrated. Like Bednodemyanovsk, Zubtsov has an attractive church, prominently situated on the bank of the Volga. Zubtsov is a medieval town and respondents said there were many archaeological relics in the surrounding countryside. However, the most striking link with the past is with the triumph of the Soviet nation in World War Two. This was a district of fierce battles, commemorated by a memorial tank on a bluff opposite the town centre. Zubtsov differs from the other towns in that it has had more housing available for incomers and this has enabled the settlement of highly skilled Russian migrants from Central Asia and Azerbaidjan.

Building a Post-communist Russian Nation

In December 1991, the inhabitants of Achit, Bednodemyanovsk and Zubtsov witnessed the end of the USSR. As citizens of its successor state, the Russian Federation, they found themselves with a new identity.

In Soviet days, Russia was just one of the USSR's 15 constituent or 'union' republics. However, because of the political imperative to subdue overt nationalist tendencies in the former imperial heartland of the Russian empire, symbolically and institutionally Russia had a less clear-cut formal identity than did Armenia,

Lithuania, Uzbekistan, and other republics. Russia, for example, unlike the other union republics of the USSR, had no Communist Party – until 1990 – and no Academy of Sciences. The old Russian symbols, such as the double-headed eagle, were discarded because of their association with the imperial dynasty.[6]

It fell to Yeltsin, the first President of the independent Russian Federation, to recreate Russia as a sovereign state with its symbolic and institutional trappings. It now had its own presidency, army and security police. Particularly in Moscow, statues of Lenin and other Soviet heroes were demolished, and cities named after revolutionaries were given back their ancient Russian names, such as Samara and Nizhnii Novgorod. Yeltsin attended Orthodox Church services and the Church began to restore buildings that had fallen into ruin or been demolished in the Soviet era. Moscow was once again full of golden domes and the chimes of church bells.

However, state building and nation building are separate processes: institutional and symbolic changes did not in themselves add up to the creation of a new national identity. In the Russian case the situation was complicated by the fact that there was political capital to be made out of claiming that there was *no* existing national identity. Since President Yeltsin's call in July 1996 for the creation of a 'Russian idea', 'the national identity market has been saturated by innumerable competing narratives claiming to describe just who the Russians are and what they should be about. Each narrative establishes its importance by confecting a "lack" or "absence" of national political identity that it has been summoned to fill' (Urban 1998: 970).

The issue was not about labelling individuals as ethnic Russians. Soviet citizens had an ethnic identity officially defined in their internal passports. There were 120 million officially defined ethnic Russians living in Russia in 1989, 81.5 per cent of the total population (Dunlop 1997: 48), plus a further 25 million residing in other parts of the USSR. However, if one looks beyond passports to examine people's actual attitudes towards their identity, assertions about lack of Russian identity seem to have had a certain basis in fact. According to Lev Gudkov of the Russian Centre for the Study of Public Opinion (VTsIOM):

> for Russians, the chief role in their self-definition was until recently played by the view of themselves as citizens of the USSR, as Soviet people. Neither language, nor culture, nor the past, nor traditions had a significance comparable to the perception of themselves as citizens of the Soviet state. From 63 per cent to 81 per cent of ethnic Russians called their homeland not Russia but precisely the USSR. (Dunlop 1997: 55)[7]

The political salience of debates about national identity was clear as Russia's foreign policy, at first highly pro-Western in orientation, became more sceptical towards the West and, from 1993–4, concentrated more intensively on relations with the 'near abroad' – other states of the former USSR.

Vera Tolz has identified five main types of definition of the Russian nation in late 1990s intellectual debates:

1. 'Union identity: the Russians defined as an imperial people or through their mission to create a supranational state';
2. 'The Russians as a nation of all eastern Slavs' (including Belorussians and Ukrainians);
3. 'The Russians as a community of Russian speakers, regardless of their ethnic origin';
4. 'The Russians defined racially';
5. 'A civic Russian (*rossiiskaya*) nation, whose members are all citizens of the RF, regardless of their ethnic and cultural background, united by loyalty to newly emerging political institutions and its constitution.'

Tolz points out that the vision of the civic nation had the shortest heritage in Russia – being essentially a Western concept – and the fewest intellectual advocates, but that it was chosen as the basis for official policy (Tolz 1998). Citizenship was open to all ethnic groups from the beginning – unlike in some other former Soviet republics. Later, in the 1990s, it became no longer mandatory to have one's ethnic identity noted in a passport.

This, then, was nation building as played out in Moscow. However, Moscow is hardly representative of the rest of Russia, being much more westernised and prosperous. For example, in May 2000 average Moscow salaries were about two-and-a-half times those in Penza region, where Bednodemyanovsk is located.[8] What sort of impact did the nation-building project have on ordinary Russians, on people who lived in towns with Soviet names and prominent Soviet symbols such as war memorials and statues of Lenin, far from any branches of Pizza Hut?

Provincial Perceptions: becoming 'more' Russian

Respondents in Achit and Bednodemyanovsk were invited to comment on the significance for them personally of the building of the Russian state since 1991 and the greater accessibility of Russian culture. They were also asked to discuss the concept of 'Mother Russia'. Much of what follows is based on these 100 responses. There were some very clear overall trends, although it is more problematic to derive statistically valid conclusions about subgroups within the total sample (men/women, Achit/Bednodemyanovsk, older/younger, core/fringe). Where I have suggested trends among sub-groups these are hypotheses only. The pilot survey in Zubtsov merely asked about national pride, but this question also produced some illuminating responses.

It was clear that Achit and Bednodemyanovsk were not intellectual communities ripped by fierce debates between Slavophiles and Westernizers or proponents of Tolz's five models. People did not make prescriptions for Russia's future. They did not talk about Russia as a superpower[9] or an empire. In fact most respondents did not even mention nationalism or issues connected with multi-ethnicity. Of those who did, only seven women and five men seemed to regret unequivocally the demise of the USSR; six other people made comments weighing up the benefits and disadvantages of the event. Their reasons for preferring the USSR were often linked to the perception that in Soviet days there had been less nationalism and more harmony between ethnic groups. In a number of cases these were women with sons who might serve in Chechnya or relatives in parts of the former USSR where Russians feel persecuted. In other words, they had personal reasons for their opinion, in addition to any views they may have absorbed from the media. Some made comments about their Soviet upbringing such as 'we are internationalists: nationality isn't important'.

Among the respondents who did not regret the demise of the USSR, two men who expressed a keen interest in Russian history pointed out that despite this interest they were 'not nationalists'. It seems possible to conclude that among these more nationality-conscious respondents, the organization of the multi-ethnic state (USSR/Russia) was seen as a moral issue: there was a strong feeling that nationalism was 'wrong'. There was no sign than any of these respondents harboured imperial aspirations.

Only five women[10] and seven men made comments that could be labelled as Russian nationalist. Most of these comments were to the effect that before 1992 Russia did not have a proper identity of its own: people did not talk about Russia as a separate nation and it did not have its own institutions. Only two people, both men, made racist comments about Jews and Germans in central and regional government. Finally, 13 people said that they did not think that Russia had really become more Russian since 1991, some on the grounds that Russians still lacked a clear identity, others saying that Russia was, as before, multi-ethnic. One person claimed that 'Russia always was Russian and still is'.

In total, then, only a minority, or 41 per cent of respondents, took up the invitation to make general assertions about the nation. It is curious that 75 per cent of the men did this, whereas only 32 per cent of the women did the same.[11] However, the total number of men is so small that perhaps one should not read too much into this. It seems more important to note that these overarching issues connected with national consciousness were not at the forefront of most people's minds when they read the question.[12] Instead, they were more interested in talking about their direct personal experience: what they liked about the Russian cultural revival. Sixty-five per cent of the respondents chose to talk about how they welcomed the publication of new history books, the availability of literary texts banned by the Soviet regime or the restoration of Orthodox churches.

Women in particular were keen to talk about the Church.[13] Only a handful defined themselves as believers; others welcomed religious toleration as a general principle, talked about the moral role of the Church in making people behave more kindly, or praised the aesthetic qualities of church architecture and music. Respondents talked about the fact that Church services were attended by different social groups and that this had a role in binding together the community. A number of women said that it was important for all churches to be restored, not just the showcase cathedrals but also all the little village ruins.

Only four people specifically did *not* welcome the Orthodox revival. In Achit this was linked to the fact that the children's arts and sports centre, located in the old church building, was faced with the prospect of eviction.

Ethnic issues were not mentioned at all in connection with the church. No one made the equation Russian = Orthodox, although this is a truism of Slavophile discourse. Nor did any of the non-ethnic Russian respondents criticize the restoration of churches and the increased status of Russian Orthodoxy. (One of them, a Bashkir, pointed to the parallel increasing visibility of Islam in the local district.) Rather, churches tended to be appreciated as a welcome manifestation of increased freedom of choice in everyday life, for beautifying the local landscape and generally exerting a positive influence on the local community.

Comments on the rewriting of Russian history were similarly couched in non-nationalist terms. Respondents rarely identified re-writing as a nationalist project, although there were some comments to the effect that 'people *ought* to know their own history' and also that one could not necessarily trust the veracity of history writing even today. Most people, however, did not problematize the issue. They 'liked' reading history or watching historical programmes on television: history was 'interesting'. The only caveats tended to be practical ones: resentment that they could not afford to buy books or travel to museums, and regret that they could not receive the Culture Channel on television. (In this latter respect most of Zubtsov was better off than the other towns.)

Russia is also becoming more ethnically Russian in that ethnic Russians living in non-Russian republics of the USSR have been returning to settle in the Russian Federation. In 1990–6, 2.4 million ethnic Russians returned to Russia, out of a total of 25.3 million (Zayonchkovskaya 1999: 119.). Settlement has not been even throughout the Russian Federation, despite some official efforts. Most of the immigrants settle where they expect to find employment, often through friends and relatives. The eight Russian and two Tatar immigrants I interviewed had all taken this informal route: it was almost a matter of chance that they had ended up in the small town.

Many of the migrants are highly educated and skilled (Zayonchkovskaya, 1999: 111–12) and their arrival can significantly enhance the local intelligentsia. This phenomenon was most marked in Zubtsov and least true of Achit. Migrants included three English teachers (a scarce and valuable commodity in rural Russia); a senior policeman; a university lecturer, now working as a government official; a family of artists, working at a children's art and music school; a piano teacher; a family of doctors; a faith healer, once a teacher; and the deputy manager of a Park of Culture and Rest. In addition to these 1990s arrivals, the ethnic Russian curator of the museum in Zubtsov, a keen historian, had chosen in the Soviet period to study not in her native Kazakhstan, but in Tver, because she wanted to be closer to her roots.

These incomers had mixed feelings about their new lifestyle. On the one hand, all were glad to 'return' to Russia. On the other hand, they had moved from large towns or cities, where they had often had a sense of being part of the local, Russian intellectual elite. As Hilary Pilkington (1998: 21, 169) demonstrates in her book on Russian migrants, they constitute a 'distinct socio-cultural group', prone to a 'superiority complex . . . *vis-à-vis* the local Russian population'. For example, one of my interviewees suggested that Russians were much 'nicer' in Uzbekistan than in Russia.

Many migrants had suffered deskilling as a result of the move. For instance, one woman had been head of a medical institute in Samarkand but was now an ordinary doctor.[14] The faith healer most bitterly expressed this sense of downward social mobility: 'We moved from a city to a town, from a town to a village [Achit], and next we'll be living in the forest.'

However bitter the migrants themselves, their arrival could be seen as a bonus by the host community. Bednodemyanovsk, for example, desperately needed doctors, so the arrival of a family of three together made a significant impact. In Zubtsov the migrants made an important contribution to local cultural life, so much so that one respondent, much exaggerating the number of teachers from Central Asia, felt that the 'Russian intelligentsia was coming home.' A Zubtsov poet (Cherednyakh 1999) commented on an exhibition by a Russian migrant from Dushanbe:

> Only superlatives will do
> Since, for Zubtsov, it's all so new.[15]

To conclude: all three communities were becoming more 'Russified' in the sense that local people had greater freedom to attend Orthodox services and greater access to Russian culture in the form of publications and television programmes. To some extent, especially in Zubtsov, the communities had also been enriched by the arrival of migrants from the 'Near Abroad'. However, respondents tended to interpret the significance of these developments as being important for them personally and for the local community; they related them to Russia's wider destiny less often.

The Remoteness of Moscow and the West and the Salience of Local Identity

The next section will discuss the dogs that did not bark in the night – the 'obvious' answers, which were not given, to the survey questions about whether Russia had become 'more Russian', and if so, how far this was connected with the emergence of Russian state institutions such as the presidency and army. These (non) answers were that Russia is not more Russian because it is more Westernized, and it is a very significant change that Russia has a democratically elected president and parliament rather than being ruled by the Communist Party.

These are replies that would seem obvious to many foreigners, Muscovites, or inhabitants of the larger and more prosperous cities, such as Samara or Yekaterinburg. However, the impact of the apparently massive transformations of the 1990s is much smaller on Russians living in small provincial towns or rural areas. This is true even for Zubtsov, just 200 kilometres from the capital.

Perhaps, therefore, it is not surprising that only two respondents said that the reason Russia was not more Russian was that it had become more Westernized or Americanized. It is true that many people did complain that there were too many violent Hollywood films on television, but they did not seem to view this as part of a wider phenomenon of Westernization. (One woman pointed out that although she hated American films, she loved French ones.) The reason for such reticence must surely be that people in Achit and Bednodemyanovsk are relatively untouched by Westernization except through the main television channels. They have no Internet access. Only six had ever travelled to the West. Many, unlike in Zubtsov, have given up reading a national newspaper, because of the expense; they will buy only the local paper, which is written in much simpler language, without the digressions into the Latin alphabet, anglicisms and references to Western practices that characterize the national papers. (For example, although a Moscow-published newspaper can use the phrase 'there's no such thing as a free lunch' – using the neologism *lanch* in place of Russian *obed* (Dunn 1999: 10) – language and context combine to make the expression incomprehensible in Achit or Bednodemyanovsk.)

Moscow, by contrast, is in many respects like a (smart) Western capital city: as one woman put it, 'for us Moscow is like England'. The more flourishing regional capitals have also become more Westernized, albeit to a lesser extent than Moscow. However, one of the clearest research findings was that people in small towns are travelling very much more rarely even to the regional capital. For most of the year, sometimes for years on end, they are marooned in their local area. The problem is partly the cost of living in the regional capital. Fares are also an issue. For many women, the bus fare for a 300- or 400-kilometre round trip is equivalent to about a week's salary. Another problem is time: the women were farming vegetable gardens and many had cows and other livestock; most depended on their farming efforts for more than half their family diet. Holidays had become impossible for many.

If people cannot travel around their native land this clearly must have some kind of impact on their sense of national identity. Moreover, it created a sense of deep frustration about the implications for the younger generation. Respondents were concerned about both their own children and also local children in general: they had not seen the art and architectural treasures of Moscow and Petersburg, and had therefore missed out on something very important. Furthermore, one of the respondents' most strongly voiced anxieties was that they would not be able to get their children to the cities to study at university: tuition fees and the cost of living in the city made this prohibitively expensive for many.

However, there is a more political aspect to this feeling of disconnectedness from the cities, particularly Moscow. Moscow was described by women in Achit and Bednodemyanovsk as being 'a different state', 'another continent'. 'Moscow doesn't know/care how we live' was a common refrain. The survey question asked people how significant they found it that 'Russia had its own president, army, etc.' Apart from a handful of positive comments about newly elected President Putin, hardly anyone found anything to say about these state institutions. Two people thought that nothing had changed. The Russian President was just like the General Secretary of Soviet times. Two others welcomed collaboration between Church and state. One woman said it was good that they could elect their President but immediately qualified this by doubting whether the elections were entirely fair.

Cultural aspects of Russification, with their personal and local impact, were clearly much more meaningful for the respondents than any institutions in Moscow. Zubtsov respondents, who were asked whether they thought they could influence Moscow politics, were in almost complete agreement that this was impossible: 'we are midges', as one of them put it. Respondents in all three towns were asked to comment on a quotation from Russian sociologist Leonid Kogan about the rupturing of affective/cultural[16] links with Moscow. Kogan (1997: 126) asserted that 'links between the centre and the regions have ruptured today even more in the affective/cultural sphere than in politics or economics'. In Zubtsov, people tended to agree with Kogan that links had snapped. Zubtsov is only 200 kilometres from Moscow, but the women most bitter about the gap between Zubtsov and the capital seemed to be those who had most direct contact with Moscow – for example because their husbands or fathers commuted there to work on a weekly basis. In Bednodemyanovsk and even more so in Achit most people misunderstood the quotation to mean that Penza or Yekaterinburg was the centre. Moscow did not occur to them. They could not have any relation to it: it was 'another world'.

If central government is not important, how about regional? Regional leaders and their education ministries have tried to build up a sense of loyalty to the region and a more powerful regional identity. For example, in Penza they have patronized a folklore revival, which a number of Bednodemyanovsk respondents felt was a positive initiative. (One man, however, saw it as a cynical exercise in manipulation from above.) One might wonder, however, how much it contributes to regional rather than local self-identity. One woman, working in the children's art centre, said that the most interesting result of schoolchildren touring the local villages to interview elderly inhabitants was that they had found out that every village had slightly different rituals, songs, embroidery patterns, and so forth. In the Urals there is and probably always has been a quite powerful sense of regional identity and pride: this is a rich region that is a net contributor to the federal budget. The school curriculum now includes a regional emphasis, such as the subject 'history of the Urals'. The governor's propaganda newspaper, *Oblastnaya gazeta*, is widely available, with, for example, 50 copies being supplied free to the local library. However, once again one has to question whether local people really identify with the regional political institutions. In neither town was there much unqualified support for the regional governor and there was quite a lot of bitterness and sense that Achit and Bednodemyanovsk – lacking as they were in industry – had been almost completely neglected by the regional centre. As for *Oblastnaya gazeta*, it is given away to pensioners who want a copy of the television schedule.

One is drawn to the conclusion that, for the vast majority of these people living in small towns, local identity is overwhelmingly important. Almost every respondent in every town read a local newspaper; usually, in Achit and Bednodemyanovsk, it was the only newspaper they read. Although a few people wanted to move, most asserted that they could not imagine living anywhere else. Only three women – who were among the most intelligent and highly educated – had more sense of the potential flexibility of identity, and claimed that if they were with their families they could live anywhere.

Motherland

The Russian word for 'homeland' or 'motherland' *(rodina)* is ambiguous: it can include the concept of the 'little' motherland (*malaya rodina*) or local area. When asked what they thought of when they heard the words 'motherland' or 'Mother Russia', many respondents said things like 'the little corner where I live', 'my family', 'my garden', 'my house, my bread, my children', 'where I live and am respected', 'local nature' or 'where my mother is'. Research in other Urals towns (described in Kogan 1997) backs up the impression that people locate themselves primarily in their 'little' motherland.[17]

The images of the motherland that respondents conjured up seemed to derive from popular Soviet songs and lessons at school, hence a certain uniformity was not surprising. It was rather paradoxical, of course, that lessons that had been intended to inspire love for the *whole* motherland resulted in a sense of attachment to the local area. With regard to 'Mother Russia' in particular, people often talked about nature – an image of fields and forests – and this corresponds to the origins of the concept as evoking the Russian soil and fertility (Hubbs 1988). Respondents also commonly took the metaphor a stage further and talked about history and the arts – culture as a manifestation of Russian fertility. In Zubtsov, where people were asked to describe their emotions about Russia, respondents spoke of their pride in Russia's rich history and cultural heritage. Some respondents talked about roots in connection with the 'mother' image and one might have expected explicit mention of the race and nation, but these were not forthcoming. People seemed to see Mother Russia as referring not so much to the nation as a whole as to them and their personal roots in culture, history and the local area. If they did have images of the whole nation, these were often located in the past, in the days when they could afford to travel around the country and read extensively about it. Although no one said 'my personal library' or 'my photographs of Leningrad' when they described Mother Russia, these too were part of the women's identity. They were anchors into a time that was perhaps to some extent a mythical Golden Age but also had some objective existence. During this time, before they became poor, the women had been more 'cultured' and more proud of themselves. Now they spent too much of their leisure time picking Colorado beetles off their potato plants.

When asked to think in more detail about why Mother Russia was a mother, respondents, both male and female, came up with the image of Russia as 'long-suffering'. One woman linked her to the Virgin Mary in this respect. Another, an ethnic Tatar, claimed that 'she and I suffer together'. The most popular response, however, was that Russia was a mother because children were closer to their mothers. Mothers were more affectionate and loveable than fathers; it was to mothers that children turned in distress. It was admitted that in Russia's case she sometimes let them down. A number of respondents, in all three towns, made the observation that you could not choose your mother and that she might not always be perfect. However, you would love her nonetheless. Only two, very bitter women, did not seem to feel so affectionate: one referred to Russia as a (wicked) stepmother and another observed that 'she used to feed us but now she's thrown us out and spat on us'.

If Russia is seen as the mother, who is the father? Joanna Hubbs, in her study of the origins and literary evocations of the myth of Mother Russia, suggests that Russian peasants did not see Mother Russia as requiring a mate. 'In the peasant tradition . . . all things are borne by the earth and derive from her fertility. The soil is the great *baba* (woman), the giant Matrioshka[18] who enfolds the historical Mother Russia . . . She seems to need no mate. She is self-moistened, self-inseminated' (Hubbs 1998: xiii–xiv).

The Russian phrase *rodina-mat'* (motherland-mother), used in Stalinist patriotic propaganda, conjures up the somewhat androgynous image of a famous war-time poster. Here, Mother Russia is a stern figure, very unlike either most Russian women or the feminine Matrioshka doll who is associated with Mother Russia. Some respondents mentioned this difference: they associated *rodina-mat'* with official patriotism and the state, and that it was different from Mother Russia. In just a few of the other responses 'mothers' were also associated with the state. One man used the expression 'stepmother' to refer to the state, as opposed to the real Mother Russia, which meant 'history and roots'. A woman in Bednodemyanovsk described Mother Russia as a figure surrounded by a brood of children – *rossiyane* of different ethnic identities. Hence Mother Russia was a unifying principle for the different ethnic groups in the Russian Federation.

To return to the issue of fatherhood, however: androgynous as Mother Russia may be to some, it is much more common to see her as feminine and to make a distinction between the mother nation and the father state. In modern Russian this is encapsulated in the two words *rodina* (motherland, literally 'the place which gave birth') and *otechestvo* (fatherland). The distinction, however, has a long history. As Hubbs (1988: 14) points out, *Matushka Rus* (Little Mother Russia) is simply the historical name of the land that the peasants perceived as 'married' to *Batiushka Tsar* (Little Father Tsar).

State and nation should coexist, like husband and wife, or state and civil society. However, the force of concepts such as Mother Russia or civil society derives from the fact that the relationship is problematized. In other words, there is a need to make the distinction between these 'good' phenomena and the state because the state is seen to be in some ways distant from or hostile to the interests of ordinary people.

Before the 1990s, only a narrow section of the Russian intelligentsia problematized the relationship between Soviet state and Russian nation. From the 1960s onwards, an environmental movement consisting largely of writers and scholars began to criticise the Soviet state for destroying the natural heritage (Mother Russia). 'Village prose' writers sometimes chose as heroines elderly village women who were seen to embody essential values of the Russian nation. Under Gorbachev, criticism of the state for destroying the Russian nation and natural heritage became more open. It was often anti-Semitic and anti-communist. To some extent this type of criticism had a strong provincial bias: Siberians were prominent because the main ecological issue was Lake Baikal.

However, the phenomenon that I have described in Achit, Bednodemyanovsk and Zubtsov is only indirectly linked to the Baikal Movement. The link is in the

Gorbachev period, when 'the centre' became, throughout the USSR, a byword for authoritarian and undemocratic rule. The USSR was ripped apart by centrifugal forces – a 'war of laws and parliaments' as the different republics, city and even borough governments asserted their 'sovereignty' and control over the local economy. The fragmentation process resulted, in Yeltsin's Russia, in a federal system that recognized the destruction of Soviet hyper-centralisation and gave the regions much more autonomy, while restoring important powers to 'the centre'. However, it seems that it was impossible to restore a sense of affection towards and connectedness with the capital or the state in general. It did not help that Russians – including most of my respondents – were extremely suspicious of the reliability of the national media, often their one link to the outside world. Although by 2000 there was a certain cautious optimism about the new President, Putin, this feeling was insufficient to overcome the sense of alienation from 'the centre'.

Zubtsov respondents who said they were ashamed of Russia uniformly mentioned the government and parliament. The Zubtsov survey was conducted in 1999, so this reflected disgust with Yeltsin in particular. In Bednodemyanovsk and Achit in 2000, when it had already become clear that the war in Chechnya was going to drag on and claim many more victims, a number of women talked about their dislike of the state's warmongering and their horror at the thought that their sons might have to serve in Chechnya (although the ostensible point of the war in Chechnya was to defend Russia's borders). In September 2000, after the Kursk affair, Achit respondents expressed their extreme mistrust of the naval authorities.[19]

A handful of women did mention the need to protect Mother Russia like one's mother, clearly echoing official propaganda, but this seemed to be an abstract position, rather than reflecting a real commitment. Only one woman, not an ethnic Russian, said that she welcomed the fact that her son would serve in the Russian army. One male respondent asserted that he could not imagine himself dying for the Russian state and government, although for the nation, the 'motherland', he was of course ready to lay down his life.

When probed about why Mother Russia was not Father Russia, one respondent, a mother of three who did all the household work, although her husband was retired, claimed that 'everything [in ordinary life] depends on women, although the government consists entirely of men'. Two other women – both colleagues, young and single – complained that men were 'spoiled' and 'unreliable'. However, many respondents expressed the opinion that fathers were more distant from their children because they were strong and strict. Real Russian men often do not match this image, but given that Mother Russia is linked implicitly to her opposite (Father Tsar, Fatherland), it was easier to understand the image of the strict father, which perhaps had more connection with the strict state than with actual fathers. It was still out of date, however. Given people's sense that Moscow had abandoned them, the 'stern but just' father figure hardly fitted reality. In the end, however, the most significant point is that fathers were seen as remote figures. As Russian peasants used to say, 'God is high in the sky and Moscow is far away'.

I would suggest that the attachment to the distant father image stems from an essentialism which is so deep-rooted in Russian society that the political and social changes of the 1990s, for all their radicalism, have had little or no impact on popular attitudes.[20] My respondents simply failed to entertain the idea that men might be as well suited for parenting as women. If men were not equal parents, this seemed to be because men were just less adequate in this sphere, rather than because in other spheres they had a more important role to play. All the women, for example, saw themselves as equally entitled to paid employment. They asserted that work played a central role in their lives and had a strong sense of professional pride. Women with 'New Russian' husbands had in some cases been asked to stay at home, but they had continued to work despite the small size of their salaries. Neither did they think it odd that women should have managerial roles at a local level. Most of the headteachers, all the hospital chief managers, all the head librarians and two of the three newspaper chief editors were women. A number of women made quite scathing remarks about men in local government.

Neither did women meekly accept that they should do most of the housework. In fact many women claimed that their husbands contributed equally to the domestic chores. When pressed for details they often conceded that 'he doesn't do the laundry' or 'I'm the one who does the pickling and jam-making'. Nonetheless, it was significant that they felt that men ought to contribute to the housework.

People associated women with motherhood partly because motherhood was so common. It is still not really socially acceptable in Russia to choose not to be a mother. Almost every woman in the sample, except the youngest respondents, was a mother; a few others mentioned that they would like or would have liked to become mothers. Proper women were mothers, just as in the Russian Empire or Soviet days. The 'women's' organizations, such as they were, reflected this assumption. In Bednodemyanovsk the women's council, a Soviet institution, had recently been revived, but its chief duty was to arrange celebrations for conscripts joining the army and to help local mothers adjust to their new status as soldiers' mothers. In Achit, a branch of the Association of Women of the Urals was just getting off the ground; a member said that if they had money she would like to be able to 'help local families'. A women's club at the Achit police force organizes birthday parties for militiamen's children.

Conclusions

Women, then, could identify with 'Mother Russia' on several levels and they perhaps used the image as a way of bolstering their own self-confidence. Their confidence as mothers did need bolstering because they felt they were failing their children by not being able to afford to give them a proper education or sufficient exposure to the national cultural heritage. Often they could not afford to buy books or travel with children to theatres and museums. Hence it was some comfort to believe that whatever the failings of the Russian state, however much Mother Russia herself suffered as a consequence, she was still always responsive, always there when her children called. This was surely how the women would have liked to think of themselves as parents.

How, though, did they think of themselves as Russians? If we return to Vera Tolz's five patterns of identity, it would seem that in some respects most of the respondents adhered to the 'civic nation' model. They were most definitely committed to democratic values such as freedom of speech and free elections, and they also believed in the multi-ethnic state. (In practice, however, the Russian respondents were more accommodating towards certain ethnic groups than others. Their Tatar and Mordvin neighbours were more part of 'Russia' than were Roma or Chechens.)

The respondents presumably inculcated values of democracy and tolerance into their children and the community at large. However, Tolz suggests that for the 'civic nation' model to function, citizens should also be 'united by loyalty to newly emerging political institutions and its constitution'. Here the definition of Russia as a 'civic nation' is less tenable. Tolz (1999: 1015), citing national poll data, also suggests that 'as far as the broad public in the RF is concerned Russian identity is largely subjective (identification with Russia as a homeland and self-identification as a Russian are key characteristics); and it is also linguistic and cultural. The question of citizenship is far less significant.' My research indicated extreme lack of trust in central state institutions and a perception of an unbridgeable gulf between Moscow and the provincial 'depths'.

Gudkov's claim, quoted above, that 'neither language, nor culture, nor the past, nor traditions had a significance comparable to the perception of themselves as citizens of the Soviet state' clearly refers to the past. What has changed? It is not, obviously, that the second part of the statement should now read that Russians overwhelmingly feel that citizenship of the *Russian* state is the most important component of their identity. Hardly any respondents used the word *rossiyanin*, a citizen of the RF, and when one woman did assert that 'we are all *rossiyane*' this was only to say 'we are multi-ethnic'. It was rather the first part of the statement that had become untrue: a consciousness of culture, the past and traditions were important components of the respondents' identity.

Timo Piirainen's case study of 30 teachers in St Petersburg in 1996 also led him to conclude that 'Russia was in the first place perceived as a cultural entity and not an ethnic or a political one' (Piirainen, 2000: 194). Moreover, the teachers in St Petersburg, by virtue of their place of residence, were able to identify themselves as well-qualified bearers of this national culture. 'The Russian heritage, it is so very vast. And I, as a person living in St Petersburg, I understand that I have an obligation to pass on this culture' (Piirainen, 2000: 169).

Teachers in small towns, however, could not so readily equate their Russian identity with the 'vastness' of the entire nation and its culture. It is tempting to add a sixth model to Vera Tolz's five. This would be a model created not by Moscow or Petersburg intellectuals but by many teachers and doctors in little provincial towns. It might be even more applicable to their children. Mother Russia = the 'little motherland' could be the name of this model. In this model, Russia as an entire geographical entity, and the Russian state, seem to become more and more distant. The provincial depths become deeper. 'We've started to live in our own little micro-world', as one headteacher expressed it. Memories of Moscow and other Russian cities are still strong and people still read history, but in the world of today, based as it is around subsistence agriculture, the 'soil which feeds us' is the most commonly experienced aspect of Mother Russia. Nonetheless, people do not reduce Mother Russia to its original peasant definition. Culture is still important, but only that culture that can be organized on a local, community level. Russia shrinks to the 'little motherland' of one's immediate community.

Notes

1. Women have much greater responsibility than men for socialization. They are almost ubiquitously regarded as the 'main' parent (see below) and they predominate in the socializing professions. In 1997, for example, women constituted 69 per cent of employees in culture and the arts and 79 per cent in education (*Rossiiskii statisticheskii ezhegodnik* 1998: 182).
2. I interviewed 40 women and 10 men in Achit; 36 women and 14 men in Bednodemyanovsk; and 31 women and 10 men in Zubtsov. Since the Zubtsov research was conducted in 1999 and based on a pilot questionnaire, it differed slightly from the Achit and Bednodemyanovsk research conducted in 2000. Most of the respondents were ethnic Russians. The rest were: five Tatars, two Ukrainians, one Bashkir, one Mari, two half-Ukrainians, one half-Pole, one half-Chuvash and one half-Mordvin. All the 'halves' were predominantly or entirely Russian speaking. One respondent claimed to be Russian, without qualification, but another respondent said that the person concerned was Mordvin.
3. For more detailed description of the research, and discussion of the terms 'core' and 'fringe intelligentsia', see White (2000).

4. Information from Achit Statistical Office, September 2000. For more information on the Mari, Tatar, Chuvash and Bashkir peoples see Frank and Wixman.
   The 'Middle Volga' region includes Bednodemyanovsk and Achit, although
   both towns are on its outer fringes (south-western and eastern).

5. Information from Penza branch of the Russian State Statistical Committee,
   Goskomstat, April 2000. The next census was in October 2002.

6. The absence of separate Russian institutions meant that Russians were directly
   subject to federal ones: a situation that could be regarded as favourable to
   Russians, because federal Soviet institutions, like the Communist Party of the
   Soviet Union, were viewed throughout the USSR as overwhelmingly *Russian*
   institutions, whereas, for example, the republican communist parties had a
   certain 'token' status.

7. Compare Drobizhaeva's (1992: 100–1) report on similar survey findings, such
   as lack of interest in history among Russians.

8. Calculated from Russian State Statistical Committee figures at website http://
   www.gks.ru/scripts/free/1c.exe?XXXX20F.3.1.1/090060R, 8.11.00.

9. The one exception said that he had liked living in a superpower in Soviet days.
   This was a businessman who in other respects did not regret the demise of
   the USSR.

10. One of these women had also regretted the demise of the USSR.

11. The numbers in the paragraphs above add up to 23 women and 18 men. N =
    76 women and 24 men. (Zubtsov respondents were not asked this question.)

12. Possibly they did not want to talk about these more political topics to a
    foreigner. However, the same people did discuss political issues in response
    to other questions.

13. Thirty women, or 39 per cent of the total, welcomed the restoration of
    churches, a sentiment expressed by only four men (17 per cent).

14. However, deskilling was less extreme than among the migrants to rural areas
    described in Pilkington, 1998.

15. The Russian is:

    I zdes', na vystavke, vysokoparnykh
    Ya ne boyus' segodnya slov.
    V foie tak neobychno, stranno,
    Ved' dlya Zubtsova eto – nov'.

16. The Russian word *dukhovnyi*, literally 'spiritual', implies everything that is
    non-material: perhaps 'affective' or 'cultural' are the best translations in this
    context.

17. That this was true elsewhere in provincial Russia was confirmed to me by
    Penza sociologist Valentin Manuilov, Penza, April 2000.

18. Russian nesting doll.

19. Mistrust was amplified by scandals about the unreliability of official inform-
    ation in the cases of both the most recent war against separatists in Chechnya
    (initiated by Putin in 1999) and the mysterious sinking of the Kursk in the
    Barents Sea in August 2000.
20. See chapters by Sue Bridger, Peggy Watson and Anne White in Bull, Diamond
    and Marsh (2000).

Bibliography

Bull, A., Diamond, H. and Marsh, R. (eds) (2000), *Feminisms and Women's Move-
    ments in Contemporary Europe*, Basingstoke: Macmillan.
Cherednyakh, G. (1999), 'Andreyu Kurbanovu', *Zubtsovskaya. zhizn'*, 16 March:
    4.
Drobizhaeva, L. (1992), 'Perestroika and the ethnic consciousness of Russians',
    in G.W. Lapidus and V. Zaslavsky with P.Goldman, *From Union to Common-
    wealth: Nationalism and Separatism in the Soviet Republics*, Cambridge:
    Cambridge University Press.
Dunlop, J. P. (1997), 'Russia: In Search of an Identity?' in I. Bremmer and R. Taras
    (eds), *New States, New Politics: Building the Post-Soviet Nations*, Cambridge:
    Cambridge University Press.
Dunn, J. A. (1999), 'The Transformation of Russian from a Language of the Soviet
    Type to a Language of the Western Type', in J.A. Dunn (ed.), *Language and
    Society in Post-Communist Europe. Selected papers from the Fifth World
    Congress of Central and East European Studies, Warsaw, 1995*, Basingstoke:
    Macmillan.
Frank, A. and Wixman, R. (1997), 'The Middle Volga: Exploring the Limits of
    Sovereignty', in I. Bremmer and R. Taras (eds), *New States, New Politics:
    Building the Post-Soviet Nations*, Cambridge: Cambridge University Press.
Hubbs, J. (1988), *Mother Russia: the Feminine Myth in Russian Culture*, Bloom-
    ington: Indiana University Press.
Kogan, L. (1997), 'Dukhovnyi potentsial provintsii vchera i segodnya', *Sotsiolog-
    icheskie issledovaniya*, 4: 122–9.
Pilkington, H.A. (1998), *Migration, Displacement and Identity in Post-Soviet
    Russia* London: Routledge.
Piirainen, T. (2000), 'The Fall of an Empire, the Birth of a Nation: Perceptions of
    the New Russian Identity' in C.J. Chulos and T. Piirainen (eds), *The Fall of an
    Empire, the Birth of a Nation: National Identities in Russia*, Aldershot: Ashgate.
Rossiiskii statisticheskii ezhegodnik (1998), Moscow: Goskomstat Rossii.
Tolz, V. (1998), 'Forging the Nation: National Identity and Nation Building in
    Post-Communist Russia', *Europe-Asia Studies* 50, (6): 993-1022.

Urban, M.(1998),'Remythologising the Russian State', *Europe-Asia Studies* 50, (6): 969–92.

White, A. (2000), 'Social Change in Provincial Russia: the Intelligentsia in a *Raion* Centre', *Europe-Asia Studies,* 52, (6): 677–94.

Yuval-Davis, N. (1997), *Gender and Nation*, London: Sage.

Zayonchkovskaya, Z. (1999), 'Recent Migration Trends in Russia', in G.J. Demko, G. Ioffe and Z. Zayonchkovskaya (eds), *Population under Duress: the Geodemography of Post-Soviet Russia*, Boulder: Westview.

–10–

Westenders: Whiteness, Women and Sexuality in Southall, UK
Raminder Kaur

In a youth club in Southall, a multi-racial area in the borough of Ealing at the outer edge of west London, a young Asian man eats a plateful of chips. A young white woman approaches him to ask him to clear up the tomato sauce he had accidentally spilt on the floor. When she turns round to walk off, he replies, 'Fucking white bitch!' The retort is partly directed at her but is also a way of recuperating his sense of machismo when scolded in the company of his male friends. She does not hear this, but later a black youth worker has a chat with him about the incident. He compares her position as a white woman in a predominately Asian area with his position as an Asian man in a predominately white society in Britain. The youth worker asks the young man whether this might feel intimidating and whether it would make him feel anxious to which the response is, 'yes'. After a protracted discussion, the young man apologizes to him rather than the woman about what he had just said. In the end, the young woman does not get to hear about the incident in case the situation gets out of control. To hear what he said would have been to spark off an incident that neither of the men relished.

This episode highlights several themes that I want to explore in this article: firstly, the perception and experiences of white women as a numerical minority in Southall. Secondly, I outline the ambivalent dynamics of gender and race in situated contexts. And thirdly, I investigate whiteness as a racial category that is produced (and often disavowed) in relation to engagement with others. Even though usages of the terms race and ethnicity have variant histories – the former being premised upon biology, the latter more so on linguistic and cultural attributes – there is also a great deal of interchangeability in their contemporary articulations. Such overlaps notwithstanding, I consider whiteness as a more racialized category and deploy white ethnicity to focus on dynamics to do with predominant understandings of English, Irish and so forth. The terms of the debate, such as white, Asian and black are of course provisional abbreviations for the complex crisscrossing of social identifications based on race, ethnicity, religion, gender and individual/family histories, but in the crucible of interethnic/racial dynamics, there might be instantiated a momentary crystallization of identities.[1] This is a crucial part in the production of knowledge about self in relation to the Other where heterogeneous categories might be reduced to one that reproduces itself *as if* homogenous, as with the expressions, white and Asian. Primarily, I consider the dynamics of women-to-men perceptions and relations between young adults taking into account such racial/ethnic dimensions.[2] All the women I encountered were heterosexual. Thus, my discussions on sexuality are orchestrated by people interested in members of the opposite sex. The key focus is the nature of engagements of white women with non-white men.

After a discussion on whiteness and gender, the first section of the article delineates the contours of the habitus that circumscribes white women's lives in Southall. Habitus, in Pierre Bourdieu's (1990) formulation, refers to a set of dispositions that generate practices and perceptions, often unconscious as a kind of 'practical sense' (*sens pratique*). The second part concerns itself more with what I have called the 'styling' of racialised and gendered selves from the women's perspectives. This latter permits us to consider white women's creative agencies in their variant negotiations of dominant discourses that constitute the habitus of the area in a way that mitigates the problematic connotations of habitus as an overarching determinant of human behaviour. It will be noted that even though the contours of habitus in Southall identify women as racially marked, women's way of dealing with their social environment is premised more on articulating gendered rather than racialised roles.

Prisms of Whiteness and Sexuality

It is only in the last decade or so that whiteness has become an area of extensive study. Much of the literature arises out of feminism, labour history, and lesbian and gay studies (Frankenberg 1993; Dyer 1997; Rutherford 1997). All invariably agree that in the West whiteness exercises a hegemony over other racial groups in its taken-for-granted invisibility and dominance.[3] Like other forms of identification, whiteness has its own dynamic constituencies and differentiation. In many situations in Southall it divides sharply into the provisional categories of English and Irish ethnicity.[4] As Gerd Baumann reports: 'To speak of a *white community* is commonplace among South Asian and Afro-Caribbean Southallians; yet it is rare among their white neighbours themselves. Their self-classification acknowledges only one internal distinction as clearly as this: that between Irish and English Southallians' (Baumann 1996: 92, his emphasis).

That it is rare to speak of whiteness is part of its hegemonic invisibility. Rather when it is articulated, it is done so along the lines of ethnicity – that is, according to region or nation. However, whiteness from the outsider's point of view, is not an invisible category. Ralph Ellison provides a cutting critique of such assumptions with his fictional work on black lives in 1940s America, *Invisible Man* (1947). He writes:

> I am an invisible man. No, I am not a spook like those who haunted Edgar Allan Poe; nor am I one of your Hollywood movie ectoplasms. I am a man of substance, of flesh and bone, fibre and liquids – and I might even be said to possess a mind. I am invisible, understand, simply because people refuse to see me. Like the bodiless heads you see sometimes in circus side shows, it is as though I have been surrounded by mirrors of hard, distorting glass. When they approach me they see only my surroundings, themselves, or figments of their imagination – indeed, everything and anything except me. (Ellison 1947: 7)

From Ellison's perspective, it is blackness that connotes invisibility in the sense of dehumanization.[5] Whiteness is associated with visibility because it is granted ostensible rights, privileges and status in the West. Thus, from a non-white perspective, whiteness was certainly not invisible. The invisibility of whiteness is better equated with ideals of humanity and the power that this enshrines. Whiteness is normalized to the point that it *appears* invisible, not that it is racially unmarked from other perspectives. Thus, at this juncture we can summarize that whiteness is not naturalized from a non-white perspective, nor is it left unquestioned in the wake of exercises in self-reflexivity and studies on whiteness. bell hooks argues 'only a few have dared to make explicit those perceptions of whiteness that they think will discomfort or antagonize readers' (hooks 1997: 166). This is part of the liberal conviction that human beings are essentially all the same – another instance of the doctrine of universal subjectivity. To hear of perceptions of whiteness from the 'other side', however uncomfortable, is often dismissed, such that they 'unwittingly invest in the sense of whiteness as mystery' (hooks 1997: 168).

The factor of gender and/or sexuality is equally crucial in considerations of whiteness. Proposing that there is a universal experience of womanhood is contentious in light of critiques of Eurocentric feminism (hooks 1991; Stephen 1989; Frankenberg 1997). Yet there are significant points of consonance when considering women as social bodies. The post-Enlightenment 'rational' individual is implicitly white, European and male – 'transcendental agents' (Hobart 1993: 7) that pervade Western patriarchy. This allows for the identification of 'blacks with the body, and whites with the mind' (Gilroy 1993: 97). White women, however, have had a more ambivalent relationship with issues to do with race and heterosexist patriarchy (Ware 1992). Their colour might connote privilege, but patriarchal assumptions posit that they are essentially emotional, sentient and biological bodies essentially for sexual relationships or reproduction (MacCormack 1980). White women are construed as bodies *subject* to external forces. This is distinct from dissolute, implicitly male, entities such as the 'all-seeing eye', and 'the hidden hand' that *subject* social phenomena. When juxtaposed with a consideration of racial relations, the finer differentiations of male and female subjectivities are all too easily effaced into a singular debate about white supremacy.

Developing Baumann's (1996) observations somewhat, white people resident in Southall do not simply consider themselves 'de-racialized', but *marked* as white – a situation that is internalized and negotiated accordingly in the environs. It is from this premise that, more often than not, they choose to disavow the perennial reminder of racial differences. Thus, despite their local specificity as white people, they tap into a wider translocal discourse premised upon the invisibility of whiteness. With the combined effects of a numerical minority status, a primarily working-class population, and the issue of women being considered as first and foremost sexual or biological bodies, white women are very conscious of their noted visibility in the area. Their perceived corporeality, being seen as 'bodies' with particular associations, forms the reciprocal basis of these social realities (Douglas 1970; Scheper-Hughes and Lock 1987). Bearing in mind the indissolubility of the psychic and physical body and that, in most cases, 'the boundaries of the body are the lived experience of differentiation' (Butler 1993: 65), women (as tends also to be the case with other categories of people) represent themselves in reaction to outsiders' perceptions of them. For white women in Southall, knowledge about how they are perceived is well known. Yet how they react to its articulation in the area corroborates the liberal logic that they should be seen first and foremost as human beings, not as part of a 'raced' collective.

The disavowal of whiteness amongst white women in this case is not simply another example of the colour- and power-evasion strategies that Ruth Frankenberg (1993) describes for white middle-class women in the US. In Frankenberg's case, white women did not want to talk about racial issues because it was seen as improper; in the process, they reproduce racialized discourses of others whilst reconstituting their own unracialized whiteness as a privileged position in social hierarchies. Rather, not conscientizing racialized whiteness in the Southall context is more orientated by the idea that if white women were to mark themselves of as singularly distinct because of their race, they would further risk the problem of being seen as 'backwards', exclusivist, and worse a racist, and thus become ostracized in the area.

As compared with former decades and the continued racist articulations in other areas, such as Southall's neighbouring districts and the East End of London (Cohen 1997), views on migrants are not expressed in terms of resenting their presence in the area. In fact, even though grievances might be aired, there is a conscious vigilance of 'not wanting to sound racist'. Many of the ardent white racists had moved out of the area from the 1950s with the onset of migration from Britain's former colonies and memories of battles between far-right elements and residents had been inscribed as markers in the late 1970s and early 1980s when Southall began to be seen as 'an Asian town' that could defend itself (Bains 1988).

Even when the brunt of racial tensions were over by the 1990s, recent incidents of racial tensions and aggression kept the memory alive. This occurred after the murder of an Asian cab driver by a white passenger in 1989 on the borders of Southall on the Golf Links estate (Gillespie 1995: 123–6), and during the time of my fieldwork, a white drug-dealer who was killed by an Asian man in 1999. Many of my white respondents were worried that the killing would spark off a racial war and were concerned about how this might affect them. Albeit a tense period, there were no untoward occurrences due to the killing. The tensions that persisted were premised largely on religious identities, particularly between Sikhs/Hindus and Muslims who trace their background to the subcontinent. This was particularly sharp at the time of India-Pakistan cricket matches and the battle over the line of control at Kargil in Kashmir, both occurring in the summer of 1999. None of these issues implicated white people who remained outside of the vitriolic lines of fire.

'Ethni-City'

Southall's main street, known as The Broadway, and its general reputation, have earned it the appellation of 'Little India/Punjab'. In reality, however, its public places are the subject of contention between dwellers of varied origins including African-Caribbeans, Somalis, Eastern Europeans, Irish, and English amongst others. Migration into the area began around the 1930s with people who came from depressed coal-mining areas such as South Wales and Durham and from the poorer rural regions of Southern Ireland. From the late 1940s until the 1960s, migration was primarily from the Caribbean islands followed by migration from Punjab (in both India and Pakistan) from the 1950s and, in the late 1960s and 1970s, Indians resident in East Africa, who were forced to abandon their homes due to 'African-ization' policies, also settled in Southall. The 1991 census data shows that 58 per cent of the population of Southall are Asian, 30 per cent white (of which 10 per cent were born in Ireland), 7 per cent black and 5 per cent described as other. These labels are nothing more than a convenient way to account for the contextual and interactive nature of Southall's multi-ethnicities in the 1990s. Furthermore, they do not fully account for temporary residences, later influxes into the area such as the Somalis and the East Europeans from the mid-1990s, or details such as mixed-race households.

As was clear from many of the discussions I had with white women in the area, despite the difficulties, there is an overwhelming acceptance that Southall is a place for migrants and a beacon for multicultural Britain. Indeed, Asian ethnicity has become normalized due to its predominance in the area. As with the term white, Asian is not to refer to a homogenous category: the majority come from a Punjabi background (also by way of East Africa) and include Sikhs, Hindus, Muslims and

Christians, categories that themselves are open to contestation. Nonetheless, this is not to mitigate the association of Asianness with the place, which, occasionally, is not marked as a category of identification due to its normative status. This 'non-ethnicization' is a dynamic that is only specific to this and other comparable areas in Britain. However, the aim of this article is not to focus primarily on these Others of the white imaginary, but to spotlight the latter, to look at 'white *qua* white' (Dyer 1997: 13) where I consider whiteness and its intersections with gender and sexuality from the point of view of white, heterosexual women who live in Southall.

Given this brief background on the area, it is instructive to consider more detailed ethnographic portraits of white women's lives in the area to illustrate my main argument. Tina (34) who had been living in Southall for three years, said: 'I felt isolated when I first came here. It's the first time I've ever felt like that. I mean I've lived in Clapham, Brixton, Harlesden, White City, and I've never felt a sense of anxiety like I did on this estate.'[6] Emma (40) comments: 'Before Somalians used to ignore me. Now they stare at me because they've become more Westernized a bit and say things like darling to me.' Some of these perceptions have come about through having brief encounters – not qualitative or protracted relationships – with the Somali men. This is compounded by a sense of anxiety, exacerbated by their minority representation in the area.

'Minority consciousness' (Baumann 1996: 138) amongst white people in Southall recalls a colonial analogy. The classificatory logics associated with practices such as the census created a self-reflexive populace conscious of other enumerated collectivities (Kaviraj 1992: 26). Such colonial discourses were also '*productive* discourses, creating new kinds of knowledge, expression, political practice and subjectivity' (Breckenridge and van der Veer 1994: 6, their emphasis). It led to the popularization of majority and minority discourses in relation to reified religious communities of the subcontinent. The Southall case is a diluted and contingent version of such historically situated discursive practices. It is watered down because if white people wish to leave the area, it immediately inverts their numerical self-recognition to one that is constitutive of a majority rather than a minority; this along with the consumption of mainstream print and audio-visual media enable the sustenance of a majority consciousness. The encounter is contingent because it only applies to the particular locale of Southall (and perhaps other areas like this elsewhere in the country even though Southall represents the highest density of Asians in Britain).[7]

Being the object of others' 'stares' is frequently mentioned. It is a stare that is not just specific to white women, for the 'watchful eyes' of relatives and neighbours also subject Asian youth to an informal network of surveillance. However, when white women become the object of such stares, it takes on a different valency: on the one hand, the women are associated with availability and sometimes a lack of moral principles; on the other hand, the women find it extremely disconcerting, not being used to such intense attention in Britain. After getting to know the women over a period of months, they began to relay such resentment to me for they saw me as a young and 'modern' Asian woman who did not appear to be constrained by orthodoxy. Such viewpoints informed their discussions amongst each other, but not ones they aired with Asians they knew in the area. Lesley (22), an Irish woman, said: 'People stare at you all the time. When we go to the shop, they all look at you and the men follow you around like you're about to steal something.' Kate (22) said: 'All the Asian men stare at you, shout at you and whistle at you. We were walking down Kings Road once and someone pulled up a car. There were two Asian men in there. They stopped and squirted water at me with a pistol.'

Being 'stared at' unnerves the women who are otherwise accustomed to assimilating in their surroundings.[8] Their feelings of discomfort arise from a combination of *being seen to be* marked out as different not only racially but also as sexually available, and anxieties to do with proximity to Others who are perceived to be 'different' and in the majority. It is instructive to compare this 'stare' to the gaze of which, in the wake of Michel Foucault's (1977) work on disciplinary surveillance, we have plentiful commentary. According to Foucault, the gaze is imbricated in bureaucratic panopticism which systematically confines and oppresses the object of the gaze. In this case, the stare is less imbricated in, and more contingent on systems of power – that is, the stare is not related to state panopticism in a straightforward manner. Rather the stare momentarily fixes the object/subject in a more discursive framework. The stare is not exactly hegemonic in being backed up by institutional sanction that lead to control or containment of the subjects, nor is it entirely about fulfilling a curiosity that simply reifies the object. It is more about exercising an *a priori* knowledge of white women as independent and 'free' – that is, physically and sexually available. Thus the stare is simultaneously sexualized – in which women are construed as subjects of their own will and yet objects of desire; and racialized – where whiteness is construed as a site of privilege, unbridled individualism and comparative freedom from social restraints. In a development of the fetishization of the black person (Bhabha 1983), this sexualized and racialized look is one that oscillates in a spectrum between the poles of disdain and desire.

Being the object of a stare that easily magnifies into a powerful gaze from the subjected women's perspective in the wider machinery of patriarchy is unsettling for the women as it is seen to lay the premises for what might become untoward behaviour against them.[9] Other than 'bitch', another term commonly used term to call white women by young non-white men was 'lady'. However, I also noted that young white women responded favourably to being called 'a lady' by other men even though the appellation probably carried as much sexual undertones as did the term 'bitch'. Whereas 'bitch' implied someone who was loose and provocative, 'lady' implied someone who was affable and available – almost like a prize object to be admired or won. Such dichotomies are parallel to whore/wife dichotomies in many male-oriented arenas such as hip hop (hooks 1991), but in this case is further differentiated by questions of race/ethnicity – that is, women of similar backgrounds are conceptualized through the lens of wife material, whereas the opposition of whore is split into two types, the lady and the bitch. An exaggerated masculinity here, as elsewhere, is correlated with an exaggerated series of dichotomies to do with female categorizations.

Asian women are overwhelmingly seen as property – they 'belong' to someone. White women at large are perceived as 'free goods':[10] men can use them in exchange without long-term commitments – that is, they are seen in terms of flings, short-term relations, and prostitution. The prevalent Asian view that marriage is a union between two families rather than individuals inflects the sense of Asian women as 'property' to be exchanged between families, even though several creative measures in taking control of a degree of the marriage arrangements and decisions have been noted as far back as the 1970s (Brah 1978). There are of course relationships that overcome the parameters of 'racial endogamy', but they are comparatively rare – a point corroborated by Avtar Brah's article on young Asian teenagers, which states 'Courtship is . . . seen to be an end in itself rather than a prelude to marriage' (Brah 1978: 199). Of the 30 or so white women with whom I had acquainted myself, only one, Tina (mentioned above), was married to a British Asian Sikh whom she had met through her work, and then moved into the area after marriage. Such exceptions notwithstanding, striking parallels can be made with Asian men's dealings with Asian and white women and debates on gift and money/commodity exchange. The former is homologous with 'transactions concerned with the reproduction of the long-term social or cosmic order' as occurs for gift exchange and the latter with 'a "sphere" of short-term transactions concerned with the arena of individual competition' as is the case for exchange of goods (Bloch and Parry 1989: 23). Women are 'gifts' when considered as marriageable, often when ethnicity (and in more regulated contexts, religion and caste) is shared by members of both sex; they are 'goods' when women are sought as part of a competitive field of match-making and breaking, where shared ethnicity is not such an issue.

Another striking feature of Southall's streets is the predominance of men, particularly after dark. Many of the women I spoke to raised the issue of the perceived machismo, aggression and potential danger to themselves as women especially at night. Emma commented: 'There's no places to go out around here. Even the pubs are really macho. It's boozy aggressive and macho. I don't feel comfortable there.' This would explain why many of the women go out of Southall for their nights out, particularly to the nearby locations of Ealing and Acton. However, going out of the area is not always a viable option every night for the largely working-class or lower middle-class population that has been attracted to Southall for its relatively inexpensive housing and rents. Considerations such as the expense of drink, club admissions, and late-night taxis, as well as early morning work or college the next day place limits on the weekly occurrence of these sojourns. Thus, for positive and negative reasons, a variable part of their evening leisure is spent in Southall.

Many of the white women also commented upon the scarcity of Asian women out and about, particularly at night. The curbs on Asian women's mobility occur primarily for two reasons. First, due to the premium placed on girls'/women's reputation if she is to maintain the *izzat* (honour, pride and respectability) of her family. Even 'if she is merely seen 'hanging around' or 'chatting', let alone 'flirting' with boys on the high street or elsewhere in public' (Gillespie 1995: 153), this is enough to compromise her reputation. Second, as a consequence, if Asian women or courting couples do want to go out, they gravitate to places outside of what they perceive to be the intense sociality of Southall.

One white woman, Susan (19), explained the dearth of women in Southall's public places as not just about limits on Asian women's mobility, but also about not sharing similar interests: 'All the Asian girls I knew at school didn't really go out that much. They were all into their education. They do their homework and that's it. Now they're all doctors and lawyers.' Another, Linda (21), who had been in Southall for two years, commented on Asian women: 'I don't mean to sound offensive but they stick to themselves. Don't get me wrong. I'd deal with anyone. But they don't deal with us, so we stick to our own.' But this notion of 'non-integration' was not always extended to the men from such categories.[11] Meryl (18) commented: '[Asian girls] are not interested in you when you're on the road. The boys are not like that. The girls just walk past. They don't want to know you especially if they're with their friends. They're stuck up!' Emma commented on Somalis, similarly seen as oppressive towards women: 'You never see their women. May be they meet at each other's houses but I do think it's weird you don't see many of them. It's probably due to the fact that they're Islamic'.

The desire to know more women in the area is disrupted by Eurocentric notions of difference – in this case, that of Islam being seen as authoritarian, particularly towards its women. I was certainly seen as an anomaly, visibly Asian but with little restrictions on my public mobility. But this was also put down to the fact that I did not grow up in the area. Nonetheless, even though I lived several miles away in south London, I was associated with the place through a kind of transplanted locality where my perceived ethnicity made me appear suited to the area. Then, in almost reverse gear, perceptions of my resettled ethnicity seemed to dissolve as other mutual interests and practices, such as playing pool, shopping, music, going out and so forth, were pursued. Women who had just moved into the area, particularly from Ireland, saw me as a repository of knowledge on Asian lifestyles and a means to find out more about the area. On one occasion, I accompanied them to the local Sikh temple, which they always saw as some kind of 'mystery place' but did not feel it was 'their place to go'. This feeling of 'not-belonging' even extended to the Indian restaurants. The so-called 'national practice' of 'curry and lager' was not as popular amongst white people in Southall even though there are numerous restaurants in the area.[12]

Prevalent in much of young white women's discussions was the question of what to wear, not just as an aesthetic concern, but also as a pragmatic issue tempered by climate, context and self-reflection on how what they might wear could effect their engagements on the streets of Southall. The concern for young women is the desire to be attractive to men whom they are attracted towards – and this need not be ethnically demarcated – but without compromising themselves as freely available to all as according to the local mythology about white women (I use the term mythology to invoke the flux between imaginaries and actuality rather than to indicate an outright falsehood). Even though there is no definitive red light area in Southall, white women who are free to move around as and when they wish, particularly after dark, tend to be equated with the notion of 'prostitute'. Tina, married to an Asian man, still felt the object of a sexualized and raced gaze in public: 'One time I was walking with my husband. It was about evening time, down the old town. And an old man said something in Punjabi – I'm not going to translate because it was really bad what he said. He implied I was a prostitute. My husband got really angry and called him everything under the sun.'

Dressing down for the occasion so as one could not be read as a 'prostitute' often warded off women's sense of sexual threats in Southall's public spaces. Thus, even though times of going out were about 'dressing up', it also necessitated 'dressing down'. Kate (20) told me about a night when they were being followed by a car. The men seemed to know their route, as they would always be ahead of them, shouting 'sexual things' to them. That time, Kate said she was glad that she had a skirt on that was below her knees. However, even dressing down might not be enough as they found out from experience. Meryl related the incident when:

> I was walking home one night and had to go down an alleyway. A man stuck out his hand, and I put my two fingers up at him. Then he followed me down the alleyway. I was shocked. I thought I was all right because I had dungarees on and it was only about 8 o'clock. It wasn't dark, and it wasn't as if I was wearing a short skirt and asking for it!

This internalization of 'asking for it' reinforces patriarchal views about women judged from bodily insignia. Heather (21) quipped as a white woman in a short skirt walked past the railway station: 'Was that a skirt or a belt? She must be a visitor around here. I'd never wear anything like that. I'm more of a jeans person. It's much more practical.'

Notions of 'prostitute' were also internalized and sometimes became a trope with which to conceptualize other women, even though they tried to be understanding of other women's predicaments. Kate and Lesley talked about an Asian woman who they saw in the pub in the company of several men. She was the only other Asian woman I had seen in the pub myself. Someone had told them that she was a prostitute, but they wanted to give her the benefit of the doubt, almost in a faint-hearted gesture of sisterly solidarity. Nonetheless, they would notice certain acts, such as the exchange of money between her and men. They also knew that she lived down the road, and that they saw 'men coming and going out of her house'. There was a hint of suspicion spurred on by the supposition that an independent Asian woman in Southall living on her own would have to be a prostitute. They seemed to accept the gossip about her because what they chose to focus on emphasized the practices of a sex worker. Kate was a little worried that she had to walk past the house every day. Another day, Kate and Lesley were playing cards in the bedroom window, and they saw a car pull up with two girls. Lesley said, 'They could have been eighteen and were very pretty. One was white, the other black and they were with an Asian man.' Kate projected her own concerns onto the women and felt sorry for the girls: 'Why did they have to do it?' She recounted how this could be potentially threatening for themselves – as white women who live on the same road as a locally known 'brothel': 'The other evening I was walking past the house, and an Asian man asked for my phone number: 'He even had a pen and paper ready to take my number. And he was about 65!'

Race/ethnicity might be normalized as a constitutive facet of the area, but what remain as oft-discussed markers are other differentiations based on age, behaviour and the physical appearance of Asian men. Kate said, 'Why is it always the old ugly ones that look at me? They're never good-looking!' Moreover, comments as to men's 'rudeness' were frequent, particularly as to women's encounters with elder men. Jenny (19) talked about the idea of 'dirty old men', which was not intended as a specific description, but one that was for anyone they did not like the look of, was physically unattractive, or was considered too old for sexual relations: 'They're really rude. When we dress up like that it's because we're going out to have a good time. Not to be letched at by dirty old men!' Jenny elaborated that these were mainly elderly Asian men. Younger men, because they are considered to have more *nous* – that is, 'know how to chat' – were not included in this generalization. This is in tandem with widespread ideas about the elder generation Asians being seen as authoritarian, orthodox and out-of-touch with modern lifestyles, and the younger generation being more Westernized, interesting and 'with it'. It is a view that overlooks the complex series of negotiations where there might be considerable variation in intergenerational communication (Brah 1978). The reception of the film, *East is East* (1999), is a case in point that further corroborates the popular demonology of an inter-generational gulf. In the movie, elder generation Asians are either seen as 'odd' or pathologized as violent, whereas members of the younger generation become points of identification for being 'trendy' and 'interesting'. Occasionally, general views about elder men are also conflated with young men's flirtatious behaviour with white women, particularly if not welcome, due to assumptions about their racial/ethnic similarities.[13] Jill reflected: 'They elbow me. One man spat on me. One time, it was after Vaisakhi,[14] a group of men in a white limo drove past and shouted out to us to join them. We said no. Then they shouted out, 'Snow-white bitches!' Jill was not sure how to respond to the invective in relating the episode, but she did assert that, because there were three of them, they started jeering at them, but not in a way that fore-fronted their race/ethnicity, a point I shall return to below.

It is evident that not only spatial considerations, but also temporal aspects inflected women's lives. Women's conceptual geography of Southall was one that changed with the dial on the clock. Thus time was less an abstract schema, and more a somatized perception tinged by anticipation of how certain places at certain times might affect them physically. The conceptual mapping was quite different for men whose out-of-bound areas, if any, were largely marked spaces where the possibility of territorial violence could flare up. Meryl recounted the time she went to a fair in Southall Park where a man groped her:

> Then he grabbed me by the arm and took me to the car park. I tried to get away but then he held on with even more force. He asked me who I was and where I lived. It was only about 9.30 so it wasn't late. I was screaming so much he let me go. Then the man got together with his mates, and when I walked past with my friend they were jeering. One of them slapped my friend's bottom.

> [I asked her whether the man was Asian?]

> No, he was weird. I don't know what he was but he was coloured.

Time plays a part in the account where even 9.30 p.m. ('before the pubs close') was not a sufficient guarantor against being harassed. This episode is revealing for a number of other reasons. On the one hand, white women, unless they were known to be related or connected to particular groups of people, were seen as goods to be taken. On the other, Asian race/ethnicity was easier to recognize and, due to their long presence in the area, was normalized. People who had grown up in the area knew who was who, and even though they might not be part of their networks of kin/friends, they were part of their mappings of knowledge of the area and its residents. But for the newer migrants into this region, renowned for transient residents, there was less certainty about 'where they were coming from' – an expression not exclusively about their cultural backgrounds, but also where they lived and their motivations in their negotiations with others.

Although a widespread phenomenon, the context of Southall as multiracial has heightened a protective instinct from white male associates. Fathers and long-term partners in particular place certain limitations on women's movements. Heather related the time when:

> I went out with a black man for a drink. I didn't fancy him. I just went for a drink as he asked me out. Then I went to Andrew's [her then boyfriend]. I was quite drunk, but it was obvious I hadn't done anything. Still, he didn't trust me when I told him who I had been out with and suspected me of all sorts.

White men's perception of Southall as populated by, on the one hand, Asian men – stereotypically understood as sexually repressed but also (in light of the unruly connotations of Southall) aggressive, or black men – considered sexual predators, seem more entrenched in racial stereotypes than amongst the women, a point I shall return to below. Whether repressed or predatory, the assumed outcome is the same – the threat of 'taking their women'. As public space is seen to 'belong' to non-whites, it appears to produce a protective trait amongst white men. It is an example of the lingering sedimentation of colonial discourse about the threat of rape of white women by the 'natives' (Dyer 1997; Ware 1992). In the majority of cases, however, young women, unless they chose otherwise, seemed to be 'mistresses of their own will' with a desire to assert their independence. They are not just frail and hapless victims of men but have learned to fend for themselves. This attitude would lead to frequent rows between 'possessive' boyfriends, and 'strict' fathers – rows that would result in an opening of negotiations or, in extreme cases, a shut-down of the relationship.

Stylistics

Until now I have concentrated on the contours of habitus that have inscribed themselves on women's bodies as gendered and raced subjects. Men's perspectives are necessarily second-hand as it is the means by which women engage with dominant tropes that concern me here. Habitus might be seen as a feature of the 'cultural non-consciousness that [they] all inhabit' (Dyer 1997: 7). However, the preceding account also highlights the blurred line between unconscious disposition and conscientized articulation of the habitus, where even though the social environment inscribes itself on people's minds and bodies, this is not to say that it is not realized, discussed and operationalized by these very people themselves. Whiteness is marked and felt particularly through the 'stare' and other conduct towards the women. Nonetheless, even though white women felt singled out for their race and sexual associations, they still did not articulate it in terms of a racial-ized discourse. This observation agrees with other research findings, as with Anne Phoenix' survey on white Londoners, where 'many young people found it difficult to talk about what white meant to them and few presented themselves as having white identities . . . Generally . . . the white young people consistently played down the significance of colour while frequently producing accounts which indicated that their lives are racialized' (Phoenix 1997: 188).

In this last section – by no means an exhaustive account – I turn to situated strategies that enable young women relatively safe channels of communication and mobility in the area. These are, of course, the very features that make the area a habitable place for women of many backgrounds. The aim of this section is also to consider the contradictory and parodic aspects of everyday negotiations as a whole that, as is the nature of these strategies, undermines reified understandings of habitus. Thus I provide a series of examples to the kinds of techniques deployed – what I prefer to describe as styling – as a response to the combined effect of public, corporeal, psychic and social spaces of gendered interactions in Southall. There are broad themes that emerge: everyday strategies of living that border on mimetic assertiveness and predatory engagements with men; accessories that enable greater mobility and security; the safety in numbers so that numerical self-recognition becomes tied in with a larger group; self-parody and the reappropriation of abusive terms that transcend the cusps of objectification and subjectivity (or agency). Variant perspectives on gender are also offered, such as, on the one hand, how women feel they have it tougher and thus themselves need to be tougher; and, on the other, the sympathetic or patronizing attitude towards younger men, or more to the point, 'boys'. Generally, it is noted that gender roles are more openly discussed and performed than racial identities.

As elsewhere, one strategy of living an independent life as a woman in Southall is 'to become like the men', particularly in public spaces. When walking the streets, I noted how many of the women walked firmly with a purposeful stride. Lesley said, 'We have to look as if we mean business.' The case of 'giving as much as you got' was also prevalent amongst the women at the youth centre I regularly visited. It became a means of asserting one's space without compromising on perceptions of them as the 'weaker sex'. One of the male regulars at a pub looked at a new woman who had come into the pub, and said, 'It's about time we had real women in here.' Jill put up one finger at him and they started jeering. In another instant, Meryl threatened to challenge a man for being obstructive in a story that is much too long-winded to rehearse here: 'He's chatting my name. If I don't get my money back, I'll bloody kill him', she asserted.

Despite such rhetoric, white women did not tend to partake of the masculinized conflicts for territory and male pride. Instead, they fought for a sense of mobile territory that they could call their own with subtler strategies than aggressive stakes on particular areas of 'defending one's patch'.[15] Familiarizing paths and places so that they become known, friendly, and even homely is a way of making them, in a sense, domestic. Domestication is not just a female-specific term, but tends to be a more 'feminine' way of asserting public space as their own. Where men might be *aggressive* in making a territorial stake, women tend to be *assertive*. Women would often domesticate public spaces so that they could call it their own – an extension of the domestic space. This could be in the form of a regular pub, by getting to know the staff and customers. Or it could be in the form of being a member of a youth centre, where they felt at home, and had played a constructive part in the running and even decorating of the place.

Kate once reflected, 'If you go in to the pub, you feel like you're back in Ireland. There are a few old men in there who are so typically Irish.' The pub invoked the comfort of hospitality 'back home'. Interestingly, elderly men of a similar ethnicity were troped as familial and quaint, rather than 'backwards' and irritating as the above discussion on elderly Asian men highlighted. Old Irish men here were entwined with nostalgia for a time and place considered remote and perhaps 'lost'. Thus, even though Southall was their immediate habitus, other places offered further geographic imaginaries. As a brief overview, this could be in terms of (1) the 'imaginary of return' for recent migrants such as the recent influx of Irish where home acts as 'a mythic place of desire' (Brah 1996: 192; see also McGarry 1990 for phases of Irish migration into Southall), (2) an 'imaginary of moving' – a phrase I use to describe the constant reference of Southall residents to move out of the area when circumstances allowed – more a desire rather than an actual fulfilment, and (3) the frequent outings to the environs of Southall for reasons to do with work or leisure.

Accessories that enhanced mobility were another mode of negotiating the public space. This could be in terms of wearing practical clothes and shoes, bikes, mobile phones, and if possible a car. Nadia (40) drove a car so did not have to encounter the streets so much when travelling to work in one of the community centres. Still, she cited the need to have a mobile phone: 'I heard of a woman being harassed at the traffic lights. That's why my husband got me a mobile. But it's not just specific to Southall. It's everywhere, don't you think?' This is a cautionary reminder of the generalized risk of violence against women that need not be specific to Southall. In 1999, mobile phones had not yet become a consumer necessity in quite the way they are nowadays. They were seen as more of a prize commodity and many of the women desired to purchase one when circumstances permitted. The phone not only afforded them communication at all times but also further enhanced their confidence in negotiating public spaces in the area.

Safety in numbers was another means of negotiating what might appear as the intimidating contours of Southall at night. It became a way of marking out their presence which mitigated the feeling that they were marked as a minority group in the locality. Most of these groups included men, and some of these groups were composed of various ethnicities and races depending on friendships (although never Asian or Somali women, for instance). Irish women who were temporary migrants, over for educational and vocational training, hung out in larger groups than the equivalent age group of English women. They also had a network of women that they could call upon due to the fact that they were all over for training purposes, and resorted to the sanctity of female camaraderie whenever they wished. Being away from the relatively strict environs of rural Ireland, living in Southall still afforded them greater freedom of choice to do what they wished.

Melissa, an English woman, said that she had been part of a girls' gang since she was little: 'We had different names. Then later we hung out with boys.' There was a mood of defiance paraded, but often only when in large groups. She continued, 'We used to wear short skirts and everything even though it was Southall. I was a hard bitch!' Melissa testified to the reappropriation of terms of customary abuse such as 'bitch' to signify a woman to be reckoned with. Such strategies were nearly always conducted in the safety of familiar, domesticated places. For instance, Meryl would often play up to expectations of herself as a 'slapper' in a parodic fashion when in the youth club. She would shake her breasts at the Asian boys in the youth club, and when they got carried away and she felt that she was losing control over the situation, she would end it with a 'Fuck off!' or 'Sharrappp!' On another occasion she was more serious and said to me, 'I'm a slapper. I mean if I want to have a good time with a man, I would.' I was reminded of the female rap artiste, Missy Elliott's single, *I'm a Bitch* (1999) where she reclaims the misogynist term, 'bitch' from the confines of the masculine ethos of hip hop, and uses it as a way of demonstrating pride in assertive femininity. Rather than being terms that objectified loose women, looseness became a resource with which to assert your agency in a pleasurable manner. Slapper need not just be a term of abuse, but also a term connoting sexual adventure, one that can be boasted about in terms of stories of sexual conquests.

Boasting about 'pulling' was rife. Meryl said to me, 'I've been out with more men than you've had hot dinners!' Another woman, Lisa (21), talked about how she and her friend 'pulled' four men each the other night at the pub. When I asked whether they were white, black or Asian, she looked annoyed and said, 'All sorts. Black, white, Asian – it doesn't matter.' Marking them as racially distinct seemed inappropriate next to the pleasures that they could afford simply by being with men. Amongst the white population, unwillingness to discuss racial matters took on a qualitatively different valency particularly if we consider that (1) white people are in the minority and do not want to be seen as backwards or racist; and that (2) white youth are born in a climate of multicultural acceptance and overwhelmingly think the 'race question' is irrelevant. A humorous incident might bring this point closer to home. On one occasion, Valerie and Meryl, one woman of African-Caribbean heritage, the other white of mixed English and Irish descent, both in their late teens, were teasing each other about 'chocolate and cream' in relation to the men that they 'got off with over the weekend'. I immediately assumed that this was another version of 'ebony and ivory' – black and white men that they had sexually experimented with. When I later decided to pursue what exactly they meant by 'chocolate and cream', and whether this included Asian men, it transpired that the sexual experiments they were discussing were of a different nature altogether: they were talking about taking a man regardless of ethnicity, stripping him down, and then covering him with melted chocolate and cream! It was not that difference was levelled out, but that it was noted and sampled for its diversity in terms of the sexual promises it might deliver. That indeed was a journey towards, or a sign of, sexual maturity.

Evidently, women themselves can be predators and Southall is not unique on this factor. Lesley said: 'Once this dishy Asian guy walked into the pub. We all fell off our stools and Denise was on the floor getting a good look at his arse. He was on his way to the toilets. It's good sitting around the gents.' In another instance at the youth club, Lisa said to a group of young men, 'I work with children [in a nursery] all day long. I want some adult conversation.' None of the young men replied, instead they looked around in embarrassment. Older men known to the women in the pub had no problem engaging in sexual banter, however. Whereas younger men would counteract sexual innuendo with either embarrassment or invective, older men were up for the challenge. These men tended to be above the age of 30/40. Pool games were saturated with innuendo about 'balls, holes and sticks', for instance. The women encouraged men in the safe environs of their regular pub where they knew nearly everyone. They responded by doing impressions of perverts, flashing their legs and coming out with corny chat-up lines, as from the second Austin Powers movie, *The Spy who Shagged Me* (1999) that was running in cinemas at the time.

Racial/ethnic demarcations could be broken down with the performance of feminine roles and the generation of sexual interest: for white women to enter into highly racialized spaces is much easier than it is for white men. For instance, Jenny recalled the time she was going out with a member of the notorious Holy Smokes 'gang', a group of Asian men who revelled in an image of toughness and masculinity, and as local legend would have it, would not entertain fools gladly particularly if they were men from rival groups, such as the Tuti Nangs, or more generally, non-Sikhs. She remembered having 'no problems' hanging out with them, and judging by her charismatic personality and her continued work in Asian community theatre where she said that she 'played the token white woman', one is led to believe her.

To briefly end with the range of white women's views on the politics of gender: when Meryl had got banned from a regular pub, she reacted aggressively due to a combination of drink and the fact that a man who she used to go out with, who was now going out with her former 'best friend', fell over coming up the steps. Her account of the events went as follows:

I was just a little high-sterical [sic]. That's all. And they ban me altogether! The bouncers just threw me out like that. I've seen men have fights in there with knives, and they were in there the next week. Why me? My sister went in there the other day, and she got pulled up because they thought she was me.

The understanding here was that women had it tougher than men did. Because women had to pay the consequences of patriarchal prejudice, they need to be strong on all fronts if they did not want to play up to images of being seen as the weaker sex.

However, another time, Meryl discussed how 'men can have it hard'. After initially laughing at her unwitting innuendo, she sympathetically considered those men that want to work in a nursery where she was being trained as treated unfairly:

All the people at work are women. They should have more men, but they don't because people think they could be [she whispers] paedophiles. I don't think all men who want to work in nurseries should be suspected of this. It's not right. I heard about a couple with a fourteen-year-old boy. It was the man and the woman who used to abuse him. They used to beat him and then have a cigarette at the bottom of the bed as he lay there battered!

On this occasion and contrary to expectations, men were subject to sympathy, and were not viewed as having superiority in all aspects of public life. They were easily pathologized as 'paedophiles' even if their intentions to work with young children were innocent, which Meryl thought was a travesty of equality. Similarly, another woman training as a nurse recalled how she felt sorry for a two-year-old Muslim boy who came into the hospital to be circumcized. The sympathy was intermingled with her assumptions that Islam was a dictatorial and non-egalitarian religion. It had not occurred to her that orthodox Jews also circumcized young boys. Judaism, after all, is not so demonized in the contemporary West, as has been the case with Islam particularly in the last few decades (Said 1995). On both counts, both females expressed how they were 'lucky' or even 'blessed' to be women.

Whither Whiteness

What has emerged in the above account is that, despite the constitutive and determining facets of habitus, it can form the basis from which white women interact in a range of creative and sometimes unexpected ways. This is in an arena of racial/ethnic interrelations, an arena that due to the unpredictable nature of such encounters makes for a dynamic flux of interfaces. After an exploration of whiteness and gender, and the characteristics of minority white presence in Southall, I then went on to explore women's sense of public, corporeal and psychic selves in relation to perceptions of them in the public realm. Part of this discussion focused on the 'stare', which was seen to subject white women in a myriad of ways. This was followed by an exploration of white women's everyday strategies of living: these emphasized male mimicry, prioritized accessories that enabled greater mobility and security, sought safety in numbers, and revelled in self-parody and the reappropriation of abusive terms that transcended the cusps of object-ification and agency. I then considered variant perspectives on gender such as how women have it tougher and thus need to be tougher, and the sympathy towards or patronizing of men or young boys by these women. It was noted that white women had a greater range of gender identities which they could assume than men who might, in this extremely heterosexist area, be open to accusations of being a 'homosexual' if they appeared to, or acted effeminately. Women's ability to per-form versions of male and female roles was seen as an empowering resource. Thus, whereas white women's experiences of Southall are tempered by the dynamic interface of gender and race – they are not just white, but white women – their strategies of coping are more premised upon the negotiation of gender identities, not so much racial identities. In other words, on balance, it is issues to do with gender that are most adaptable for women and allows for interventions in racial-ized encounters that might otherwise not be possible. This is for a range of reasons. First, the women did not want to be seen as 'backwards' or branded as racists. This is in an area where white people are in a minority and where Asianness is the normative condition due to their established residence in the place since at least the 1960s. Second, women were interested more in sexual encounters with men they liked (even if this was a temporary adventure in tasting difference). Finally, there are the enduring effects of the lingering residue of the normalization of whiteness, which is lent succour by going out of the area for work/leisure and mainstream media consumption – a situation that leads to their discomfort at being marked as raced white women in Southall. One wonders, in the light of this dis-cussion and if we were to return to the opening scenario, what the white woman would have done had she actually heard the Asian man's retort. Would she have responded, or even retaliated, to the aggregate invectives of 'fucking' and 'bitch' and swallowed the 'white' referent as part of its recurrent disavowal? Responses, after all, are framed within the contingencies of the available cultural grammar. Perhaps such questioning is where the project to reconfigure whiteness as text, feeling and ontology might begin in Southall and beyond.

Acknowledgement

The research for this paper was conducted as part of a Brunel University research project, 'Reconsidering Ethnicity: A Study of Non-Ethnic People in the Midst of

Ethnicity'. It was funded by the Economic and Social Research Council, 1997–99 in the Department of Human Sciences. The project included Ian Robinson, Ronald Frankenberg and Aaron Turner. Thanks in particular to Ronald Frankenburg for comments and reconstructive suggestions for this article and also to Brian Axel for his incisive feedback. All shortcomings in the article, however, remain my own. The names of individuals cited in the text are altered to protect their anonymity.

Notes

1. Frederik Barth (1969) has discussed such phenomena in relation to the creation of boundaries but Ian Robinson et al. (1999) take this further to note that such boundaries might be too rigid and what is required is a fluid, processual understanding of social dialectics. My perspectives on this are that both kinds of effects are possible – that is, processes might well lead to the momentary reification of identities. See Kaur and Kalra on 'latticed identities' between embedded and de-essentialized categories (1996: 220).

2. I cannot do justice to men-to-women relations in the limited space of this article. For male perspectives, see my co-researcher's, Aaron Turner's, forthcoming work. The findings in this article have arisen out of participant-observation and informal interviews in women's homes, youth clubs, pubs and other social centres located mainly in the Old Town of Southall over a period of nine months in 1999, although my previous residence in the area from 1991–2 was also of great benefit to the research proceedings. During this time I got to know about 30 white women, the majority in the 18-to-early-30s age range. There is no one place where white women congregate, but various scattered locations in and around Southall. To some extent, it reflects the scattered residences of white populations in the area and their diversity of backgrounds and interests. The Golf Links estate on the outskirts of Southall's New Town is a stronghold for white residents. Even though it is administratively part of Southall, residents (and even those who live outside the estate) tend to describe the estate as part of Greenford, the next district to the north-west of Southall proper. I did not engage with white women on this estate for two main reasons: firstly, resentment against Asians is prevalent amongst residents of this deprived estate, and secondly, the social landscape was not conducive to considering the dynamics I was interested in – white women as a numerical minority in a locality resided by non-white people.

3. I follow Stuart Hall's outline of the West as a concept that (1) characterizes societies into different categories; (2) describes a set of images; (3) provides a model of comparison; and (4) functions as an ideology (Hall 1992: 277).

4. The relations between notions of the English and the Irish is itself a complex arena, particularly for mixed families, second- or third-generation Irish. How these impinge upon race or cultural ethnicity is a further complication (see McGarry 1990).
5. In the book, black invisibility also provides the potential for a kind of spectral power.
6. Clapham and Brixton are multiracial areas in South London, Harlesden and White City in West London. These areas are marked for their predominant African-Caribbean populations.
7. Governance of Southall is not qualitatively distinct from the rest of the nation even though the respective institutions and agencies might have a more ostensible multicultural directive. Thus if there are severe violations, for instance, legislative and policing bodies would not act that differently from other white-dominated areas in Britain. However, Baumann states that 'minority consciousness' might manifest itself in the following ways: (1) where whites generalize a shared marginality in which it is felt that public policies, events and outdoor spaces favour those that are 'ethnic' – that is, those who are non-white; and (2) where whites generalize about surrounding categories of communities in which they make reified assumptions about their culture (Baumann 1996: 138).
8. It is not only white women who are the focus of male attention. Marie Gillespie reports, for instance: 'Young males can often be seen conspicuously 'cruising' up and down the Broadway in red Ford Capris and white Triumph Stags, sound systems at full volume pumping bhangra or reggae beats, trying to catch the eyes of girls walking by, shouting provocative and flirtatious remarks' (Gillespie 1995: 35).
9. This is in fact an ungrounded fear for the incident of rape in the area is no higher than elsewhere in the city. Asian men's responses are not so extreme as to risk a possible backlash in neighbouring white-dominated districts such as Greenford (Gillespie 1995: 126).
10. Thanks to Ronnie Frankenberg for the suggestive phrase of 'free goods'.
11. This sense of 'not mixing' is also reported by Les Back (1996: 64–5) for the case of south-east London, and provides a convenient means of propagating popular imaginaries of cultural difference.
12. Overwhelmingly, the popularity of 'curry and lager' is consonant with the depersonalized and non-committal nature of the consumptive act. Whilst consumption might be about something that is different from the self in order to constitute the self, it is also conducted in a commoditized arena conceived as distinct from the 'gritty reality' of everyday living – that is, for local white people, away from Southall. If Asians are normalized as part of that 'gritty reality' in the area, then their cultural commodities do not seem to carry that

cachet of alterity to the same extent and are not consumed with as much relish
as perhaps by a tourist to the area. This also extends to the current penchant
for Indian saris, bindis and other forms of dress in popular culture (Sharma,
Hutnyk and Sharma 1996). I met no white women resident in Southall wearing
tokens of Indian fashion. It was seen as too much of an 'Indian thing', and as
one woman asserted, 'it felt phoney wearing them next to Asian women'. In
a place where Asianness characterizes popular conceptions of the place as the
norm, consumption of its commercial features is not so attractive for local
whites, but can be for those white people not from the area who are touring
the area out of interest.

13. See Claire Alexander's book, *The Asian Gang* (2000), for a compelling critique
of the pathologization of Asian men to which some of the white women were
also partial.

14. Vaisakhi is traditionally an Indian harvest festival celebrated in April.

15. For white male perspectives, see Aaron Turner's forthcoming Ph.D. at Brunel
University.

Bibliography

Alexander, C. (2000), *The Asian Gang*, Oxford: Berg.

Back, L. (1996), *New Ethnicities and Urban Culture: Racisms and Multiculture
in Young Lives*, London: UCL Press.

Bains, H. S. (1988), 'Southall Youth: An Old-Fashioned Story', in P. Cohen and
H.S. Bains (eds) *Multi-Racist Britain*, London: Macmillan.

Barth, F. (1969), *Ethnic Groups and Boundaries: The Social Organisation of
Cultural Difference*, London: George Allen & Unwin.

Baumann, G. (1996), *Contesting Culture: Discourses of Identity in Multi-Ethnic
London*, Cambridge: Cambridge University Press.

Bhabha, H. (1983), 'The Other Question', *Screen* 24, (6): 18–35.

Bloch, M. and Parry, J. (1989), 'Money and the Morality of Exchange', in M.
Bloch and J. Parrey (eds) *Money and the Morality of Exchange*, Cambridge:
Cambridge University Press.

Bourdieu, P. (1990), *The Logic of Practice*, Cambridge: Polity.

Brah, A. (1978), 'South Asian Teenagers in Southall: their Perceptions of Marriage,
Family and Ethnic Identity', *New Community*, 6: 197–206.

Brah, A. (1996), *Cartographies of Desire*, London: Routledge.

Breckenridge, C. A. and van der Veer, P. (1994), *Orientalism and the Post-colonial
Predicament: Perspectives on South Asia*, Delhi: Oxford University Press.

Butler, J. (1993), *Bodies that Matter: On the Discursive Limits of 'Sex'*, London:
Routledge.

Cohen, P. (1997), 'Labouring under Whiteness', in R. Frankenberg (ed.) *Displacing Whiteness: Essays in Social and Cultural Criticism*, Durham: Duke University Press.

Douglas, M. (1970), *Natural Symbols: Explorations in Cosmology*, London: Barrie & Rockcliff.

Dyer, R. (1997), *White*, London: Routledge.

Ellison, R. (1947), *Invisible Man*, Harmondsworth: Penguin.

Foucault, M. (1977), *Discipline and Punish: The Birth of the Prison*, London: Penguin Books.

Frankenberg, R. (1993), *The Social Construction of Whiteness: White Women, Race Matters*, Cambridge: Cambridge University Press.

Frankenberg, R. (ed.) (1997), *Displacing Whiteness: Essays in Social and Cultural Criticism*, Durham: Duke University Press.

Gillespie, M. (1995), *Television, Ethnicity, and Cultural Change*, London: Routledge.

Gilroy, P. (1993), *The Black Atlantic*, London: Verso.

Hall, S. (1992), 'The West and the Rest: Discourse and Power' in S. Hall and B. Gieben (eds) *Formations of Modernity*, Oxford: Polity.

Hobart, M. (ed.) (1993), *An Anthropological Critique of Development: The Growth of Ignorance*, London: Routledge.

hooks, b. (1991), *Yearning: Race, Gender, and Cultural Politics*, Boston: South End Press.

hooks, b. (1997), 'Whiteness in the Black Imagination', in R. Frankenberg (ed.) *Displacing Whiteness: Essays in Social and Cultural Criticism*, Durham: Duke University Press.

Kaur, R. and Kalra, V. (1996), 'New Paths for South Asian Identity and Musical Creativity', in S. Sharma, J. Hutnyk and A. Sharma (eds) *Dis-Orienting Rhythms: The Politics of the New Asian Dance Music*, London: Zed Books.

Kaviraj, S. (1992), 'The Imaginary Institution of India', in P. Chatterjee and G. Pandey (eds) *Subaltern Studies VII: Writings on South Asian History and Society*, Delhi: Oxford University Press.

MacCormack, C.P. (1980), 'Nature, Culture and Gender: A Critique', in C. MacCormack and M. Strathem (eds) *Nature, Culture and Gender*, Cambridge: Cambridge University Press.

McGarry, T. (1990), *A Study of the 'Irish' in Southall*, Department of Human Sciences BA Dissertation, Brunel University.

Phoenix, A. (1997), 'I'm White! So What?' The Construction of Whiteness for Young Londoners', in M. Fine, L.Weis, L.C. Powell and C. Mun Wong (eds), *Off-White: Readings on Race, Power and Society*, London: Routledge.

Pratt, M.B. (1992) 'Identity: Skin, Blood, Heart', in H. Crowley and S. Himmelweit (eds) *Knowing Women*, London: Polity.

Robinson, I., Frankenberg, R. and Turner, A. (1999), 'Ethnicity: What's the Idea?' unpublished paper, Department of Human Sciences, Brunel University.

Rutherford, J. (1997), *Forever England: Reflections on Masculinity and Empire,* London: Lawrence & Wishart.

Said, E. (1995), *Orientalism,* New York: Pantheon.

Scheper-Hughes, N. and Lock, M. (1987), 'The Mindful Body: A Prolegomenon to Future Work in Medical Anthropology', *Medical Anthropology Quaterly,* 1(1): 6–41.

Stephen, J. (1989), 'Feminist Fictions: A Critique of the Category "Non-Western Women" in Feminist Writings on India', in R. Guha (ed.) *Subaltern Studies VI: Writings on South Asian History and Society,* Delhi: Oxford University Press.

Sharma, S., Hutnyk, J. and Sharma, A. (1996), *Dis-Orienting Rhythms: The Politics of the New Asian Dance Music,* London: Zed Books.

Ware, V. (1992), *Beyond the Pale: White Women, Racism and History,* London: Verso.

Index